Wel

THESE HANDY, PORTABLE BOOKS are designed to be the perfect traveling companions.

THESE HANDY, PORTABLE BOOKS are designed to be the perfect traveling companions. Whether you're traveling within a tight family budget or feeling the urge to splurge, you will find all you need to create a memorable family vacation.

Use these books to plan your trips, and then take them along with you for easy reference. Does Jimmy want to go sailing? Or maybe Jane wants to go to the local hobby shop. *The Everything® Family Guides* offer many ways to entertain kids of all ages while also ensuring you get the most out of your time away from home.

Review this book cover to cover to give you great ideas before you travel, and stick it in your backpack or diaper bag to use as a quick reference guide for activities, attractions, and excursions you want to experience. Let *The Everything® Family Guides* help you travel the world, and you'll discover that vacationing with the whole family can be filled with fun and exciting adventures.

 TRAVEL TIP

Quick, handy tips

 RAINY DAY

Plan ahead for fun without sun

FAST FACT

Details to make your trip more enjoyable

 JUST FOR PARENTS

Appealing Information for moms and dads

THE EVERYTHING
— Family Guides —

Dear Reader,

Thanks for picking up this copy of *The Everything® Family Guide to Mexico*. I've written this book in order to help you and your family get the most out of your trip to Mexico, whether it's your first or one of many. As one of the only family guides to Mexico on the market, it's an important tool in helping your family experience Mexico's culture together and bring back memories to cherish forever.

This book is a culmination of twenty-one years of traveling to Mexico. Throughout all my trips, I've gathered a knowledge about the country that shows you, in as much detail as a book allows, how much I enjoy it. Keeping your family in mind, I discuss some of the most popular places, as well as some off-the-beaten-track destinations if you're more adventurous.

It's hard to keep information current about Mexico. Phone numbers and Internet addresses change constantly. I've tried to make sure that the information in this book was up to date when I wrote it.

In order for you to keep up with the latest information on Mexico, please visit my Mexico Web site, *www.therealmexico .com*. If you'd like to share your Mexico experiences with me, drop me a line at *bobbrooke@bobbrooke.com*. To learn more about me, visit my main Web site at *www.bobbrooke.com*. My goal has been to provide a comprehensive and informative book on Mexico. Only after you've returned with suitcases full of happy memories will I be able to know if I've succeeded.

Adiós, and *buen viaje*!

Bob Brooke

THE
EVERYTHING®
FAMILY GUIDE TO
MEXICO

From *pesos* to parasailing, all you
need for the whole family to *fiesta*!

Bob Brooke

Adams Media
Avon, Massachusetts

Dedication

I'd like to dedicate this book to my good friend Michael, who has been with me every step of the way, encouraging me to do the best that I could.

Publishing Director: Gary M. Krebs
Associate Managing Editor: Laura M. Daly
Associate Copy Chief: Brett Palana-Shanahan
Acquisitions Editor: Lisa Laing
Development Editor: Meredith O'Hayre
Associate Production Editor: Casey Ebert

Director of Manufacturing: Susan Beale
Associate Director of Production:
Michelle Roy Kelly
Cover Design: Paul Beatrice, Matt LeBlanc,
Erick DaCosta
Design and Layout: Brewster Brownville,
Colleen Cunningham, Jennifer Oliveira

An Everything® Series Book.
Everything® and everything.com® are registered trademarks of F+W Publications, Inc.

Published by Adams Media, an F+W Publications Company
57 Littlefield Street, Avon, MA 02322 U.S.A.

www.adamsmedia.com

ISBN 10: 1-59337-658-8
ISBN 13: 978-1-59337-658-1

Printed in the United States of America

J I H G F E D C B A

**Library of Congress Cataloging-in-Publication Data
available from publisher**

This publication is designed to provide accurate and authoritative information with regard to the subject matter covered. It is sold with the understanding that the publisher is not engaged in rendering legal, accounting, or other professional advice. If legal advice or other expert assistance is required, the services of a competent professional person should be sought.

—From a *Declaration of Principles* jointly adopted by a Committee of the American Bar Association and a Committee of Publishers and Associations

Many of the designations used by manufacturers and sellers to distinguish their products are claimed as trademarks. Where those designations appear in this book and Adams Media was aware of a trademark claim, the designations have been printed with initial capital letters.

Visit the entire Everything® series at *www.everything.com*

Contents

Top Ten Family-friendly Activities to Experience in Mexco

1. **Beaches:** Talcum-soft sands beckon you to soak up the Mexican sun.

2. **Climbing the pyramids:** Ancient Mexico comes to life.

3. **Exploring the deep:** Another world exists below the surface of Mexico's seas.

4. **Shopping the markets:** Wandering through a Mexican market is a great way to find treasures.

5. **Taking part in a callejonada:** Nothing compares to following a group of musicians down a narrow street.

6. **Mariachi serenade:** The sound of mariachis will give you an exhilarating feeling that makes you want to sing along.

7. **Folkloric dancing:** Your feet will tap to the Mexican rhythms of traditional dances.

8. **Watching fireworks:** A Mexican fiesta isn't a fiesta without pyrotechnics.

9. **Visiting museums:** No longer dark and boring places.

10. **Eating, eating, eating:** Tasting real Mexican food may surprise and delight you.

Acknowledgments

Thanks to all the Mexicans who made this book possible, from the hotel clerk who suggested a special place to eat to the guides who pointed out special details on my travels. And particular thanks goes to all the state and local tourism offices throughout Mexico for their help in gathering information about their destinations.

Introduction

It used to be that when you traveled to Mexico, everything was different than at home. And although families did travel together, it was only the wealthy that took long trips. Today, jet planes and package travel have put Mexico within the reach of many families. But with travel geared more toward individuals, whether alone or together, it's hard to know just where to go, where to stay, and, most importantly, what to do as a family. This book will help with all those things.

Unlike the glitzy new beach resorts found along Mexico's coasts, the culture found in its cities and towns is family based. Sure, you'll see American discount stores and fast-food restaurants, but even though they may look like the ones at home, they're different. That's because most of the people who patronize them do so as families.

Mexico is a complex culture. Not only is it different, for the most part, from what you're used to at home, it's different from other cultures in that it goes down many levels into history. Today's Mexicans, no matter whether they're talking on a cell phone or tapping on a laptop computer, carry on traditions of their ancient past—even if it's only in the food they eat. They've created a special culture, a blend of European Spanish and Mesoamerican Indian, that celebrates its past in so many ways. You'll find a little piece of it just about anywhere.

Go to the main square of any Mexican town, and you'll experience Mexico. It's there that everyone comes to wait, to meet, to do business, and to relax. You'll see children running around the fountains while their proud parents discuss the latest news with friends. Or stroll through any Mexican market—with aisle after aisle filled with sweet-smelling baskets of breads, golden deep-fried pork rinds, herbs of all kinds, tropical fruits by the truckload, and an endless selection of handicrafts—and you'll experience Mexico.

Even though the title of this book is *The Everything® Family Guide to Mexico*, it's impossible to tell you everything about this fascinating country—to do so would take volumes. But these pages will tell what you need to know to plan your family's vacation to Mexico, and in such a way that you'll begin to experience Mexican culture as you read.

If you're going to travel to Mexico, you should look beyond the luxurious beach resorts and search for the real Mexico—the Mexico that, in many instances, has been hidden by a veneer of modern innovations. You'll find it in the faces of the Indians of the country-side, the *mestizos* of the cities, and families just like yours.

CHAPTER 1

Welcome to Mexico

HISTORY, TRADITION, AND SUPERB scenery combine to make Mexico a unique vacation destination for your family. This is a culture that is neither Indian nor Spanish. The Mexicans have modified Castilian Spanish to their own softer tongue. They've created their own piquant cuisine, based on maize, the corn of the Indians. And they've combined church celebration and market into their own fiesta. The culture is drenched with Aztec, Toltec, and Olmec survivals mixed with Spanish importations. Whether exploring Mayan ruins, penetrating tropical jungles while exploring placid lagoons, or getting to know Mexico's history by exploring its colonial towns, you'll get to experience Mexican hospitality and the friendliness of its people.

What Does Mexico Have to Offer Your Family?

Until a few years ago, Mexico attracted mostly adults looking for fun in the sun and a different type of cultural experience. With the opening of special children's attractions and resorts with special children's programs, the adults who used to come to Mexico alone are now taking their kids along. Besides the warm climate, beautiful beaches, and cultural activities that everyone can enjoy, you and your children can explore special children's museums, zoos, theme parks, underwater caves, and archaeological sites—you can even swim with the dolphins. These attractions weren't built for just tourists, so as an added bonus, you'll be mixing with the Mexicans and their families.

 TRAVEL TIP

If you're traveling with a baby or toddler, you'll find just about anything you may need, including disposable diapers and baby food. Just keep in mind that few hotels offer baby cribs. Since Mexicans travel with their families, you'll find family accommodations in Mexico's major cities and resorts.

Ecotourism

Ecotourism has become a popular alternative to traditional tours in Mexico. With diverse terrain and an abundance of natural resources, you'll find Mexico an ideal destination for experiencing nature firsthand. Until recently, only traditional camping and hiking tours were available. Now, however, integrated tours encompassing not only nature but the cultures of Mexico's many indigenous peoples make it possible for you and your family to experience unique adventures.

Beginning as a grassroots movement, ecotourism now includes many small tour operators who have the support of the Mexican government. Generally, you'll find ecotours are less expensive in Mexico than elsewhere; they also offer a true cultural immersion. Ecotours allow you to experience another ethnic culture, integrating local traditions and festivals. Tour operators conduct their tours with small groups of eight or ten people. Each includes the local foods of the region, along with explanations about how they're prepared.

 FAST FACT

An ecotour offers a true Mexican experience while making you more aware of the local plants and animals by having experts on hand to explain them. They also promote the real traditional folk art designs, as tours help provide a market for almost-extinct handicrafts.

Sporting Activities

Mexico offers numerous sporting opportunities for your family, both as a spectator and a participant, including some of the best snorkeling and diving, fishing, and golf in the Western hemisphere, as well as horseback riding, sailing, and parasailing.

For Those Who Just Like to Watch

If you're planning a short vacation in Mexico or you're not much for jumping in and joining in the fun, then perhaps your family might enjoy attending a game of soccer, Mexico's national sport. Most large cities have a soccer stadium with regular matches throughout the year.

If you're in the mind for more traditional Mexican sport, you might attend a *charreada*, or Mexican rodeo. Held on Sunday mornings, these events feature *charros*, or gentlemen riders dressed in traditional outfits complete with large sombrero, competing in exhibitions of skilled riding.

And if the *charreada* is too tame for you, attend a *corrida*, or bullfight. But bullfights aren't for the faint of heart. They're usually gory spectacles full of pomp and circumstance in which up to six bulls are slain as the crowd yells, *"Ole!"*

Snorkeling and Diving

You'll discover some of the best snorkeling, skin-, and scuba-diving spots in the world off Mexico's 6,000 miles of coastline. Prime underwater sites in Mexico fall into three main categories: the west coast/ Sea of Cortés, the Caribbean, and the unique *cenotes* of the Yucatan

Peninsula. On the Caribbean, the clear, warm lagoons of Cozumel, Cancún, and Isla Mujeres teem with tropical fish and incredible coral deposits of intricate formation and colorful hues. Those resorts on the west coast also offer ideal conditions.

Fishing

Anglers from the world over have fallen in love with Mexico. Its coasts offer some of the best deep-sea fishing in the world, and fishermen travel the Baja and Pacific Coasts as well as the eastern Gulf and Caribbean coasts looking for snook, sea bass, dorado, striped marlin, sailfish, red snapper, billfish, and shark. Some experts believe that the southern tip of the Baja Peninsula at Los Cabos offers some of the best game fishing in the world.

Golf

Mexico has become a golfer's paradise. With ideal weather and scenery in both the Pacific Coastal area and the temperate central highlands, golf is a year-round sport, with many exciting and challenging courses laid out by top-name designers.

With more professionally designed courses completed and dozens in development, visitors can putt from Mexico City to Los Cabos and Cancún. The degree of difficulty on Mexico's greens also varies dramatically. From the short, fun courses of Club de Golf Acapulco to Baja's Cabo del Sol Golf Club, there's a golf game for everyone.

Horseback Riding

If you like to ride horses, Mexico offers your family a long tradition dating back to the conquest by the Spaniards. Mexicans are enthusiastic riders—in some cases, a bit *too* enthusiastic. Unlike gentle group rides that you may have taken on vacations in the United States, you'll find a horseback ride in Mexico to be a more independent affair. Though you may be part of a group, you'll find that your Mexican leaders aren't as watchful as those in the States since accident lawsuits are nonexistent under Mexican law. If you or any of your family members doesn't know how to ride or ride very little, then maybe you should save this activity for another vacation. But if you have riding experience, then there's nothing like a family ride along the beach.

Sailing and Parasailing

The major Mexican beach resorts all offer water-sports activities, including sailing and parasailing. Again, Mexico generally isn't the place to learn these sports. Many Pacific beaches have dangerous lateral currents and undertows, and few have lifeguards. The beaches at Acapulco, Mazatlán, and Puerto Vallarta on the Pacific, as well as Cancún on the Caribbean offer parasailing, in which you participate at your own risk.

What Are Your Family Vacation Options?

Every major all-inclusive company has one or more resorts in Mexico, many offering facilities and programs for children. Though this type of vacation isn't for everyone, it's often the most economical for families and will give you the best value for your travel dollar.

JUST FOR PARENTS

The legal drinking age in Mexico is eighteen.

Of course, you can also rent condos or efficiency suites in all-suite style resorts, where you have to pay separately for food and activities.

When Should You Visit?

Mexico has two distinct tourist seasons, so when you go depends on where you go. If you live in the cold, snowy north, then you'll want to visit Mexico's beaches in the winter. But if you're looking for colonial charm, then summer is the best time to visit. However, that coincides with the rainy season, which runs from May to October. No, it doesn't rain constantly, just in the late afternoons, leaving you plenty of time to explore.

TRAVEL TIP

Seaside resorts can be downright steamy during the summer, especially those along the Pacific Coast. And Cancún and Cozumel on the Caribbean side can get hit with severe tropical storms and hurricanes, though not often.

But more than the weather, you may want to take advantage of the peak and off-peak tourist seasons. At the beach resorts, the peak of winter season begins on December 15 and ends at the end of April or after Easter, whichever comes first. At both times, many Mexicans take a two-week vacation, usually visiting or traveling with family. This can be a problem, as hotels in some areas fill up with Mexican families. Off-peak season begins around April 15 and lasts until December 14. During this time, you can save as much as 25 to 50 percent on resort hotels. Of course, sometimes you can save just as much with family packages during the rest of the year. Unfortunately, you won't find any seasonal rates at any hotels in Mexico's interior.

The Climate of Mexico

Most people associate Mexico with winter suntans and beautiful seaside resorts. While the Pacific and Caribbean coasts are just about the all-time favorite escape for those trapped by winter's blows, they're only part of the story. With agreeable temperatures most of the year throughout its regions, Mexico offers a climatic variety that's unsurpassed.

The country's nearly perfect weather is as welcoming and diverse as its colorful geography. There are two seasons: rainy and dry. Generally, rains fall and temperatures rise from June through October, leaving November through May as the more temperate, drier season. Annual average high temperatures range in the 80s and 90s, while average lows range between 40 and 60°F.

Most of the country lies south of the Tropic of Cancer, and the influence of the mountains, seas, and ocean plays a great role in the varying conditions.

Much of the country is dry and balmy, particularly the northern and Baja California regions. Southern Mexico and the Yucatan Peninsula experience significant rainfall from June to September, but the rest of the year this region is pleasantly dry and temperate. On the Pacific Coast, from Puerto Vallarta south, the sun shines for at least part of every day, even during most of the rainy season.

Average Temperature Ranges

Beginning in Baja California, with its desert landscape, you'll find average winter temperatures of 68°F. The Sea of Cortés side of Baja tends to be warmer than the Pacific side. Rainfall of less than ten inches occurs between December and April. Farther south, you can bask in the sun 350 days a year. The desert brings cool winter evenings. Low humidity and refreshing sea breezes make even the highest summer temperatures, often near 100°F, comfortable. In the spring and fall, temperatures cool off to 77°F.

What's known as "The Mexican Riviera" begins at Mazatlán and continues south along the Pacific Coast. Here, the months from November to May are a sure bet for warm, dry days and balmy evenings. The rainy season runs from June through October, with daily rain showers and warm temperatures. The average winter temperature ranges from 70 to 80°F, but in summer it climbs to 85 to 95°F with high humidity.

 **TRAVEL TIP**

Allow yourself a day to acclimate to the high altitude of Mexico City. Plan a bus tour of the city, eat light, and go to bed early.

From Mexico City to Guadalajara, the higher elevations of the central plateau yield springlike conditions much of the year, though evenings can be quite cool in the winter. Afternoon showers aren't uncommon during the May-to-September rainy season. December and January are the coolest months, with an average annual high of 81°F and a low of 41°F. Guadalajara and Cuernavaca, at a mere 5,000 feet, offer balmy daytime temperatures in the 70s year round.

Winter is the most popular time to visit the Yucatan, but the climate is mild year-round with an average temperature of 80°F. In the summer, trade winds keep the Gulf Coast and Caribbean areas somewhat cooler, while interior jungles can be hot and humid, with higher temperatures. Rainfall is frequent in April and May and from September to January.

Mexico's Gulf Coast is somewhat humid, with warmer temperatures averaging around 72°F. Rainfall increases the farther south you travel. Cool, northerly winds blow from September through February.

Mountains, Desert, or Coast?

Spanning 2,000 miles—from the western Pacific Coast to the Gulf of Mexico in the east—Mexico's extremely diverse geography encompasses nearly every geological form found in the Western Hemisphere: low plains, rolling hills, rugged mountains and deserts to the north; 6,000 miles of seacoast; tropical lowland jungles; snow-capped mountains; and awe-inspiring gorges.

The Sierra Madre Oriental and Sierra Madre Occidental mountain ranges on the east and west and a row of towering, widely spaced volcanoes enclose the central highlands, comprising 60 percent of the country's land mass.

Mexico's terrain touches four distinct bodies of water, which accounts for the country's unmatched array of sunny seaside destinations. The Sea of Cortés (also called the Gulf of California) to the northwest, and the Caribbean to the southeast, contain some of the world's richest marine life. The Gulf of Mexico borders Mexico's northeastern coast, and the Pacific Ocean meets the western shore. Nearly half the country is more than 5,000 feet above sea level.

CHAPTER 2

Mexico: An Overview

LIKE THE UNITED STATES, Mexico encompasses a variety of cultures and peoples, and the country has been described as the world's most successful melting pot of peoples, races, and cultures. Like their country, the Mexican people are complex and often mysterious.

The Mexicans

Of its more than 96 million inhabitants, between 75 and 83 percent are *mestizos,* or people of mixed Indian and Spanish blood. Ten percent of the people are *criollos,* or creoles, of old Spanish descent, and 10 to 15 percent are Indian.

While the great majority of Mexicans speak Spanish, 25 percent of the Indians speak only their native languages—Nahuatl, the tongue of the Aztecs, and Mayan are the two most prevalent. Before the Spanish conquest, there were at least 120 different Indian languages, and fifty-six still survive.

Mexican Architecture

When the first Spaniards arrived in Mexico, they couldn't believe the magnificence of the Aztec cities such as Tenochtitlán, the capital, which showed a thorough understanding of city planning, design, and well-coordinated land use and waterworks. You'll discover much of this architectural legacy preserved in Mexico's numerous pre-Columbian archaeological sites, museums, and parks.

The wide variety of colonial architecture in Mexico reflects the overwhelming influence of religious-inspired Spanish design. Many of these first churches and convents occupy former sites of indigenous buildings. In many cases they used materials and even the walls of the former structures. Strong Romanesque and Gothic features characterize the thick walls and massive buttresses of these early structures. You'll find atriums and *capillas fosas*—small processional chapels at the four corners of the courtyards—only in Mexico.

The sixteenth century also witnessed the arrival from Spain of the plateresque style, which features intricately carved stone doorways and decorative patterns of flowers and arabesques. You'll see the Indian plateresque style, combining a local interpretation with pre-Columbian building techniques, in some parish churches.

The seventeenth century brought baroque styles of architecture to Mexico. You can see restrained forms of this in the great cathedrals of Mexico City, Puebla, Morelia, Guadalajara, and Oaxaca. These magnificent buildings reflect not only the growing patronage of the Spanish crown, but the development of a more elaborate Mexican high baroque style called churrigueresque, reflecting the growing power of Mexican-born *criollos*.

═FAST FACT

Estilo churrigueresco, named after the Spanish architect Jose Benito Churiguera, is eighteenth-century Mexican high baroque, featuring gold-encrusted altars covered with heavenly beings. The Mexico City cathedral shows some of the finest examples.

Some of the churches in Puebla and Oaxaca show a uniquely Mexican variation of this style, called the Poblano style, which combines stucco ornamentation with colored tiles and red brick. The

Casa de los Azulejos, or House of Tiles, in Mexico City features this style of ornamentation.

After the 1910 revolution, the functional style of the Bauhaus school began to take shape. It wasn't until the 1950s and 1960s that Mexican architecture showed the influence of Le Corbusier and his International School. Today, Mexican architects are striving to create their own unique style of contemporary architecture, examples of which you can see in the southern suburbs of Mexico City and in Monterrey.

Arts and Crafts

Leaving a place as fascinating as Mexico is hard to do, but you'll find that you can take a little bit of it home in the form of arts and crafts that personify the country's warmth, imagination, and varied culture.

Though distinctive handicrafts flourish in every region, central and southern Mexico are especially noted for the variety and sheer number of their artisans. The black pottery of Oaxaca, the Talavera pottery of Puebla, the woven pine baskets of the Copper Canyon, and carved ironwood animals of the Pacific Coast are but a few examples.

 TRAVEL TIP

If you're short on shopping time, look for FONART stores, run by the Mexican government and found in most major tourist areas. Each offers a sampling of folk art from different regions at reasonable fixed prices.

Many towns and cities in craft-producing regions have shops sponsored by local and state governments as well, often under the name of Casa de Las Artesanias. Since such stores seek to display the variety and quality of their region's works, they make excellent places to study the types of crafts available and their prices.

Mexican Music

Music, like eating, is an integral part of Mexican life. You won't go far without hearing someone singing or music blaring from a boom box in a corner *tienda* (store). But for many North Americans, the blaring trumpets, mellow guitars, and soft violins of *mariachi* music symbolize Mexico. This type of music originated during the French occupation of Mexico during the nineteenth century, when weddings called for large musical ensembles. Originally performed by *campesinos* or field hands playing guitars, the 1920s brought fancier *charro* outfits and the addition of other stringed instruments and trumpets. And while *mariachi* music has become known all over the world, it is, in fact, only played at weddings, fiestas, and other special occasions. The word *mariachi* comes from the French word *mariage,* meaning marriage. The players, dressed in tight pants and dark jackets with silver buttons and wearing large sombreros decorated in a similar manner, perform in groups of eight to ten. Today, *mariachi* music is especially popular in the state of Jalisco. The annual Mariachi Festival, held in Guadalajara at the beginning of September, is known far and wide.

 TRAVEL TIP

If you're in Veracruz over a Saturday night, you can join the locals as they dance to Cuban danzon ryhthms played by an orchestra in the main square.

In the states of Chiapas, Tabasco, Oaxaca, and Veracruz, you'll also hear the lilting sounds of the marimba, a xylophone-type instrument with large wooden keys played by four people using rubber-tipped batons. One carries the melody, while the others play a secondary melody in counterpoint.

Mexican Dance

The Aztecs believed that dance kept the world in motion. It was an integral part of their religious rituals. They danced to win the favor of their gods so that they would find good fortune in war, harvest, and marriage. Though most Mexican dances began as religious rites, today they're performed at fiestas and at folkloric shows throughout the country. Specific styles have developed in each region. One of the most well known is the *baile venado,* or deer dance, of the Yaqui Indians of Sonora. Originally performed for good fortune in hunting, it's a part of every folkloric dance troupe's repetoire. A male dancer pantomimes a deer being chased and eventually killed. Another popular folkloric dance is the *jarabe tapatio,* or Mexican hat dance from Guadalajara. You'll recognize this national folk dance, with its heel-to-toe movement, as one you may have learned in elementary school.

≡FAST FACT

While folkloric groups perform dance shows all over Mexico, especially at the resort destinations on "Mexican Nights," the granddaddy of them all is the Ballet Folklórico de Mexico, performed at the Belles Artes in Mexico City on Sundays and Wednesdays. It's an experience your family shouldn't miss.

Other folkloric dances include the languorous *huapango* and sassy *la bamba* of Veracruz, the comical *baile viejito,* or the dance of the old men, from Michoacán, and the sedate *jarana* of Yucatán, in which male dancers perform while balancing beer bottles on their heads. All of Mexico's regional dances have their own special costumes and music.

A Tradition of Good Eating

Ever since the arrival of the Spaniards in Mexico, travelers have been astonished to find that Mexican food isn't what they thought it was. Far beyond the simple tacos and burritos of fast-food Tex-Mex eateries, it's a cornucopia of delights with a 3,000-year-old legacy and rich cultural traditions.

The origins of Mexican food began with ancient Indian civilizations. They cultivated maize, commonly referred to as corn, which became the raw material for tortillas, the flat unleavened dough baked in a pan that functions like bread. They ate a red fruit called a *tomatl* (tomato), which the Spaniards thought poisonous. And they drank a muddy brew called *chocoatl* (chocolate), that the Dutch later refined with milk and sugar.

≡FAST FACT

The Spanish conquistadors first came into contact with chocolate in sixteenth-century Mexico, where Moctezuma and his followers mixed hot water with ground beans and a variety of spices to produce a favorite drink.

Mexican cuisine is extremely varied. Though menus throughout the country often show the same dishes, these are mere variations on a theme. Each is changed slightly by the ingredients of the region where it is made. There are the traditional dishes made from tortillas—tacos, enchiladas, tostadas. In addition, there are rich sauces like *mole poblano,* a concoction of sixty-one herbs and spices (one of which is often unsweetened chocolate) served over boiled chicken.

One of the main ingredients found everywhere in Mexico is *chiles* (peppers). Often confused with Tex-Mex chili (a meat-and-bean stew), over 100 different kinds of chiles in Mexico are served in a variety of ways, from stuffed to chopped in *salsa verde* (green sauce).

Eating As a Social Event

Mexico's unique gastronomy doesn't begin and end in the kitchen. Colorful, noisy, and hospitable, the Mexican meal is just as important to Mexican cuisine as is preparation of the food. Food is just the excuse for sharing and exchanging companionship and news. Restaurants, which tend to get crowded between 2 and 5 P.M., during the Mexican's main meal, are as diverse as the food they serve.

Getting Around in Mexico

You'll find getting around Mexico relatively easy if you know a little Spanish. Doing so will definitely give you an edge in negotiations for taxi fares and making reservations for buses and ferries. If you speak no Spanish, stick to English-speaking deluxe buses and taxis for hire.

By Bus

Traveling by bus in Mexico can be an adventure, but it can also be extremely pleasant. It all depends on the class of travel you choose. While bus travel is probably the least expensive way to get around the country—buses connect nearly every town and village—it's a good idea to buy your tickets in advance, especially if you're planning to ride around the major holidays.

 **TRAVEL TIP**

When calling Mexico from the United States, dial 011 before the area code.

You can purchase your tickets for cash on a first-come, first-serve basis at bus stations, which resemble airport terminals. Classes available include first, second, and deluxe, and can be labeled in Spanish with a variety of names, such as *primera plus*, *ejecutivo*, *plus*, or *de lujo.* Often there's little difference between these classes, though first class usually means you'll ride in air-conditioned comfort. It also means a toilet on board and comfortable, less-crowded seating. The new deluxe buses are air-conditioned, usually seat only twenty-six or so passengers, show movies en route, have onboard stewards serving snacks, clean restrooms, and make few stops or may run express from city of origin to their final destination. There's little difference in the price from first class to deluxe, so the extra cost is worth it.

≡FAST FACT

You should begin your informational search for buses in Mexico at ✑*www.ticketbus.com.mx*. It lists your choices of lines, cost of your ticket, how long your trip will take, and departure times.

Though you can depend on deluxe and first-class bus schedules, their routes and times can change. You can get current information from local bus stations since there is no national bus directory.

By Taxi

Mexico has a variety of taxis. Before getting into one, however, you should tell the driver your destination and ask the fare—just say "*¿Cuánto cuesta?*" To get an idea of what local fares may be, ask the desk clerk or concierge at your hotel. If the fare quoted you isn't what you had been told, or if negotiations aren't going well, just say "*No, gracias,*" and try another.

Mexico City has had problems with its taxis in recent years, mostly kidnaps and robberies. Even though the situation has improved, it's a good idea to avoid flagging down a taxi. Instead, take those either lined up at a taxi stand (called *sitio* taxis) or parked in front of a hotel. While the hotel taxis can cost as much as those in the United States, it's better to be safe than sorry.

 **TRAVEL TIP**

Make sure the taxi you choose has a meter and a driver's ID hanging in plain sight from the dashboard or visor. The ID indicates the driver has been licensed by the city government.

You can also hire a taxi for a guided tour at an hourly rate. Just make sure the driver speaks English clearly enough for you to understand.

By Rental Car

Renting a car in Mexico is rarely as simple as signing on the dotted line and roaring off into the sunset. The process can go off without a hitch, or it can be an adventure.

You'll probably rent your car from an international car rental firm, either directly or through your travel agent as part of a package. Or you may rent on-site, thinking you'll get a better deal. No matter what your choice is, renting a car in Mexico can be expensive if you don't shop around.

Rates vary greatly from city to city and even from location to location within the same city. Lower prices are generally found with smaller local companies, where the ability to speak Spanish is a definite asset. Discounts are available for smaller cars rented for longer periods and sometimes if you reserve a certain number of days before your arrival—usually seven to fourteen days. You'll also get a break by paying at the time of booking, renting by the week, and returning the car to the same location.

The actual rental procedure is the same as anywhere else in the world. However, the implied meaning may be slightly different. You must have a valid driver's license and be able to convince the rental agency of two things: that you are personally creditworthy (a valid credit card in your name usually will do), and that you will return the car on time.

In addition, the minimum renter age, ranging from twenty-one to twenty-five years, differs from one company to another, even though the minimum driving age in Mexico is eighteen. There may also be an upper age limit of sixty-nine to seventy-five years.

By Ferry

If you're planning to drive down the Baja Peninsula and then continue driving on the mainland, you'll have to take one of the ferries that sail between Baja California and the mainland through the Sea of Cortés. The trip usually takes about twenty-four hours, so you'll need to make advance reservations for your car and your onboard accommodations at the ferry offices. You'll have a choice of three different classes of accommodations: *cabina,* private cabin with bath; *turista,* shared bunk beds; and *salón,* the least expensive, with unreserved reclining seats. Some ferries offer an *classe especial,* with larger deluxe cabins.

Ferries base their vehicle fares on the length of your vehicle. Passenger fares are separate, with children sailing for half the adult fare. Though *salón* fares are sold on a first-come, first-serve basis, *turista* fares can be reserved three or more days in advance and *cabina* fares a month or more in advance.

The ferry between La Paz in Baja California Sur and Mazatlán in the state of Sinaloa offers the most service. The three ferries that sail this route offer all classes of service, including *especial,* plus a cafeteria, restaurant with bar, video lounge, and disco. They sail daily in the late afternoon from Mazatlán, except Sunday.

Passenger-only ferries also run between the island of Cozumel and Playa del Carmen on the mainland below Cancún and between the island of Isla Mujeres and Cancún.

Dollar or Peso?

Within the last few years, the value of the Mexican peso to the dollar has remained fairly stable, around 10 pesos to the dollar, which makes it easy to figure out prices. The official currency of Mexico is the *nuevo peso* (new peso), designated by a N$. Notes come in 10-, 20-, 50-, 100-, 500-, and 1,000-peso denominations while coins come in 1-, 2-, 5-, 10-, and 20-peso amounts. Be sure to check the amount on any coin or bill before handing it over. They can be confusing.

 TRAVEL TIP

It's wise to exchange your money in increments of $20 U.S.—perhaps up to $100 at a time. Keep your pesos in your wallet or purse and your dollars in a safe place, so if you're robbed or lose your wallet, you won't lose everything.

Many merchants and restaurant owners in border towns and beach resorts like Cancún and Los Cabos often will take U.S. dollars, but they'll give you pesos as change. Pemex stations take only pesos.

Understanding Exchange Rates

You can exchange U.S. or Canadian dollars at any Mexican bank or at an independent exchange kiosk called a *casa de cambio*. Surprisingly, these places give very good rates, sometimes even better than the banks. You'll need your passport as identification, whether you're exchanging cash or cashing traveler's checks. You can usually obtain the best rates at the *casas de cambios* at the Mexico City airport. For small amounts (around $20 or so), it's best to just exchange your money at the hotel desk. The difference in the exchange rate will be marginal. Remember, you cannot exchange Mexican peso coins back into U.S. currency.

TRAVEL TIP

It's a good idea to exchange a small amount of money at your home airport before you depart for Mexico. This way you'll have some Mexican currency on hand in case you don't have time or can't find a place to exchange money on arrival.

Using Credit Cards, Debit Cards, Traveler's Checks

While the ads tell you to protect your money by carrying traveler's checks, you may find that some places in Mexico won't cash them. The best known brands, Bank of America and American Express, are the easiest to cash and the fastest to be replaced if lost or stolen. Many Mexican banks won't cash Canadian traveler's checks.

Credit cards are probably the safest way to spend. Visa and MasterCard are widely accepted throughout Mexico. Many merchants shy away from American Express cards because of their high fees. Be aware, however, that many hotels, restaurants, and merchants will add a 3- to 6-percent surcharge to credit card purchases. Many Mexican banks, as well as the airports, have ATM machines from which you can get pesos with your card. In addition, you'll pay a 15-percent value added tax on all goods and services, including all hotel and restaurants bills and international telephone calls.

Bargaining Tips

Bargaining anywhere is fun. But the Mexicans have made it an art. You'll find that bargaining usually applies only to markets. Retail stores have set prices. While you may find it tempting to bargain for every item you purchase, it's better to bargain only for higher-priced items. Here are some tips:

- To begin bargaining, offer half the price of the item.
- If the seller says no, offer a bit more. Keep this up until you reach a price you can both agree upon.
- *Never* successfully bargain for an item and not buy it.
- If you don't like the offered price, walk away. Often the seller will follow and give you a lower price.
- Offer to buy two or more items and ask for the best price for all.
- Be sure to express your gratitude for the excellent price you received.
- When bargaining in Mexico, do it in Spanish if possible, no matter how bad.

Tipping

Major resorts in Mexico often add service charges to your bill, so there's no need to tip. However, you should tip everywhere else. For waiters, leave at least 15 percent. Give porters and bellboys between 5 to 10 pesos (50 cents to $1) per bag, depending on the size of the bags. If you have large, heavy bags, it's worth a few dollars to have someone put them on a cart, especially in the Mexico City airport. Leave 3 to 4 pesos a day for chambermaids. Normally, taxi drivers don't expect tips.

CHAPTER 3

The Land of Mexico

MEXICO IS A COMPLEX country, a land of surprises, a land of beauty, a land of mystery. The variety of landscapes and cultures will astound you. Mexico is timeless, a land where time can go forward to the future and backward to the past at the same moment. It's no wonder her people cry, "*Que Viva Mexico!*" (Long live Mexico!)

The States of Mexico

Mexico has thirty-one states and a federal district—Mexico City— much like Washington, D.C. The states and their capitals can be grouped by geographic regions as follows:

TABLE 3-1
THE STATES OF MEXICO AND THEIR CAPITAL CITIES

Region	State	Capital City
North	Chihuahua	Chihuahua
	Coahuila	Saltillo
	Durango	Durango
	Sonora	Hermosillo
Central Highlands	Aguascalientes	Aguascalientes
	Guanajuato	Guanajuato
	Hidalgo	Pachua

Region	State	Capital City
	Morelos	Cuernavaca
	Nuevo León	Monterrey
	Puebla	Puebla
	Querétaro	Querétaro
	San Luis Potosí	San Luis Potosí
	State of Mexico	Toluca
	Tlaxcala	Tlaxcala
	Zacatecas	Zacatecas
Pacific Coast	Colima	Colima
	Guerrero	Chilpancingo
	Jalisco	Guadalajara
	Michoacán	Morelia
	Nayarit	Tepic
	Sinaloa	Culiacán
Gulf Coast	Tabasco	Villahermosa
	Tamaulipas	Ciudad Victoria
	Veracruz	Jalapa
Yucatán Peninsula	Campeche	Campeche
	Quintana Roo	Chetumal
	State of Yucatán	Mérida
Southern Mexico	Chiapas	Tuxtla Gutiérrez
	Oaxaca	Oaxaca
Baja California	Baja California Norte	Mexicali
	Baja California Sur	La Paz
Distrito Federal (abbreviated D.F.)	Mexico City	

The Regions of Mexico

From the pastel-colored caves, striking desert landscapes, and reddish-orange mountains of Baja California to the lush green jungles and turquoise waters of the Yucatán Peninsula, from the magnificent series of gorges of Copper Canyon to miles of sun-drenched white sandy beaches and clear azure waters of the Pacific Coast, nature has created Mexico from her rich palette of colors. It's unfortunate that most other North Americans don't know much about the country's geographic diversity and what it has to offer.

Essentially, Mexico can be divided into eight regions:

1. Northern Mexico
2. Baja California
3. Pacific Coast
4. Valley of Mexico
5. Colonial Mexico
6. Southern Mexico
7. Gulf Coast
8. Yucatán Peninsula

You'll find countless ways to experience Mexico. Whether you choose to explore small villages or sophisticated cities, or lounge by a sparkling pool in one of the country's hundreds of resort hotels, or rough it on a jungle safari, you'll make new friends and cherish your time in this colorful land.

Northern Mexico

Mexico's geographically northern region, comprising the states of Sonora, Sinaloa, Durango, Chihuahua, Coahuila, Nuevo Leon, and most of Tamaulipas, offers you a chance to experience some of the country's most spectacular landscapes, set in an area of semidesert and pine- forested highlands known as El Norte.

The most spectacular natural wonder here is the Barranca de Cobre, or Copper Canyon. The Canyon itself—actually a maze of more than twenty smaller canyons that form a series of five inter-connecting canyons or *barrancas* covering 900 square miles—offers you an outdoor experience so pure and majestic that you'll feel as if you've entered an undiscovered civilization. Located in the state of Chihuahua, the Copper Canyon is four times larger and 280 feet deeper than the Grand Canyon.

▐ TRAVEL TIP

If natural wonders aren't your thing, you might want to follow in the steps of one of Mexico's most famous revolutionaries, Pancho Villa. His haunts are clustered around the city of Chihuahua and the nearby town of Parral.

The next biggest attraction in the North is Monterrey, often called "The Pittsburgh of Mexico." Here, mighty steel mills, now silent, forged the steel that built many of Mexico's buildings. Today, Monterrey offers a modern city with some of the best museums in the country.

The state of Sinaloa is home to Mazatlán, Mexico's northernmost beach resort on the Pacific. Originally game fishing brought visitors here, but the leisurely sport of sun-worshipping has taken hold. A young, lively resort, Mazatlán boasts the least expensive section of beach in Mexico with the most variety.

If you like to "hang ten," then you'll love Mazatlán, Mexico's surfing capital. But you'll enjoy parasailing—being towed high in a parachute behind a motorboat—from its wide beaches just as much. You can also try Jet-skiing and boogie-boarding or play tennis at one of eighty courts or golf on three eighteen-hole courses. And shopping is a pastime only exceeded by partying.

The states of Sonora, Durango, Coahuila, and Tamaulipas, catering more to sportsmen, don't offer much for family vacationers.

Baja California

Running 876 miles from Mexico's border with Southern California to its tip at Los Cabos, the Baja Peninsula presents a land of desert and semidesert separating the Pacific Ocean from the Sea of Cortés. Until 1973, only the most adventurous risked the severity of its terrain for the pleasure of hunting, fishing, rock hunting, fossil collecting, bird watching, and surfing in an almost pure natural environment. In 1973, the 1,050-mile Transpeninsular Highway, officially called the Benito Juárez Highway, opened.

With an 800-plus-mile coast on the Pacific and the Sea of Cortés, Baja, as it's affectionately known, offers a paradise for anglers, swimmers, and surfers. Huge clams and oysters wash up on its miles of beaches, and the emerald-green waters of the gulf and the deep-blue waters of the Pacific support an incredible variety of big-game fish. As the highway traverses Baja, the dry landscape breaks into sudden oases, while fishing villages dot the coast.

❧ FAST FACT

Whale watching has become a favorite activity as California gray whales mate and calve every winter along Baja's west coast.

Despite the land's wild nature and seeming remoteness, Baja California has experienced a tremendous surge in tourism growth, especially in Los Cabos. In the 1980s, Los Cabos became a government-sponsored and planned resort. Here, you'll find luxurious resorts catering to golfers, but most visitors come for the pleasant dry, desert climate and the sparkling blue sea.

If you like to dive, Los Cabos features dives on its North and South Walls and the Shipwreck. There's good snorkeling among the tidal pools and reefs just offshore, in Cabo San Lucas. If you're lucky, you may get to enjoy an exhilarating encounter with a forty-ton whale. Divers tell how these gentle giants lift their heads to look in curiosity at them and their tanks and then swim away.

Pacific Coast

All of Mexico's Pacific beach resorts offer a variety of sun and fun pleasures, including a smorgasbord of sports, from golf and tennis to fishing and sailing. Perhaps you'd like the exhilarating feeling of parasailing, an activity not for the faint of heart. At the beaches in Acapulco and Puerto Vallarta, all you need do is wait your turn and pay the man.

In Manzanillo, Puerto Vallarta, and San Jose del Cabo, you can feel the thrill of excitement as you ride side by side on horseback through the surf, horses' manes flying in the wind. Stop for a cool drink and some tasty grilled shrimp at an oceanside restaurant, and then jump into the surf for a refreshing dip.

If you're a deep-sea fishing enthusiast, you'll find all you can handle at Mexico's Pacific Coast resorts. Sailfish are quite prevalent, as are marlin, wahoo, yellowtail, dorado, mackerel, and bonito. Manzanillo claims to be the sailfish capital of the world, but Mazatlán offers a similar claim. January through April is marlin season.

In Los Cabos, fishing is numero uno. For years, the Sea of Cortés has held a special place in the hearts of fishermen. With more than 650 varieties of game fish in its teeming waters, it's a veritable paradise if you're a deep-sea fishing enthusiast.

The Valley of Mexico

The majority of visitors who come to Mexico never get to see its greatest wonder, Mexico City. Unfortunately, most of the hype goes to the country's beach resorts, leaving many to miss the superb museums, history, culture, and excitement of one of the world's largest cities. Here, you can stroll the broad Avenida de Reforma leading down to the city's Centro Historico, or historic district, filled with newly restored seventeenth- and eighteenth-century buildings.

Mexico City sits on the foundations of the Aztec capital of Tenochtitlán. It's the cultural center of the country, offering a bountiful number of sites to explore. The city's three most popular attractions are the Ballet Folklorico, the bullfights, and the floating gardens of Xochimilco.

You might also want to visit Coyoacan, the former suburb that is now a district of the capital, where artist Frida Kahlo lived and painted. Casa Azul, or Blue House, now houses the Frida Kahlo Museum, established in the artist's home and studio. Nearby, you'll find the Leon Trotsky Museum, where Leon Trotsky lived after fleeing to Mexico from the Soviet Union.

Teotihuacán, easily seen in half a day, lies twenty-five miles northeast of Mexico City. This archaeological site is so majestic that the Aztecs named it the City of the Gods. Covering nine square miles, this magnificent ceremonial center and some of the outlying palaces and priestly dwellings have been restored.

Known for its year-round spring-like temperatures, Cuernavaca has also become one of Mexico's prime commercial cities. Long a favorite getaway for residents of Mexico City, including Cortés and Maxmilian and Carlotta, Cuernavaca also offers interesting sites in and around town, including the Museum of Cauhnahuac in the former Palace of Cortés on the *zócalo,* the town's main square.

Colonial Mexico

Mexico's colonial cities are virtual living museums to a vanished way of life. The charm of secluded courtyards, white walls accented by wrought iron balconies, red tile roofs gleaming in the sun, and recessed windows guarded by ornate metal filigrees make visits to Mexico's colonial cities a must. These cities, built during the viceregal period, are monuments to a gracious yet unsettling age—an age when greed drove men to search out riches, not for themselves but for the glory of Spain.

Guanajuato, a city built on the riches from silver mines, is made for walking. Its narrow, cobbled streets, lined with balconied houses and winding up the hillsides, will draw you in. Like Venice, you'll find yourself diverted into unexpected squares that seem almost like stage settings in an opera. In fact, the entire city becomes a great outdoor stage during the International Cervantino Festival held in October and November.

Much of Querétaro's charm lies in its history. Part of the Aztec empire and later overcome by the Spaniards, it became a hotbed of revolutionary sentiment for independence from Spain. Colonial Querétaro offers some intriguing buildings surrounded by colorful parks and plazas. At the heart of town is the Plaza Obregon, dominated by the Church of San Francisco and convent of the same name, housing the state regional museum.

📖 TRAVEL TIP

For a taste of the real Mexico, visit Tequisquiapan, a spa town located two hours north of Mexico City in the dairy region of Mexico. Be sure to visit the local market and taste the varieties of cheese and nuts that are available.

About an hour northwest of Querétaro lies San Miguel de Allende, the consummate Mexican colonial town. The city's narrow cobblestone streets climb the slopes in gradual stages. Plaques mounted on the walls of fine old colonial houses tell what famous figure lived inside or what important event took place there. The centerpiece of San Miguel is its *el jardin,* or *zócalo,* with its unusual parish church built to look like a French Gothic cathedral. Other buildings provide a potpourri of photogenic domes, steeples, niches, and scalloped roofs. Here, your family can sign up for art or language classes at the Instituto Allende, housed in the former estate of the Counts of Canal. Now a division of the University of Guadalajara, it's the perfect place to learn or improve your Spanish.

The heart of Guadalajara, Mexico's second-largest city, boasts grand pedestrian malls ideal for strolling and shopping. Plaza Tapatia, the largest, is a good place to begin exploring the old city. A visit to the cathedral and the Government Palace, to see the dramatic murals, is a must.

There's also plenty to see nearby. Guadalajara has sprawled east to merge with San Pedro Tlaquepaque. Though the town is best known for its ceramics and glassblowing, more than 300 shops now sell everything from fine silver jewelry to antiques and leather. A former colonial villa now houses the Ceramic Museum, displaying works from around the state of Jalisco.

Southern Mexico

The Sierra Madre del Sur encircles the state of Oaxaca and, together with its neighboring state of Chiapas, contains the largest diversity of indigenous cultures and peoples in Mexico. This explains Oaxaca's richness and variety in handicrafts, folklore, culture, and cuisine. With its mix of indigenous cultures, plus its colonial grandeur and numerous archaeological sites, Oaxaca is a unique educational family destination.

The southernmost state of Mexico, Chiapas, is probably its most complex. Since thick rainforests cover a large part of its highlands, the state and its people, descendants of the Maya and other tribes, remained fairly isolated until recent years. Indigenous uprisings in the mid-1990s caused much concern, but even though peace has returned, there are many other places in Mexico with more to interest families.

The Gulf Coast

An attractive state capital little known by tourists, Villahermosa in the state of Tabasco is noted for its La Venta Museum, a vast outdoor archaeological display located east of the city. This unique tropical park reproduces the original site of La Venta using massive stone Olmec Indian heads, stone altars, and sculpted animals. There's even a zoo for children, featuring local animals.

But most visitors head southeast to the ruins of Palenque in the Chiapas jungle. Considered by many to be the most beautiful pre-Hispanic site in Mexico, Palenque was a Mayan center, inhabited from A.D. 100 to 900. The mummy of Lord Pacal, who died in A.D. 683, still lies in its original resting place.

The state of Veracruz, with more ecotourism companies than any other region, has become the adventure capital of Mexico. You can go river rafting, mountain climbing, hiking, and camping in the tropical forests throughout the state. You'll enjoy the *joie de vivre* (or joy of life) of Veracruz, Mexico's hot and sultry principal port city and the nation's oldest. The atmosphere here is relaxed and unhurried. Perhaps you'll want to stroll the *malecón* to watch the activity of the harbor, then take a harbor cruise, after which you can step into one of Veracruz's many cafés. At night, the main square comes alive with marimba bands playing to the crowds who come to listen and eat freshly caught seafood.

The Yucatán Peninsula

The Yucatán Peninsula, comprising the states of Yucatán, Campeche, and Quintana Roo, offers ancient history, as well as coral-lined shores, sparkling powdery sands, and azure-blue seas.

If you're into history, then you'll want to explore the Mayan sites of Uxmal, Chichén Itzá, Coba, and Tulum. But if you like to explore underwater, the Mexico's Caribbean offers world-class conditions for both scuba-diving and snorkeling. Like a bejeweled necklace, the world's second-longest reef system, with visibility ranging up to 200 feet, stretches about 250 miles south from Cancún to Belize.

Diving is the sport on the island of Cozumel, just offshore in the turquoise-blue Caribbean, and diving experts agree that there's nowhere else like it for submarine scenery. If you're not into diving, then perhaps snorkeling at Chankanaab Reef, where giant lobsters dwell under rocky ledges, will be more to your liking.

If you like to sun, swim, and party, then Cancún should be your choice. The most popular of Mexico's Caribbean resorts, it's a family resort where water sports from windsurfing to boogie-boarding to snorkeling top the list. You can also tee off at several fine golf courses or play tennis at smooth courts at all the larger hotels.

If you get weary of the sun and sand, you can take an excursion to one of the ancient Mayan ruins on the mainland. Tulum—a time-softened ceremonial center towering above the Caribbean—is the most beautiful. Nearby, the ancient city of Coba rises from the tropical jungle to look more like something out of Indiana Jones, while the most spectacular site, Chichén Itzá, a two-hour drive overland, is the most famous.

Or maybe you'd prefer to boat over to the sleepy island of Isla Mujeres, where you can eat lunch at a small seaside restaurant then snorkel off the south end of the island.

Mérida, capital of Yucatán state, makes an excellent base for exploring the Mayan ruins of Uxmal. Mérida, itself, a charming blend of large, white colonial buildings downtown and modern homes on the outskirts, developed a more European atmosphere. Before going out to explore the Mayan ruins, you'll want to visit the Museum of Archaeology and History housed in a former mansion.

Appreciating Local Culture

Too many people go to Mexico and never experience the local culture. Some eat only in chain or fast-food restaurants and don't experience Mexican food or culture. If you go to Mexico, you'll want to experience the local culture whenever you can.

To Market, to Market

One of the best places to soak up local culture is in *el mercado* or the Mexican market. Every town and many villages have one, sometimes held in a special building or held informally in the *zócalo*. Some occur daily, while others are held weekly on a particular day. You'll wander through a maze of stalls overflowing with exotic fruits, fragrant flowers, aromatic cheeses, colorful clothing, plucked chickens, and hanging meat.

 TRAVEL TIP

Many indoor markets have a food section called a *comedor*. While the food may look and smell delicious, and while most cubicles are clean, it's wise not to eat here. This type of service is similar to street vendors, who may not follow the best food-service health practices.

Hanging Out in the *Zócalo*

Every town and city in Mexico has a *zócalo* or main square. It's here that the local people gather to visit and gossip. Old or young, single or in couples, people take the time to sit on Victorian iron benches and talk or watch the children scampering about. Artists also gather here to paint portraits of people or town scenes. A favorite pastime in any Mexican city *zócalo* is to get your shoes shined and attended to by a professional shoe shiner.

A wrought-iron Victorian gazebo bandstand stands in the middle of many *zócalo*s. Here, you can sit and listen to band concerts on Saturday afternoons. Most *zócalo*s have been planted with large old, manicured trees, their trunks painted white to ward off insects, so everyone can find refuge from the afternoon heat. Some have fountains, also, and beautiful gardens. A colorful fixture on any *zócalo* is the balloon man, with his hundreds of multicolored balloons in the shapes of animals, a delight to all the children.

The largest *zócalo* in Mexico is Plaza de la Constitución in Mexico City. In fact, it's the second largest plaza in the world after Tiananmen Square in Beijing, China. Once known as the Plaza Mayor and later as the Plaza de Armas, Plaza de la Contitución isn't named for any of the constitutions that have governed Mexico but instead for the Cadiz Constitution that was signed in Spain in 1812.

Every Day Is a Fiesta

There's a fiesta just about every day in Mexico. The Mexican government estimates there are over 6,000 held annually in towns and villages all over Mexico. Of these, twenty-seven are considered major, lasting for several days and attracting thousands of people. In addition to these are the *carnavals* held before Lent in the cities of Veracruz and Mazatlán and a myriad of *ferias,* or agricultural fairs, held throughout the country.

═FAST FACT

Food is a main ingredient of every fiesta. It's a time when everyone forgets about dieting and enjoys themselves. *Los antojitos mexicanos,* the special dishes served at fiestas, are favorites of Mexican cooking. Most are made of corn, spicy, and cooked in a variety of ways. Other popular dishes served at fiestas include tamales, tacos, pozole, tostadas, enchiladas, and quesadillas.

The pre-Columbian people of Mexico worshiped many gods. When the Spanish missionaries forced Catholicism on them, they saw similarities between the rituals their own high priests performed and those of the Catholic Church. Today, the fiestas held all over Mexico are a blending of these two types of rituals, and nearly all have a basis in Catholicism. Processions, masses, and the reciting of rosaries are all part of the festivities. The Spaniards also introduced activities that gave a more entertaining side to the indigenous rituals. Besides music and dance and lots of good food, fiestas may have *charreadas*, bullfights, parades and gambling. Fiestas usually take place around the main square of a town or village.

Suggested Itineraries Within Mexico

Mexico is a big country with a lot to offer. You can't take it all in on one trip. Here are some suggested itineraries that focus on particular areas. You can travel each in approximately seven to ten days, or you can shorten or combine them according to your needs.

Mexico City Solo

Take the time and concentrate your trip on Mexico City. Explore its historic area, visit its museums, especially the Museum of Anthropology, and take in the Ballet Folklorico. Take a day tour to the ruins at Teotihuácan.

Mexico City, Guadalajara, Monterrey

If you like exploring cities, then you'll love visiting Mexico's three largest. There's plenty for your family to do in each. Begin in Mexico City, taking in its historic district and a museum or two, then it's off to Guadalajara to explore the huge downtown plaza and pedestrian mall. While you're there, browse through the Libertad Market. Last stop on this tour is Monterrey, a city with lots of things to do—rock-climbing north of the city, visiting Fundidora Park on the site of a former steel mill, or exploring Barrio Antiguo in the old part of the city.

Copper Canyon—Los Mochis to Chihuahua

To see one of the natural and man-made wonders of the Western Hemisphere, you can ride the Chihuahua al Pacifico Railway through Copper Canyon country in northern Mexico. It's been called the world's most scenic train ride. You'll ride through the Sierra Tarahumara, home of the Tarahumara Indians, traversing thirty-nine bridges and passing through eighty-six tunnels. The trip from either Los Mochis to Chihuahua takes approximately thirteen hours, with a stop about halfway at Divisadero so that you can get off the train briefly and take in the view.

Beach and City Combo

If your family likes the beach but also likes to delve into the history and culture of a place, why not split a week between the beach and Mexico City? Convenient flights make it possible to combine a stay in Mexico's capital with a stay in either Puerto Vallarta, Ixtapa, Mazatlán, Los Cabos, Acapulco, or Cancún.

Colonial Cities—Querétaro, San Miguel de Allende, Guanajuato

Located in Mexico's rich Bajio region north of Mexico City, these three colonial cities are rich in history. In Querétaro, visit the State Regional Museum, housed in a former convent, to get a glimpse of what life was like in the sixteenthth century and browse through jewelry shops showcasing locally mined opals. Next stop is San Miguel de Allende, home to a large U.S. expatriate population. This town bubbles over with charm. Why not take a Spanish or art course at the Intituto Allende while you're there? Your final stop is Guanajuato, a city built on the riches of silver mines, and a political hotbed during Mexico's fight for independence from Spain. Be sure to see a performance in the Teatro Juárez, a beautiful theater from the Belle Epoque era.

Budgeting Your Trip

When planning a trip to Mexico, it helps to know how much you can afford to spend. Put a dollar limit on your budget before you begin to make plans, and plan to stay within your allotted amount. The total amount you will spend will be determined by how far you want to travel, what type of accommodations you choose, what you want to see and do, and how you want to see things, either independently or in a group. While group travel may work for adults, it doesn't work well for families.

To figure a budget for your trip, you'll need to decide how many days you can travel based on the total amount you can afford to spend. If you want to travel in luxury, plan on spending $500 or more per day for each adult and half that for children. More moderate accommodations will cost $250 to $350 per day per adult if kids can stay free in their parents' room and more if they don't. Budget travel will cost $75 to $150 a day per adult, but only if your family camps in an RV. These figures apply to a-la-carte travel. Using travel packages can substantially reduce the total amount.

Budgeting for Your Family's Comfort Level

Unlike traveling in the United States or Canada, where budget hotels may provide good traveling comfort and amenities for your family, Mexican hotels in this category cater mostly to traveling Mexican salespeople, and they offer few amenities. You should travel at a comfort level that your family is used to at home; otherwise, your family members may find themselves quarreling a lot due to lack of rest and general dissatisfaction.

All-Inclusive or Pay as You Go?

The all-inclusive concept has taken off like a rocket in Mexico. While regular resorts often have the same facilities, nothing but accommodations can be paid for in advance. You need to carry lots of cash, traveler's checks, or credit cards to pay for all the extras, especially food, which is usually expensive. At an all-inclusive resort, like the Allegro Resorts in Mexico, about the only thing you'll have to watch is your weight and the sun. The all-inclusive price includes unlimited alcohol, soft drinks, and juices, the manager's cocktail party, entertainment, a kids' activity program, some scheduled on-site sports and activities, and clinics for all sports. Baby-sitting and other sports and activities may also be available for an additional fee.

Keeping Your Family Safe in Mexico

Based on media reports in the last few years, you may think traveling in Mexico is dangerous. While problems have arisen in certain areas, the majority of cities and towns in Mexico are very safe. However, there are those who prey on tourists—thieves, pickpockets, and scam artists. A little common sense goes a long way to keeping your family safe while traveling in Mexico.

First and foremost, guard your money and valuables. Many of the better hotels have safes in the room. If not, ask if you can keep your valuables in the hotel safe. If you're carrying traveler's checks, keep the receipts in a safe place and not with the checks. Don't carry your wallet in an obvious place, and don't leave it anywhere. The same goes for cameras. When you leave your room, put any item that's important either in the safe or in your suitcase, and lock it.

If you're driving, park your car in an enclosure or parking garage at night. Place any valuables in the trunk. Don't tempt fate.

CHAPTER 4

Getting There

EVERYONE PLANNING TO VISIT Mexico must obtain a *tarjeta de turista* (tourist card). If you're flying to Mexico, the stewards on your plane will hand out tourist cards and customs-and-immigration forms on the plane before you land. If you're driving into Mexico, you can obtain one at the border or at any AAA office in the border states—California, Arizona, New Mexico, and Texas. Tourist cards are free and valid for ninety days. When you arrive in Mexico, the immigration officer who validates the card will ask you your destination in Mexico and how long you plan to stay, then he or she will tear off a portion and give that back to you. You should carry that portion with you at all times. It's a good idea to keep it inside your passport. If you lose your tourist card, it's a hassle to get another, and you may have to pay a fine. When you leave Mexico, you must turn it in.

It's Time to Go

It's imperative to plan your trip to Mexico. This section will cover what you need to know about planning a safe and relaxing vacation.

Pack Light or Heavy?

The kind of clothes you pack depends on where you go and the weather. Generally, Mexico is an informal country, so casual clothes are fine. Larger cities like Mexico, Monterrey, and Guadalajara may require something a little nicer for dining out in better restaurants. And don't forget to pack an umbrella and a lightweight raincoat if you plan on being in Mexico from May to October, during the rainy season.

If your travels take you to Mexico City or the central highlands during the winter months, the temperature can drop to the mid-20s at night. You'll want to dress in layers since the sun can warm things up during the afternoons.

TRAVEL TIP

Make a list of valuables you're carrying with you, including jewelry, serial numbers of cameras, serial numbers on your traveler's checks, and credit card numbers. Leave one copy at home and pack one in your luggage, and carry a third in your wallet or purse. Also, make a copy of your passport photo page and put that in your luggage.

Traveling with Little Ones

Mexicans love children and take their own everywhere. The family is the cornerstone of Mexican life. So hotels and restaurants gladly welcome little ones. Pace your travels keeping your child in mind. Avoid fast-paced tours, and keep travel time as short as possible. Kids love to visit zoos, markets, plazas, aquariums, and the like, so be sure to include some in your itinerary.

FAST FACT

You must have notarized permission from your spouse or a guardianship document, divorce papers, or death certificate if you're traveling alone with your child in Mexico. Your child won't be able to board the plane without it.

And don't forget that packing for your kids, especially toddlers, requires some additional items. While you'll find disposable diapers, baby food, and medicines available in larger towns and cities, you should remember to pack a lightweight folding stroller, papoose-style backpack, a life jacket and beach toys, and a car seat if you're going to drive anywhere. And don't forget some handwipes and extra plastic bags for dirty diapers.

Can You Drink the Water?

It used to be that just about everyone that traveled to Mexico got a case of Moctezuma's revenge, commonly called *turista,* from drinking water tainted with a form of E. coli bacteria. But in recent years, the Mexican congress has passed laws requiring anyone serving the public to serve purified water. However, according to a recent study by the Office of Medical Applications of Research, 20 to 50 percent of travelers to Mexico are still getting sick. Is it just the water? The answer is a complicated no.

The leading cause of discomfort, *Escherichia coli,* otherwise known as E. coli bacteria, can be ingested in food as well as water. While many attacks can be blamed on unpurified water, just as many can be caused by unsanitary food-handling and unfamiliar spices.

TRAVEL TIP

Abstain from eating purely Mexican food—especially anything made with *chiles*—as well as any tropical fruit for the first twenty-four hours you're in Mexico to give your digestive system time to acclimate. Papaya fruit and juice is especially bad and should be avoided for a couple of days.

You should also refrain from drinking fancy alcoholic drinks and eating rich foods for the first few days. If you have to drink, Mexican beers and wines are best, served cold without ice. Remember that tequila sold and enjoyed in the United States isn't as strong as it is in Mexico. Plus, Mexicans drink slower than visitors, who often drink at the speed they're used to back home, not realizing the heat can affect them.

Even the Mexicans agree that one of the best solutions to *turista* is common Pepto Bismol (bismuth subsalicylate), either in liquid or tablet form. However, recent tests have shown that there can be severe side effects if this medication is taken too often. Another product, Imodium D, seems to work better and faster, without the accompanying side effects.

Episodes of *turista* begin abruptly, often without warning. They can occur during travel as well as after returning home and aren't contagious. The most common day of onset is the third day after arrival in Mexico, but onset may occur at any time during the visit and even after returning home.

Both cooked and uncooked foods may be implicated if improperly handled. Especially risky foods include raw vegetables, raw meat, and raw seafood. Tap water, ice, unpasteurized milk and dairy products, and unpeeled fruits are also associated with an increased risk of *turista.*

Depending on how long you go without treatment after the infectious bacteria have entered your digestive tract, the effects can be severe. So if it strikes, head for the nearest First Class pharmacy, with a pharmacist who speaks English or with a Mexican to interpret for you. This is no time to practice your Spanish. One of the best local medicines is a green chalky liquid sold under the name of Diarim.

 TRAVEL TIP

One of the best ways to prevent *turista* is to take acidophilus (the bacteria in yogurt) tablets several days before going to Mexico. This builds up the bacteria in your digestive tract and helps prevent or at least lessen *turista's* effects. You'll find acidophilus sold in capsule and chewable tablet form at all health-food stores, drugstores, and supermarkets. There are no side effects.

Bottled water is available just about anywhere, even in the smallest *tienda* (shop). When in doubt, ask for *agua purificada* or *agua minerale*. Today, just about all restaurants serve bottled water. Better restaurants also use purified water for ice. And while the law requires all hotels to leave sealed bottles of purified water for their guests, you should know that five-star hotels will add as much as $3 a bottle to your bill if you open them.

Using purified water applies not only to drinking but to brushing your teeth and rinsing your contact lenses. Above all, wash your hands as often as possible, especially before meals. Always carry some disposable antibacterial handwipes for when you can't. It doesn't pay to get paranoid about getting a case of *turista*, but a little common sense goes a long way.

Getting to Mexico by Air

The fastest, most convenient way to travel to Mexico is by air. At least eight different commercial airlines fly into Mexico on regularly scheduled flights. All fly to Mexico City and many fly directly to other destinations as well. Depending on where you're flying from, it may be difficult to find a nonstop flight, and the flight may take many hours. Be prepared to allow a full day for travel in both directions.

If you're planning on traveling during the winter, you might consider taking a charter flight, usually sold as a package. Apple Vacations, Gogo Tours, and Friendly Holidays all operate charters to Mexican beach resorts.

Domestic flights are available to all larger and many smaller cities in Mexico on either of the national airlines, Mexicana or Aeromexico, or their subsidiaries. Generally, costs for domestic flights remain higher, so it's best to plan your itinerary carefully and book your flights in advance before leaving home to save money.

Prepackaged Trips

Travel packages, generally priced per person, offer you the best way to save money on the high cost of travel to Mexico. Some include only flights and hotel accommodations, while others may include car rentals or sightseeing options. Packages to the beach resorts offer the best value during the high season, from mid-December until after Easter. However, you may find off-season packages to be downright bargains.

TRAVEL TIP

To know if you're getting a good deal on a package, call or check the airline's Web site for the cost of a round-trip flight, then do the same for a hotel, car rental, and so on. Don't forget to add in the cost of round-trip airport transfers, which can be as high as $25 per person. If the total cost is more than the package, then you've got a good deal.

Airport Information

In the last several years, Mexico's Federal Airport Administration (ASA) has embarked on a major improvement program for the twenty-eight major airports in the country. Besides new seating, new concessions, and overall facelifts, the behind-the-scenes services have also been improved for better security and more efficient operations. For information in English on any of Mexico's airports, go to ✍*www .aeropuertosmexico.com/Ingles*.

Mexico City Airport

The Benito Juárez International Airport, as the Mexico City airport is officially known, handles over 5,000 passengers an hour. Located just eight miles east of the city center, it's convenient enough to the downtown area to catch a taxi and visit a museum if you have a long enough layover.

Though the airport has just one long terminal with six different concourses, new improvements are making it not only beautiful but extremely easy to get around. Currently, eleven airlines from the United States and Canada fly into Mexico City.

If you're renting a car, the airport has all the major U.S. companies. If not, the best way to get into the city is by Taxi Autorizado, whose white-and-mustard-yellow taxis can be found on the ground floor at the end of Concourse A. Trips on this taxi are prepaid. You can also catch one of the many hotel shuttle buses.

Flying into Regional Airports

You can now fly directly to many of Mexico's regional airports. Private companies now run the Monterrey, Guadalajara, and Cancún international airports, and all facilities have been renovated to provide excellent services. Aeropuerto del Sureste, the private company that operates the Cancún Airport, has invested nearly $45 million to upgrade security, expand check-in facilities, and open additional restaurants. With improvements like this happening all over the country, it's wiser to fly directly into Mexico's smaller regional airports if possible rather than to connect through Mexico City.

Driving to Mexico?

Driving is the best way to explore out-of-the-way places in Mexico. Today, it's easier to drive in Mexico since a $5-billion highway improvement program has added thousands of miles of new highways called *autopistas* (freeways) and *autopistas de cuota* (toll roads), which connect Mexico's cities with each other and the beach resorts. However, you'll miss a lot if you drive these exclusively. Also, these roads usually have no shoulders or places to pull off if you have an emergency. Be aware that rural roads may be in poor condition with ruts and deep potholes. Remember to drive at a slower speed than at home and always with caution, no matter what kind of road you're traveling.

One thing you will run into or over in Mexico are *topes* (speed control bumps). You'll find them on many two-lane highways in a variety of sizes, from slight to gigantic. The Mexicans use these "silent policemen" to slow down traffic before and in towns and villages. Unfortunately, many aren't marked with warning signs. They're a part of driving in Mexico, and you won't go far without experiencing them. If traveling by car, bring the following along:

- Your driver's license
- Car title
- Vehicle registration
- Insurance card
- Maps
- Flashlight with extra batteries
- Tire jack and pump
- Spare tire
- Spare radiator hoses
- Spare fan belts
- Emergency flasher
- Gallon gas can
- Tire pressure gauge
- Jumper cables
- First-aid kit
- Extra car keys
- Sunglasses (plus an extra pair)
- Extra water

Never drive at night in Mexico, except on four-lane toll roads and then with extreme caution. Mexicans often drive with broken headlamps or forget to turn them on. Animals stray onto the roads. Also, rural roads are poorly marked and badly lit, if at all.

If you're in a serious accident, contact the local police and file a report with your Mexican insurance company. You and your car will be held by the Mexican police, whether you're guilty or not, until payment of claims and damages is received.

Taking Your Car

Before driving your vehicle into Mexico, you must obtain a free temporary car importation permit and purchase auto insurance from a Mexican company. You may be delayed if you don't adhere to these simple entry requirements:

- Bring along proof of U.S. citizenship, such as your passport or birth certificate.
- Obtain a Mexican tourist card (a form all travelers to Mexico must fill out before entering Mexico) and get it stamped at immigration.
- Provide U.S. proof of vehicle ownership, such as your car's original title or registration. Photocopies aren't sufficient.
- You'll also need an international credit card such as Visa, Mastercard, or American Express, in the name of the car owner, along with a valid driver's license. A $27 fee will be charged on your card to the Banco Nacional del Ejercito.
- If you lease or finance your car, you must also bring a notarized letter from the bank or finance company giving you permission to take your car into Mexico.

A slip for your credit card will be filled out in the amount of a bond—as much as $400—in case you fail to return your car to the United States within the specified time period. You need to present all these documents at the Mexican customs office at the border, where you'll be given a temporary permit, valid for up to six months. Your driver's license is valid in Mexico as long as you drive your own or a rented car.

≡FAST FACT

More than a thousand Los Angeles Verdes (Green Angels) operate service centers, radio-equipped vehicles, mobile repair vans, and radio bases throughout Mexico. They patrol 234 designated routes in green-and-white trucks from 8 A.M. to 8 P.M. Service is free, but you'll have to pay for gas, oil, and spare parts. All are trained paramedics. In case of emergency, just raise your car hood and wait.

Though you can take two vehicles into Mexico, such as a car and a motorhome, a separate permit and charge is required for each vehicle. If you need assistance in preparing your materials to enter Mexico by car, you can stop into any AAA office in Texas, Arizona, New Mexico, or California. Finally, you must leave Mexico with your car and turn in your permit at the end of your trip. Leaving the country without your car, should you have an emergency, is difficult.

Insurance

Even though your auto insurance is not valid in Mexico, Mexican law requires you to carry your insurance card or a copy of the declaration page of your policy with you. In addition, you'll have to purchase special insurance from a Mexican insurance company at the border or a company that can write a Mexican policy covering the length of your stay in Mexico (such as Sanborn's Mexico Insurance Service of McAllen, Texas; ☎800-222-0158 or on the Web at ✐*www.sanborns insurance.com*). Make sure you're covered for liability and property damage, as well as theft, at a minimum. Though this insurance is more expensive than in the United States, get as much as you can afford. Most policies come with instructions in case you have an accident.

≡FAST FACT

Special car insurance is essential for driving in Mexico because the country bases its laws on the Napoleonic Code—guilty until proven innocent.

If you have an accident, you could spend time in jail until the police establish whose fault it is. If you have this insurance, damages will be paid regardless of whose fault it is. Above all, don't stop to assist if you witness an accident. Instead, contact the nearest Green Angel patrol. Red tape in Mexico can tie you up for a long time.

Taking Your RV

More and more families are taking their RVs or campers to Mexico. It's possible to pull off the road and camp just about anywhere. Steep, narrow mountain roads and sharp curves can present problems for large trailers. However, a well-equipped camper like a Winnebago, complete with a portable toilet, propane stove and refrigerator, bed, and two five-gallon water containers will let you travel independently anywhere in the country. It also helps to install oversized tires on your vehicle for better traction and shocks to handle heavy loads when driving over rough roads. If you're towing a small car behind your rig, you'll need to get a separate permit for it.

CHAPTER 5

Hotel or Five-Star Spa?

MEXICO OFFERS A VARIETY of hotels to suit every need and budget, ranging from budget accommodations to posh resorts. You can even stay in an old hacienda. Today, practically all hotels catering to families offer modern accommodations and American-style service. But underneath it all, it's the hospitality of the Mexicans that makes the difference. This seems to show off best in low-rise rather than high-rise hotels and in Mexican and European chains rather than American ones. The country has experienced enormous tourism growth in the last decade, and with that has come an increase in the number and types of hotels.

It's extremely important to make reservations even if you're traveling in the off-peak season. But it's doubly important if you plan on staying in Mexico either before Christmas or two weeks before and after Easter; in those cases, book four to six months ahead. Make sure you have a confirmation in writing from the hotel. If you book through a travel agency, be sure to ask for a copy of the confirmation they received.

How to Know Your Family's Needs

Before you book a hotel in Mexico, it's important to know your family's needs. While there are many chain hotels that offer standardized accommodations and services you've come to know and trust, you also have a myriad of resorts, inns, and spas from which to choose. The Mexican government has divided hotels into the following seven categories according to the level of service:

- *Categoria Especial* (Special Category), reserved for hotels with distinct features or locations
- *Gran Turismo* (Grand Tourist—deluxe), for those hotels offering the most amenities and superior service
- Five- to one-star, based on the number of amenities offered— number of restaurants, pools, spa, exercise rooms, air conditioning, and so on.

In Mexico, you should book your family into nothing less than a three-star hotel. Most packages feature three-star hotels and above.

Today, just about all Mexican resort hotels feature a high level of service, as well as beautifully landscaped grounds with gardens, swimming pools, tennis courts, several restaurants, discos, and game rooms for the kids. Some also come with full eighteen-hole golf courses. While it used to be that most travelers could afford to stay in a luxurious resort, sipping margaritas by a bright blue pool, today these same resorts can be pricey for families, even with packaged travel. Even though most Mexican hotels allow children under twelve years of age to stay free in their parents' room, you need to decide what sort of amenities your family will be comfortable with. If you're not sure, then perhaps booking a week at an all-inclusive resort might be the answer. Ultimately, the age and interests of your children will determine what sort of hotel you choose.

Are There Programs for Children?

Since the Mexicans travel with their own families, you'll find programs for children at many hotels and resorts throughout Mexico. These can range from simple baby-sitting services to full-blown day-care programs with classes, various types of lessons, and field trips. The latter is fine if you and your spouse want to take your children along but want some time for yourselves.

While many three-star hotels have playgrounds and children's pools and perhaps a game room, you'll usually find supervised programs for children at four-stars and above.

Mexico's leading hotel chain, Posadas de Mexico, offers a weekend "Fiesta Kids" program for kids aged four to twelve at its Fiesta Americana Hotels. Both Fiesta Americana resorts in Cancún offer the same program daily. Another Mexican chain, Camino Real Hotels, offers its "Club Travesuras" program, including crafts, movies, games, and food for kids during holiday seasons (Christmas and Spring Break/Easter) to children whose parents purchase a vacation package. Marriott Casa Magna Hotels features its "Club Amigos" program, with field trips and activities for younger children.

You'll find the best programs for kids at Mexico's all-inclusive hotels. The premiere program belongs to Club Med. Its "Kids Club" for kids aged four through twelve features all sorts of activities geared to kids. Allegro Resorts offers a unique program, "Rookies," which helps to make traveling with kids affordable. Club Maeva, a Mexican all-inclusive that caters to American and Canadian families in winter and Mexican families in summer, offers a daily comprehensive kids program, including horseback riding, clay sculpture, video games, and pretend camping, for children aged two through twelve.

Activities for Older Kids?

Unfortunately, you'll find few organized programs for teens. Club Med has a "Junior's Club," available during school holidays, for those thirteen to nineteen. But if you're traveling with teens, you should plan a trip that actively includes them. Mexico has plenty to offer the inquisitive teenager. Adventure travel has become big business, so you'll find many activities suited to your active teens, like hiking, river rafting, and climbing—even climbing around ancient ruins. Find out what they're interested in, and let them be a part of the planning process.

Keeping It Affordable

As stated above, children stay free in their parents' room at most hotels in Mexico. But that only applies to those under twelve. If you're going to be traveling with teenagers, then you'll have to pay extra for them. Some families choose to reserve adjoining rooms so that the kids can stay in one and the parents in the other. Because Mexicans travel with their families, you'll discover that most Mexican hotels have adjoining rooms.

The best way to keep costs down is to either book a package or stay for at least seven days. Often hotel owners will give you a discount if you stay a week or longer. Staying at a three- or four-star hotel on a package will usually be less expensive than at a five-star (though not always), but it will have fewer amenities.

Picking the Right Vacation Scenario

How you choose to travel on your vacation with your family depends on the ages of your children. If you have kids six and under, you should consider staying at one hotel and exploring the area around it rather than traveling from one to another. The more you pack and unpack, the more younger children get agitated. Younger children are also affected more by the heat and humidity, as well as altitude, so you'll need to give them time to acclimate.

Bedrooms Versus Fully Equipped Suites

If you're traveling with younger children, it may be best to stay in a fully equipped suite. Similar to a small apartment, they offer your children a place that seems more like home. A standard hotel room can be limiting. With its small kitchen, this type of accommodation also allows you to prepare snacks or food just for the kids. While some people may not consider cooking part of a vacation, it can get expensive to eat out for every meal with young children. Preparing a simple breakfast and picnic lunches will go a long way to keeping your younger kids content.

Condo/Villa Rentals

If you don't like the controlled environment of an all-inclusive resort, you may want to consider renting a villa or condominium at Akumal along the Riviera Maya, in Ixtapa, or in Puerto Vallarta. Most villas come with four to six bedrooms, so your extended family can come along, too.

All-Inclusive Resorts

One of Mexico's most popular all-inclusives, the El Cozumeleño Bounty, on the island of Cozumel, advertises, "Bring nothing. Get everything." Sounds good, doesn't it, especially if you have two or more kids in tow—one price, no surprises, leave your wallet at home. That's an irresistible combination, especially to families with kids, since many also include day care and other activities.

But you shouldn't take the term "all-inclusive" at face value. In Mexico, all-inclusive generally means all meals, most on-site land-based activities, and alcoholic drinks at meals and sometimes between. Most charge for imported liquor and some charge for wine with meals. Likewise, some charge for water sports, while others include everything as long as it is part of a scheduled activity. Spanish companies, including Iberostar, Barceló, Occidental-Allegro, and Sol Melia, own and operate many of them. The following is a list of the main all-inclusive chains operating in Mexico:

- Allegro Resorts (*www.allegroresorts.com*)
- Barceló (*www.barcelo.com*)
- Blue Bay All-Inclusive Resorts (*www.bluebayresorts.com*)
- Club Maeva (*www.clubmaeva.com.mx*)
- Club Med (*www.clubmed.com*)
- Iberostar (*www.iberostar.com*)
- Palace Resorts (*www.palaceresorts.com*)
- Qualton Hotels and Resorts (*www.qualton.com*)
- Riu Hotels (*www.riu.com*)
- Sol Melia (*www.solmelia.com*)

The per-person price at all-inclusive resorts provides not only accommodations, but often airfare in some sort of package, besides meals, drinks, and activities, so usually they offer good value for families. They operate on the same concept as cruise ships. But there are many versions of all-inclusives, and some include more than others. And many cater to a particular type of guest. Not all cater to families. Out of more than 100 all-inclusive resorts in Mexico, thirty-four cater to families.

While in the Caribbean, it's often difficult to go out for meals, so you end up eating most of them at your hotel. Because you're a captive audience, food is often high priced and of poor quality. This isn't so in Mexico. All-inclusive resorts here are usually located in resort areas with lots of restaurants and attractions. The main reason families choose to stay at all-inclusives is the affordable price. And when you're traveling with ever-hungry kids, having food available all day for one price is a definite plus.

Club Med was the pioneer of the all-inclusive concept. Originally, it had an image of a swinging singles resort, but now that's all changed, with many catering to families—those in Mexico are some of the best in the chain. Unlike other Mexican all-inclusives, Club Med resorts all follow the same routine, regardless of where they're located, but only Club Med Ixtapa caters to families in Mexico with four kids programs—Baby Club Med (for infants four to twenty-three months), Petit Club Med (for kids two to three), Mini Club Med (for kids four to ten), and Junior Club Med (for kids eleven to seventeen). Club Med's all-inclusive price includes all meals, snacks, drinks—premium alcohol, as well as sodas, coffees, and teas—all water sports, entertainment, and tips, giving you a true wallet-free vacation. But Club Med vacations can be regimented, and therefore they're not to everyone's taste.

The popularity of all-inclusive resorts makes it imperative that you book well in advance. Winter weekly rates range from $1,470 per person plus airfare at Allegro Resorts to $1,505 per person for a week at Club Med, including airfare.

New or Converted All-Inclusives

Many of the all-inclusives that have opened in Mexico are newly built, but some were formerly resorts that didn't prosper. After converting to the all-inclusive concept, all have become successful. However, a converted hotel may not be as good as one built as an all-inclusive.

Many converted properties are beachfront hotels—especially in Cancún—that don't have the physical space of all-inclusives in other parts of the Caribbean. While some all-inclusive hotels are isolated, in places like Cancún there's a lot to do outside the hotel.

Kitchens of a 1,000-room converted hotel may be designed to feed only 40 percent of the guests. This can cause long waiting times and poor service.

TRAVEL TIP

In Mexico, be careful of hotels that offer a mix of all-inclusive and standard European plans. It's hard for a bartender not to wait first on the customer he knows will tip him rather than on the all-inclusive guest whose identifying ribbon or armband announces "no tip."

Before you book an all-inclusive resort, do your homework. Your family will thank you for it.

Where Are They?

Though you'll find all-inclusive resorts in Puerto Vallarta, Ixtapa, Cozumel, and Manzanillo, the majority of them are in Cancún and along the Riviera Maya.

What Is There to Do and See Nearby?

Limiting your family to spending time only at the resort will detract from your enjoyment of Mexico. Plan on excursions to nearby towns or attractions, often highlighted in the resort brochures. Once you are at the resort, ask the concierge about local attractions.

Mexico's Top Ten Family Resorts/Destinations

Mexico has so much to offer families that it's hard to pick the top destinations. As you will see below, however, some offer more for families than others.

Acapulco

Acapulco is now one of Mexico's true family resorts. The magnificent beach that frames Acapulco Bay has calm water, though you may want to swim in beachside pools instead. Since the four-lane toll road opened from Mexico City, Mexican families come here by the droves on weekends. The resort has responded with affordable restaurants and lots for kids to do. One of the biggest family attractions is the fifty-two-acre Papagayo Park, with carnival rides, an aviary, and a replica of a Spanish galleon—all for free. Ci Ci Aquatic Park, with aquarium, animal show, wave-maker and water slide, plus Mágic Mundo Marino, another splendid water park, provide fun for the entire family. Fort San Diego, one of the oldest attractions, is suddenly new since the installation of an excellent exhibit telling the story of the trade route from Spain to China. Your kids will love climbing the ramparts while you and your spouse learn about history. And let's not forget Acapulco's famous cliff divers.

Cancún

One of Mexico's newest resorts, this beach destination has everything you need to make your vacation complete—lots of restaurants, loads of shopping, and a variety of sporting facilities. It's a great place to use as a base for exploration of nearby sites. You can take a quick ferry ride over to the island of Isla Mujeres for the day to snorkel or just sit by the waterfront and watch the boats come in and out. Or you might want to take a tour to Tulum or Coba, two nearby archaeological sites, and Chichén Itzá, one a bit further away. If you're interested in nature, then you'll enjoy a boat trip to Isla Contoy, a bird sanctuary. To complete the marine theme, there are also excursions aboard the floating submarines *Nautilus I* and *II,* the Atlantis Submarine, and the minisub Sub Sea Explorer. If you enjoy water parks, then head for Aquaworld, a fully equipped water sports center and theme park.

Colonial Cities

Though most families head to one of Mexico's beach resorts for their vacation, some have discovered the charm and rich history of its colonial cities, most of which you'll find in central Mexico. The most popular of these cities, San Miguel de Allende and Guanajuato, attract visitors for entirely different reasons. The first has a large American and Canadian expatriate community, with opportunities for learning Spanish and various arts and crafts. The second, Mexico's most successful mining town, gives you a chance to explore Mexican culture to the fullest. Both these cities, as well as a number of others, offer fine museums with artistic and historical treasures, superb architecture, murals, and historic monuments. Three learning institutions in San Miguel focus on the arts, literature, and language instruction. Its most famous structure, La Parroquia Church, dominates the central square of El Jardin. Guanajuato, on the other hand, features a labyrinth of winding streets and an underground highway built on a former riverbed. As one of Mexico's most Spanish-looking cities, Guanajuato offers you a chance to visit a silver mine or attend a performance in a Victorian-style theater.

Copper Canyon

The city of Chihuahua sits in the middle of the Chihuahua Desert. Begin at Qunita Luz, Pancho Villa's home, now the Museo de la Revolución (Museum of the Revolution), to see the bullet-ridden car he was driving when he was assassinated. Then catch the Chihuahua al Pacifico Railroad train for a ride through the Barranca de Cobre (Copper Canyon), four times larger than the Grand Canyon. Many consider the rail line to be one of the greatest engineering feats of the twentieth century. Two hundred gorges link to form a series of six interconnected canyons. You should stop along the way to visit Creel and see the culture of the Tarahumara Indians and further on, stop at Bahuichivo to take a wild ride to the bottom of one of the canyons to visit the former mining town of Batopilas. If your family loves adventure, this is the place.

Cozumel

Though Cozumel is known for its excellent diving and snorkeling opportunities, it also offers other attractions. Its main town, San Miguel, offers a variety of restaurants and shops lining its *malecón*, or pier. A must-see stop is the Museum of the Island of Cozumel, which houses exhibits on the natural and anthropological history of the island. It also offers Mayan language classes and crafts demonstrations. If you like to snorkel, then you should immediately head to Chankanaab Park, a beachside paradise for sunning and snorkeling with a botanical garden and archaeological park. Beyond Chankanaab, you'll find Punta Sur, an ecological reserve with mangrove swamps and a lighthouse, plus a turtle reserve where your family can learn about sea turtles. The island is not without several Mayan sites. The best preserved is San Gervasio, with its temples to the Mayan goddess of medicine and El Cedral; the oldest have remnants of Mayan wall paintings. Your children will enjoy taking a Jeep tour along the island's back roads, a ride in a catamaran, or a glass-bottomed boat cruise. You'll also find a carbon copy of Cancún's Aquaworld, as well as Atlantis and Sub Sea Explorer underwater excursions.

Ixtapa/Zihuatanejo

This dual destination offers both sunny beaches as well as the charm of a fishing village. Like Cancún, the Mexican government created Ixtapa in the 1970s. About the only thing to see or do besides lounging under a palapa on the beach is to take advantage of the Marina Ixtapa's boat, tennis, and golf facilities. The eighteen-hole golf course is of a unique links design similar to golfing between grass-covered dunes much as they originally did in Scotland. But you'll want to head for the village of Zihuatanejo to see more of the real Mexico. Here, you'll find unusual shops, affordable eateries, a traditional marketplace, and seaside cafés serving grilled shrimp. Beautiful beaches line Zihuatanejo Bay. From here, you can take short boat trips to either Isla Ixtapa, with its four beaches, or to Playa Las Gatas on the outermost tip of the bay, where you'll discover great snorkeling and seafood served at open-air seaside restaurants. Ixtapa also has its own water park, Magic World Aquatic Park, featuring a giant pirate ship with water slides. But your family might also enjoy cycling on the six-mile bike path, horseback riding along the beaches in Zihuatanejo, deep-sea fishing, diving at over fifty dive sites, or playing golf on either of two excellent eighteen-hole courses.

Mazatlán

This active beach town is Mexico's answer to Daytona Beach. While Spring Break partiers descend upon it from March to May, it's a great place to bring your family the rest of the year. Broad sandy beaches are just one attraction. You'll enjoy taking your family to the aquarium and botanical gardens, where your children can learn about undersea life. A trained seal show and tanks containing over 250 species will captivate your children. To see Mazatlán at its best, you can take a harbor tour, visiting Old Mazatlán and the city market en route. You can also stroll along the malecón, the seaside promenade that connects Mazatlán's Zona Dorada (tourist zone) with the old part of town. To get a glimpse of Mexico's colonial past, you can take an all-day tour traveling along a scenic highway to the towns of Concordia and Copala.

Mexico City

As one of the most exciting and vibrant cities in the world, Mexico City has a lot to offer families. Beginning at the *zócalo* with a visit to the National Palace to see the murals by Diego Rivera, you can wander around this historic area taking in the cathedral and the Templo Mayor, the remains of the main pyramid of Tenochtitlán.

Or you can all hop aboard a sightseeing trolley to get an overview of the area. You can spend an entire day exploring the sights from the *zócalo* to the Monument to the Revolution. On your other days, you can visit Chapultepec Park and the must-see National Museum of Anthropology, Chapultepec Castle, and the zoo to see a family of Chinese panda bears. Further out are the Shrine to the Virgin of Guadalupe, the floating gardens of Xochimilco and the new ecological park, and the pyramids of Teotihuacán.

Puerto Vallarta

One of the best all-round Mexican beach resorts, Puerto Vallarta has something for everyone. If you've never been to Mexico or have experienced Cancún and are looking for a place that's more Mexican, Puerto Vallarta may be for you. Originally a fishing village, the town received international notoriety when John Houston chose it as the site for his film, *Night of the Iguana.* Since then, development hasn't stopped. The *malecón* is the center of life in Old Vallarta. You can either eat in a balconied restaurant overlooking the sea or watch the fishermen cleaning their catch along the beach. Or you might choose to visit the local market. You'll find lots of interesting shops on Cuale River Island in the center of town. And the town of Vallarta has enough good family restaurants that you can eat in a different one for every meal. You can also take a horseback tour inland to visit small villages or eat and play in exotic restaurants set in the nearby jungle. If you want to get away from the hustle and bustle of Puerto Vallarta, you can take a boat trip down the coast to Yelapa, a romantic seaside cove where you can swim, eat, or have your photo taken with an iguana. During the winter months, you can go whale watching along the coast to look for humpback whales.

Riviera Maya

The newest development in Mexico is taking place along the coast of the state of Quintana Roo, south of Cancún. Known as the Riviera Maya, it once offered a string of secluded beaches looking out on the turquoise-blue Caribbean Sea. But the popularity of Cancún and its tremendous growth in the 1990s brought in a younger crowd, spurring the development of chic, upscale resorts and all-inclusives along the coast south toward Tulum. Today, a four-lane highway links Cancún to the region. The once sleepy town of Playa del Carmen has become a tourist boomtown overnight. Besides its main archaeological site of Tulum, you can also visit the one at nearby Coba. To further enhance your Riviera Maya experience, you'll enjoy a visit to Xcaret, a former ranch converted into an ecological park, with theme park, zoo, two rivers for floating or snorkeling, and a lagoon for swimming with dolphins. Be aware that this *is not* a budget attraction.

Further down the coast is Xel-Há, a natural aquarium fed by springs and underground rivers that offers excellent snorkeling. Because the archaeological site of Tulum is the most accessible to tourists from Cancún and the Riviera Maya, it's overrun with tour buses much of the time. The only seaside Mayan site, it features over sixty buildings, most of them small temples. One of the most unique attractions along the coast is Sian Ka'an Biosphere Reserve, a 1.3-million-acre ecological park traversed by canals built by the Maya. You'll enjoy taking a boat trip through its lagoons and canals to experience one of the Western Hemisphere's great wilderness areas.

CHAPTER 6

Taking a Cruise Ship to Mexico

FOR SOME PEOPLE, the best vacation is a cruise. And what better way to get to Mexico than on a luxurious ship with all sorts of activities to keep your family happy en route. Today's cruise ships are like floating hotels, offering a variety of activities and fine food, all at a moderate cost. And cruising to Mexico allows you time to relax between sightseeing, all for an all-inclusive price.

What to Expect

Cruising is a great way to travel with your family. It keeps everyone together while providing a variety of activities to keep everyone happy. Your kids will find lots to keep them occupied while you relax reading by the pool or in the spa. And with hungry kids along, having all meals and entertainment included is a definite plus. But what many people like most about a cruise is that they only have to pack and unpack once—it's like staying in the same resort for your entire vacation. And one of the greatest advantages to cruising is that you can go swimming, play games, hit golf balls, and climb walls, all while you're traveling to your destination.

But if you've never taken a cruise, there are a few things you should know. While your cruise price includes accommodations, meals, and entertainment, it doesn't include port charges, ports-of-call tours, photographs taken by the ship's photographer, drinks (including alcoholic beverages, sodas, and specialty coffees), spa treatments, exercise classes, medical services, and gratuities. While you'll be able to use your credit cards for shipboard purchases, it's a good idea to bring along some cash to use when exploring your ports of call. And today's ships all have ATMs onboard.

 TRAVEL TIP

When booking your cruise, ask about a guaranteed upgrade. You reserve and pay for whatever cabin you choose, but on the day of departure, if the ship isn't fully booked, you'll be upgraded to the next highest priced cabin. Not all cruise lines offer this option, and those that do offer it only on certain sailings.

Tipping on your cruise can become an expensive affair for your family if you follow most cruise lines's guidelines. Most suggest you leave a total tip of $10 per person per day. For a seven-day cruise for a family of four, that would add up to $280. Many lines provide envelopes addressed to various types of personnel into which you can deposit your tip. It's usual to tip your cabin steward the most since he or she does the most for you. Next comes your waiter. Since your waiter will be serving you only at dinner, tip accordingly. Other than that, you should tip anyone who provides you with exceptional service after they perform the service—baby-sitters, salon staff, tour guides, and so on. Some lines insist you tip the maitre'd in the dining room. If that person goes out of their way to seat you at a special table or provides some other service, then by all means leave a tip.

Cruising today is an informal affair for the most part, so you won't have to bring along formal clothes, especially on the family-friendly ships. For dress-up nights, men should bring along a coat and tie and women a dress. Children should look dressed up, too. If you're not into dressing up for dinner, many ships have casual dining areas where you can have a more relaxed meal.

Today's cruise ships have three types of accommodations—inside cabins with no windows, outside cabins with windows, and suites. Most regular cabins are the same size on the newer ships, though inside cabins may be smaller. While most cabins will accommodate four people, you'll find them a bit cramped. Cabins usually come with twin, double, or queen-sized beds, a fold-out sleeper sofa, and another single bed that folds out of the wall or ceiling. Family-friendly ships, like those of the Disney Cruise Line, offer family cabins that sleep six but would be comfortable for four (two adults and two small children). Children must be at least six months old to sail.

Before, dining on a cruise ship meant eating with the same people at your table for all three meals every day. Today, while you'll usually have an assigned table for dinner, you can eat at other venues onboard, including twenty-four-hour room service, for other meals. Some ships allow their adult passengers the option of eating at a more upscale restaurant for an additional fee of $10 or $20.

All modern cruise ships feature some sort of theater for showing movies and putting on Broadway-style shows, several pools, a variety of restaurants, including casual eateries serving pizza and burgers, elegant spas, Internet cafés, libraries, coffee bars, cocktail lounges, shopping promenades, and sports facilities like rock-climbing walls, driving ranges, and exercise rooms.

On the day your ship sails, you'll want to board the ship at least three hours before departure so that you have time to get comfortable, make dining or spa reservations, and set up your onboard account using a credit card. Snacks are usually available.

Where Do They Leave From?

Most Pacific Coast cruises depart from either Los Angeles, Long Beach, or San Diego, California, stopping at Mexican ports along the way. Those stopping at Playa del Carmen, the coast south of Cancún, and the island of Cozumel depart from Miami, Port Canaveral, and

Tampa, Florida, and Galveston, Texas. All, for the most part, are round-trip sailings, returning in four to seven days to the port of departure. Some cruises last as long as ten days, but these aren't really suitable for families, because of both the time and cost involved.

Cruise Line Flights Versus Reserving Your Own

Unless you live near the departure port city, you'll most likely fly to your cruise departure point. You have the option of letting the cruise line book your plane reservation using the blocked seats that they have for this purpose, or you can book your own flights. Both offer advantages.

If you let the cruise line book your flights, you'll receive complimentary round-trip shuttle transfers between the airport and your ship. But you won't have a choice of flights. If mechanical problems delay your flight, the cruise line will try to get you to the first port of call to join the cruise, but they often don't do this when bad weather causes delays.

By reserving your own flights, you have a choice of flights and can use any bonus miles if you choose. However, you'll have to find your own way to the ship from the airport. And if the flight is delayed due to mechanical problems, the cruise line isn't obligated to help you get to the cruise.

Considering Your Shore Excursions

The amount of time your cruise ship stays in port varies from seven to ten hours. If you're going to explore on your own, you need to ask when the ship will be leaving port and be sure to be onboard at least an hour before so as not to miss it.

If you decide to explore on your own, be careful of booking a day-trip with anyone other than a company recommended by the ship. You could end up on a deserted beach with your wallet missing and no way to get back to the ship.

 **TRAVEL TIP**

Book your port excursions either in advance, when you book your cruise, or as soon as possible after arrival onboard ship. There's limited space. Also, if you have any kids under five, you should plan to explore the port on your own since they're not allowed on the organized tours.

Popular Cruises to Mexico

Of the eleven cruise lines that sail to Mexico, only five—Carnival, Disney, Norwegian Caribbean, Princess, and Royal Caribbean Cruise Lines—welcome families. All have special programs for kids as well as activities for parents who feel the need to have some private time.

Carnival Cruise Line

📞888-227-6482, ✏️*www.carnival.com*

Carnival Cruise Line offers you four ships to choose from on Mexican Pacific Coast cruises—Carnival *Spirit,* Carnival *Pride,* Carnival *Paradise,* and Carnival *Ecstasy.* All four ships offer a variety of facilities, including three or four pools, an Internet café, a full casino, various lounges and bars, and a complete fitness center. You'll take meals from the regular or reduced-calorie spa menu in the main dining room, or you may choose to dine more casually in the seaview bistro. Kids love the twenty-four-hour pizzeria and ice cream bar. In addition, you can make reservations and pay an extra fee to dine in the elegant Supper Club or the Sushi Bar.

Carnival Cruises are also famous for their midnight buffets. Free evening entertainment includes shows with singers and comedy acts, as well as music played by three bands and an orchestra. Billed as "Fun Cruises," Carnival focuses on a Las Vegas–style atmosphere.

For Kids

"Camp Carnival," Carnival Cruise Line's program for kids, features activities for four age groups: Toddler (ages two to five), Junior (ages six to eight), Intermediate (ages nine to twelve), and Teens (ages thirteen to fifteen). Those in the Toddler group get to watch cartoons, practice their numbers and colors, decorate cookies, and do sponge and face painting. Staff members help Juniors make puppets and put on a show, play Disney trivia games, paint T-shirts, have a beach party, learn about sea animals, and decorate cookies. Kids in the Intermediate group get to paint T-shirts, attend dance classes, play board games, make jewelry, go on scavenger hunts, put on a talent show, and take part in volleyball and ping-pong tournaments and a photography workshop. Teens have a pool party, attend midnight movies and a teen dance, take dance lessons, learn about skin and hair care, have a pizza and indoor beach party, play volleyball, and take part in a photography workshop.

Departure Ports/Ports of Call

The 88,500-ton, 2,124-passenger ship Carnival *Pride* departs Long Beach, California, every Sunday, stopping in the Mexican ports of Puerto Vallarta, Mazatlán, and Cabo San Lucas. Its sister ship, Carnival *Spirit*, departs from San Diego for a nine-day cruise to Acapulco, Ixtapa/Zihuatanejo, and Mazatlán.

Carnival's 70,367-ton, 2,052-passenger ship, *Paradise*, also sails from Long Beach on Fridays for a four-day weekend cruise to Ensenada. During the week, the *Paradise* sails on a five-day cruise to Ensenada and also stops at Catalina Island.

The 101,519-ton ship, Carnival *Victory*, sails the Western Caribbean, departing Miami and stopping at Cozumel, Grand Cayman, Cayman Islands, and Ocho Rios, Jamaica.

The following tables show sample itineraries for Carnival Cruises.

TABLE 6-1
CARNIVAL *PRIDE* 7-NIGHT MEXICAN RIVIERA/BAJA CRUISE

Day	Port	Arrives	Departs
1	Long Beach		Sunday 5:30 P.M.
2	At Sea		
3	At Sea		
4	Puerto Vallarta	8:00 A.M.	10:00 P.M.
5	Mazatlán	9:00 A.M.	4:00 P.M.
6	Cabo San Lucas	7:00 A.M.	4:00 P.M.
7	At Sea		
8	Long Beach		Sunday 9:00 P.M.

TABLE 6-2
CARNIVAL *SPIRIT* 8-NIGHT MEXICAN RIVIERA CRUISE

Day	Port	Arrives	Departs
1	San Diego		Wednesday 4:00 P.M.
2	At Sea		
3	At Sea		
4	Acapulco	1:00 P.M.	
5	Acapulco		2:00 P.M.
6	Ixtapa/Zihuatanejo	9:00 A.M.	6:00 P.M.
7	Manzanillo	7:00 A.M.	4:00 P.M.
8	At Sea		
9	Los Angeles	Tuesday 7:00 A.M.	

TABLE 6-3
CARNIVAL *PARADISE* 4-DAY BAJA MEXICO CRUISE

Day	Port	Arrives	Departs
1	Long Beach		Fridays 5:30 P.M.
2	Ensenada	9:00 A.M.	6:00 P.M.
3	At Sea		
4	Long Beach	Mondays 8:00 A.M.	

TABLE 6-4
CARNIVAL *VICTORY* 7-DAY WESTERN CARIBBEAN CRUISE

Day	Port	Arrives	Departs
1	Miami		Saturday 4:00 P.M.
2	Cozumel, Mexico	7:00 A.M.	6:00 P.M.
3	At Sea		
4	Grand Cayman Island	7:30 A.M.	4:30 P.M.
5	Ocho Rios, Jamaica	8:00 A.M.	3:30 P.M.
6	At Sea		
7	Miami		Saturday 8:00 P.M.

Table 6-5 outlines costs per person of each of the cruises listed above.

TABLE 6-5
CARNIVAL CRUISES COST

Cruise	Low Season	High Season
7-Night Mexican Riviera/Baja	$699–1419	$1089–1869
3-Night Baja Mexico	$319–369	$439–779
8-Night Mexican Riviera/Baja	$729–$1569	&729–1569
3-Night/4-Day Baja Mexico	$319–$369	$439–$779
7-Day Western Caribbean	$499–$1349	$729–$1829

Disney Cruise Lines

☎800-951-3532, ✐*www.disneycruise.com*

Younger children enjoy sailing on a Disney ship with its themepark atmosphere, but parents do as well because of the line's high level of service and family-friendly environment. Disney imagination permeates the line's 83,000-ton, 1,754-passenger ship, Disney *Magic,* which cruises the Caribbean and Mexican Riviera. It resembles a luxurious ocean liner of the past, providing both a friendly atmosphere for kids and an elegant one for adults. Cabins feature a bath and a half, allowing more than one family member to use them at the same time. Another interesting innovation is Disney's rotating dining schedule.

You'll dine in three different restaurants—Parrot Cay with a Caribbean theme, Lumières with a *Beauty and the Beast* theme, and Animator's Palate with a cartoon studio theme—but will always keep your same table assignment and waiter. The dining staff puts on interactive performances as they serve to Disney music, making meals fun. And sodas are free, either in the restaurants or at a self-serve beverage station by the pool. Breakfast and lunch buffets are also available poolside.

 JUST FOR PARENTS

For those times when you may want to be away from your children, Disney ships offer adults-only facilities, including a pool, a luxurious spa with a rain-forest steam room, a jazz nightclub and a dance club, a coffee bar with Internet access and televisions, a sports bar, and a posh art deco, reservations-only restaurant with a $10 per-person charge, serving Northern Italian cuisine as you look out on magnificent ocean views.

Your kids will enjoy meeting their favorite Disney characters for photos and autographs and watching the combination animated and live shows that feature Disney characters and songs. Character breakfasts like those at Disney's theme parks give kids a chance to pose with Mickey and Minnie Mouse.

For Kids

The Disney *Magic* features all sorts of well-supervised activities for kids, all based on Disney stories and characters. If you have younger children, ages three and four, they'll love creating a new animal species while exploring the world of *The Lion King*. Or perhaps they'll get wrapped up in a flying carpet as they rub a magic lamp and are whisked off on an *Aladdin*-style Arabian adventure to find the hidden genie. At King Triton's Court, your children will learn about ocean life. They'll also create special crafts and learn the Dance of the Seven Dwarfs. The kids' counselors invite all the little ones to

Never Land for a birthday party with Peter Pan and Captain Hook. And what child wouldn't want to become a Mouseketeer-in-Training?

Children five to seven begin the cruise with a special Aloa Luau kick-off party. During the cruise, they'll train to be a junior detective and then solve a mystery, learn simple animation techniques, conduct experiments with an ordinary egg, participate in a late-night pajama party, bake chocolate chip cookies, create a special photo frame, and listen to pirate stories.

If your children are eight and nine years old, they'll enjoy becoming a sorcerer's apprentice and making their own goo or making their own tasty drinks and afterward camping out on deck under the stars. Activities for this group are a little more challenging as they solve puzzles and test their knowledge of Disney trivia or build a volcano, then attend a special party wearing their own glow-in-the-dark bracelets where they try their hands at karaoke. These kids can also produce crazy TV spots, participate in a soap-boat regatta, and make their own pair of 3-D glasses. They even get to make their own mouse pad, featuring a photo of themselves or another they've taken on the cruise.

Older children aged ten to twelve years get to do all the above as well as learn about different cultures and all about sharks, participate in a scavenger hunt while trying to solve a mystery, and produce their own radio commercials.

Disney provides special places on board where kids can be kids. Ocean Quest, a kids'-size ship's bridge, allows them to take turns playing captain and steering the ship. Here, also, older kids can play video games, watch movies, and create arts and crafts. The Oceaneer Lab provides a perfect place for kids to conduct scientific experiments, and the Stack/Aloft gives teens their own place to chill out away from adults.

Departure Ports/Ports of Call

Disney's Western Caribbean cruises depart from Port Canaveral, Florida, and stop at Key West, Grand Cayman Island, Cozumel, and Castaway Cay.

The following table shows a sample itinerary for a Disney Cruise.

TABLE 6-6
DISNEY *MAGIC* 7-DAY WESTERN CARIBBEAN CRUISE

Day	Port	Arrives	Departs
1	Port Canaveral, Florida		Saturdays 4:00 P.M.
2	Key West	11:30 A.M.	9:30 P.M.
3	At Sea		
4	Grand Cayman Island	7:30 A.M..	4:30 P.M.
5	Cozumel, Mexico	9:30 A.M..	10:00 P.M.
6	Castaway Cay	10:00 A.M.	7:00 P.M.
7	Miami		Saturday 7:35 A.M.

Table 6-7 outlines costs of a Disney cruise.

TABLE 6-7
DISNEY CRUISE COST

Cruise	Low Season	High Season
7-Day Western Caribbean Cruise	$1018–2018	$1862–3368

Norwegian Cruise Line

☎888-625-4292, ✒*www.ncl.com*

The Norwegian Cruise Line has developed a concept called "freestyle cruising," which allows you the freedom to have more accommodation and restaurant choices, more entertainment, and more activities. The Norwegian *Star* offers over thirty cabin categories, from budget to deluxe. This family-friendly ship also offers ten restaurants to choose from, open from 5:30 A.M. to midnight, serving everything from American to Italian, French, and Spanish cuisine.

For Kids

NCL's free "Kids Crew" program includes a variety of activities. Each morning, your kids will receive their own copy of "Kids Cruise News," highlighting the events of the day. They can take part in supervised games, design and paint their own T-shirts, and join creative cooking classes in which they'll learn to make decorative cookies and pizzas and for which they'll receive their own chef's hat. They'll even be able to keep a record of their shipboard experiences in their very own scrapbook.

A specially trained staff supervises four age groups: Junior Sailors (ages two to five), First Mates (ages six to eight), Navigators (ages nine to twelve), and Teens (ages thirteen to seventeen). They keep Junior Sailors busy painting T-shirts, doing arts and crafts, having their faces painted, listening to stories, watching magic shows, and participating in the Circus at Sea. First Mates participate in sing-alongs, creative cooking classes, decorative T-shirt painting, and rootbeer-float parties by the pool. Navigators get to go on scavenger hunts and play video games, have fun at pajama parties, watch movies, and camp out in tents with flashlights. Teens enjoy playing basketball and volleyball and participating in pool parties and trivia contests, as well as dancing in a special teen disco and attending special theme parties.

Departure Ports/Ports of Call

The 91,000-ton, 2,240-passenger Norwegian *Star* departs Los Angeles and stops at four Mexican ports— Acapulco, Ixtapa, Puerto Vallarta, Cabo San Lucas.

The 78,309-ton, 2,002-passenger Norwegian *Sun* sets sail from Miami and stops at Costa Maya, Santo Tomas de Castilla, Belize City, and Cozumel.

The following tables show sample itineraries for Norwegian Cruise Lines.

Princess Cruises

✆800-774-6237, ✍*www.princesscruises.com*

Long the leader in cruises to the Mexican Riviera, Princess Cruises also has the most sailings in this region, offering some unique activities, such as its ScholarShip@Sea life-enhancement lectures. You can dine anytime in a selection of dining rooms with traditional seating, or you have the option of dining in six alternative restaurants ranging from a steakhouse to an Italian trattoria for an additional charge.

TABLE 6-8
NORWEGIAN *STAR* 8-DAY MEXICAN RIVIERA CRUISE

Day	Port	Arrives	Departs
1	Los Angeles		Saturday 4:00 P.M.
2	At Sea		
3	At Sea		
4	Acapulco	11:00 A.M.	
5	Acapulco		12:30 A.M.
6	Zihuatanejo/Ixtapa	7:00 A.M.	2:00 P.M.
7	Puerto Vallarta	9:00 A.M.	5:00 P.M.
8	Cabo San Lucas	8:00 A.M.	4:00 P.M. (for flight back)

TABLE 6-9
THE NORWEGIAN *SUN* 8-DAY WESTERN CARIBBEAN CRUISE

Day	Port	Arrives	Departs
1	Miami		Saturday 5:00 P.M.
2	At Sea		
3	Costa Maya	8:00 A.M.	6:00 P.M.
4	Santo Tomas de Castilla	8:00 A.M.	6:00 P.M.
5	Belize City	8:00 A.M.	6:00 P.M.
6	Cozumel, Mexico	10:00 A.M.	7:00 P.M.
7	At Sea		
8	Miami	Saturday 7:00 A.M.	

Table 6-10 outlines costs of each of the cruises listed above.

TABLE 6-10
NORWEGIAN CARIBBEAN CRUISES COST

Cruise	Low Season	High Season
8-Day Mexican Riviera Cruise	$579–1099	$1089–1869
8-Day Western Caribbean Cruise	$479–934	$549–1319

For Kids

Though not as comprehensive as some other cruise lines' kids programs, Princess Cruise Line's "Princess Kids" features activities for three age groups: Princess Pelicans (ages three to seven), Princess Pirateers (ages eight to twelve), and Off Limits (ages ten to seventeen). Staff members take Princess Pelicans and Princess Pirateers on galley and backstage tours, as well as have afternoon ice cream parties, watch movies and cartoons, go on scavenger hunts, and make arts and crafts with them. Those in the Off Limits group get to dance in the teen-only disco, take part in shipboard Olympics and basketball tournaments, paint T-shirts, have a pizza party, have fun with karaoke, have their own casino night, and play the dating game.

Departure Ports/Ports of Call

Departing Los Angeles, the 113,000-ton, 2,670-passenger *Diamond Princess* stops at the Mexican ports of Puerto Vallarta, Mazatlán, and Cabo San Lucas and also spends three days at sea. On its Costa Maya Cruise, the 109,000-ton, 2,600-passenger *Grand Princess,* departs from Galveston, Texas, spends two days at sea and docks at Costa Maya, Mexico, Belize City, Grand Cayman Island, and Cozumel.

The following tables show sample itineraries for Princess Cruises.

TABLE 6-11
DIAMOND PRINCESS **8-DAY MEXICAN RIVIERA CRUISE**

Day	Port	Arrives	Departs
1	Los Angeles		Saturday 5:00 P.M.
2	At Sea		
3	At Sea		
4	Puerto Vallarta	7:00 A.M.	6:00 P.M.
5	Mazatlán	7:00 A.M.	5:00 P.M.
6	Cabo San Lucas	7:00 A.M.	4:00 P.M.
7	At Sea		
8	Los Angeles	Saturday 6:00 P.M.	

TABLE 6-12
***GRAND PRINCESS* 8-DAY COSTA MAYA CRUISE**

Day	Port	Arrives	Departs
1	Galveston		Saturday 4:00 P.M.
2	At Sea		
3	Costa Maya	10:00 A.M.	7:00 P.M.
4	Belize City	6:30 A.M.	1:00 P.M.
5	Grand Cayman	12:00 A.M.	7:00 P.M.
6	Cozumel	10:00 A.M.	7:00 P.M.
7	At Sea		
8	Los Angeles	Saturday 7:00 A.M.	

Table 6-13 outlines costs of each of the cruises listed above.

TABLE 6-13
PRINCESS CRUISES COST

Cruise	Low Season	High Season
8-Day Mexican Riviera Cruise	$576–1051	$624–1052
8-Day Costa Maya Cruise	$481–861	$737–1134

Royal Caribbean Cruise Line

📞800-722-5941, ✎*www.royalcaribbean.com*

Besides offering fine service, Royal Caribbean Cruise Line prides itself on offering shipboard innovations like rock-climbing walls. And on selected sailings, the line also offers Murder Mystery Cruises that your entire family will enjoy.

For Kids

Royal Caribbean Line's "Adventure Ocean" program for kids, the most complete among the lines sailing to Mexico, offers activities for five age groups: Aquanauts (ages three to five), Explorers (ages six to eight), Voyagers (ages nine to eleven), Navigators (twelve to fourteen), and Guests (fifteen to seventeen). Those in the Aquanauts group get to finger- and face-paint, participate in adventure science and art programs, listen to stories, and attend a Pajamarama movie night. Explorers also participate in adventure science and art programs, have ice cream parties, play sports and take part in the Wacky Olympics, and have a Western hoedown and pirate night. Kids in the Voyagers group play X-games, put on a talent show and do karaoke, play sports, attend movie mania nights, and enjoy putting on skits in the adventure theater. Navigators have similar activities to the Voyagers, except they go on a backstage tour, have themed and pool parties, and go on scavenger hunts. The older teens in the Guests program have pool parties, play Battle of the Sexes, watch late-night movies, chat over coffee, play sports, and take DJ-ing classes.

If you bring along kids from six months to three years, you and they will be able to participate in Royal Caribbean's innovative Fisher-Price Aqua Babies and Aqua Tots Programs. Both feature a series of daily, forty-five-minute playgroups with fun activities for kids ages six months to three years along with their parents. The groups help to build skills through storytelling, music, and creative arts, using Fisher-Price learning toys and games.

Departure Ports/Ports of Call

While Royal Caribbean Cruise Line offers the usual seven-night cruises to the Mexican Riviera aboard their 78,491-ton, 2,435-passenger ship *Vision of the Seas,* stopping at Cabo San Lucas, Mazatlán, and Puerto Vallarta, they also offer shorter four- and five-day Baja Mexico cruises aboard the 73,941-ton, 2,744-passenger ship *Monarch of the Seas,* stopping at Ensenada on the former and San Diego and Catalina Island on the latter.

The following tables show sample itineraries for Royal Caribbean Cruise Line cruises.

TABLE 6-14
***VISION OF THE SEAS* 7-NIGHT MEXICAN RIVIERA CRUISE**

Day	Port	Arrives	Departs
1	Los Angeles		Sunday 5:30 P.M.

2	At Sea		
3	Cabo San Lucas	10:30 A.M.	6:00 P.M.
4	Mazatlán	8:00 A.M.	5:30 P.M.
5	Puerto Vallarta	8:00 A.M.	11:00 P.M.
6	At Sea		
7	At Sea		
8	Los Angeles	Sunday 7:00 A.M.	

TABLE 6-15
MONARCH OF THE SEAS 4-DAY MEXICO/BAJA CRUISE

Day	Port	Arrives	Departs
1	Los Angeles		Fridays 5:30 P.M.
2	Ensenada	8:00 A.M.	5:00 P.M.
3	At Sea		
4	Los Angeles	Mondays 8:00 A.M.	

TABLE 6-16
MONARCH OF THE SEAS 5-DAY MEXICO/BAJA CRUISE

Day	Port	Arrives	Departs
1	Los Angeles		Monday 5:00 P.M.
2	San Diego	8:00 A.M.	6:00 P.M.
3	Catalina Island	8:00 A.M.	5:00 P.M.
4	Ensenada	8:00 A.M.	5:00 P.M.
5	Los Angeles	Friday 8:00 A.M.	

TABLE 6-17
VOYAGER OF THE SEAS 8-DAY WESTERN CARIBBEAN CRUISE

Day	Port	Arrives	Departs
1	Miami		Saturdays 5:00 P.M.
2	At Sea		
3	Labadee, Haiti	8:00 A.M.	4:00 P.M.
4	Ocho Rios, Jamaica	9:00 A.M.	5:00 P.M.
5	Grand Cayman Island	8:00 A.M.	5:00 P.M.
6	Cozumel, Mexico	10:00 A.M.	7:00 P.M.
7	At Sea		

Day	Port	Arrives	Departs
8	Miami	Saturday	8:30 A.M.

Table 6-18 outlines costs of each of the cruises listed above.

TABLE 6-18
ROYAL CARIBBEAN CRUISES COST

Cruise	Low Season	High Season
8-Day Mexican Riviera Cruise	$499–1899	$609–1159
4-Day Baja Mexico	$299–329	$359–709
5-Day Baja Mexico	$279–619	$379–829
7-Night Western Caribbean Cruise	$599–1599	$749–1499

Murder Mystery Cruises to Ensenada aboard the *Monarch of the Seas* cost approximately $274 to $314 per person, including the cruise, port charges, and murder mystery fee, depending on the sailing date.

CHAPTER 7

Family Activities in Mexico

YOU'VE PROBABLY FOUND THAT when your family engages in activities they're interested in, your vacations are all the more enjoyable. Some people enjoy just soaking up the sun and sipping margaritas, but Mexico offers much more than that. First, you can learn about this fascinating culture and the history of some of the richest civilizations in the world. Or perhaps you want to pursue a hobby like photography or cooking—Mexico's cuisine is way more then just tacos. Or maybe you'd like to learn to scuba dive or, if you're already a diver, to explore old shipwrecks and coral reefs. Your biggest problem will be finding the time to do all that you want to do.

Water Sports

At Mexico's larger beach resorts you can indulge in a wide choice of water sports, from windsurfing to parasailing to waterskiing, snorkeling, and "banana boat" riding. If you like diving, you'll discover many great sites beneath Mexico's tropical waters. At several resorts, fishing is especially good.

═FAST FACT

Mazatlán is Mexico's surfing capital. The best waves are at Los Pinos Beach.

Fishing

If you're a deep-sea fishing enthusiast, you'll find all you can handle at Mexico's Pacific Coast resorts. Fishing charter companies provide half- and full-day fishing excursions, most including tackle and bait. You can obtain a spot on a boat with other anglers, or you can charter an entire boat for your family. Longer-range cabin-class cruisers cost between $250 and $300 a day, including equipment and a guide, while small local boats (called *pangas*) go for about $80 to $100 a day. Prices and service varies from one resort to another and from company to company, so be sure you establish what's included—drinks, bait, snacks, equipment, and so on. Some companies charge to release the fish. Find out first. And it's customary to tip the boat captain 10 to 15 percent of the charter cost upon returning. Sailfish are quite prevalent, as are marlin, wahoo, yellowtail, dorado, mackerel, and bonito. But you can also hook sea bass, striped marlin, red snapper, swordfish, albacore, halibut, and shark. While Manzanillo claims to be the sailfish capital of the world, Mazatlán makes a similar claim.

All Cabo outfitters request that you release billfish back into the water, and some even require it. *Pangas* here rent for $200 a day, twice the going rate, while cabin cruisers go for $350 to $450 per day.

If you're traveling to Cancún or Cozumel, you'll also find good deep-sea and lagoon fishing. Cancún's Nichupte Lagoon, where you can catch needlefish, barracuda, and occasionally sharks, is excellent for off-shore fishing. Charters leave from several marinas and start at $240 per boat per day.

Fishing Gear

There's no problem bringing any kind of fishing gear into the country, and every major port has charter boats and gear for hire. But you will need a permit to fish in Mexico, which you can easily obtain by writing or calling the Government of Mexico, Secretariat of Fisheries (2550 Fifth Avenue, Suite 101, San Diego, CA 92103-6622; ✆619-233-6956). You can also get a permit at the United States-Mexico border, from local fish and game wardens, and from outfitters. Licenses sell for $10 daily, $25 weekly, and $35 monthly and are good in any state in Mexico.

TRAVEL TIP

If you're planning on sailing your own boat into Mexican waters, you must obtain a boat permit from a Mexican consulate or customs broker. Permits, issued for six months, can be extended through your local automobile club or the closest Mexican consulate or tourist office.

Swimming, Scuba Diving, Snorkeling

Mexico's 6,000 miles of shoreline offer some of the best snorkeling, skin-, and scuba-diving spots in the world. The clear, warm lagoons off Cozumel, Cancún and Isla Mujeres barely conceal brilliant coral, tropical fish, and exotic marine plants and animals. At 80 to 100 feet, you can swim among magnificent coral gardens and fish, as well as see guns, anchors, and sealed chests remaining from fifteenth-century shipwrecks.

If you like to dive and party, too, then Cancún should be your choice. All the larger hotels can make arrangements for both instruction and equipment. Most of the best dive sites lie off Punta Nizuc at the southern end of the island. At Las Cuevitas (Little Caves), the resident big fish and small tropicals love to pose among the corals for photographers. Both snorkelers and divers head to El Garrafon Beach, at the end of the five-mile-long island of Isla Mujeres to view the beautiful coral gardens. In the Cave of the Sleeping Sharks, also on Isla Mujeres, you can observe the razor-toothed predators as they doze in a stupor caused by the area's low salinity.

South of Cancún at Akumal is Xcaret, a water-sports theme park. If you've never snorkeled before, you can float on a river through an underground cavern and out into the inlet. The natural aquarium there is considered one of the most beautiful in Mexico.

▐ TRAVEL TIP

If you want to learn to scuba dive, be sure to look for instructors sanctioned by the Professional Association of Dive Instructors (PADI) or the National Association of Underwater Instructors (NAUI).

You'll find innumerable beaches and lagoons with great scuba diving along Baja's Pacific Coast, but you'll need a wet suit if you plan on diving as far north as Ensenada.

In the Sea of Cortés, you'll experience the clearest of conditions during the summer and fall, with visibility of 100 feet and water temperatures in the 80s. Because its waters are temperate, this area lacks the bright tropical coral of the Caribbean. What will attract you to dive here is the opportunity to swim with such large creatures as whales, sea lions, dolphins, manta rays, groupers, and dozens of other giants of the deep. Los Cabos features dives on the North and South Walls, the Shipwreck, Land's End, and the Blowhole. Ixtapa/Zihuatanejo, the only resort where you can dive on the Mexican Riviera, offers good diving and snorkeling in its shallow bay waters.

Lessons/Gear Rental

The following diving fees are typical at Mexican beach resorts:

Lessons:
- Multilevel diver instruction: $150
- Discover Scuba course: $50–$80
- PADI Scuba Certification Course: $350
- Advanced Scuba Certification: $250
- Refresher Course: $50–$60, including equipment

Dives:
- One-tank afternoon dive: $35–$43

- Two-tank dive from large boat: $60–$65, including two tanks, weights and belt, dive master, small snack and beverages.

Snorkeling:
- Snorkel trip: $25–$40

Equipment Rental:
- Tanks: $6–$15
- Wet suit: $6
- Regulator with octopus console: $7
- Dive light: $5
- Buoyancy compensator: $8
- Dive computer: $10
- Mask/snorkel/fins: $5
- Nitrox: $8

Personal Watercraft (PWC) Rentals

Hobie Cats are a fun way to get on the water when the wind kicks up. And Jet- or water skiing offers an exhilarating alternative. Or perhaps you prefer to skim the surf in a WaveRunner. Your hotel concierge or activity desk will be happy to make arrangements for you.

Sailing

Over the last fifteen years, the Mexican government has built a series of marinas from Ensenada south to Acapulco and beyond. What better way to see the Pacific coastline than to spend a day sailing aboard a luxurious sailboat? Whale-watch in winter and observe dolphins, turtles, and manta rays throughout the year. Luxury day sails include open bar, lunch, snacks, tropical fruit, snorkeling and fishing equipment, and lifejackets. If you're an experienced sailor, then you'll want to rent a boat for a few hours and sail around the bays of Puerto Vallarta, Zihuatanejo, or Acapulco.

Along the Caribbean coast, you'll find two marinas in Cancún, one on Isla Mujeres, and another at Puerto Aventuras, below Cancún at Akumal.

Golf

The lush scenery at most of Mexico's more than 120 golf courses will make it hard for you to concentrate on your golf game. Mexico has become a golfer's paradise. The weather and scenery are ideal in both the Pacific coastal area and the temperate central highlands. Here, golf is a year-round sport, with many exciting and challenging courses laid out by top-name designers.

Available Courses

With the opening of challenging world-class golf clubs in Mexico in the last decade, new standards have been set in integrating spectacular settings with challenging golf and first-class amenities. Several championship courses, including the target-style desert layout of the Palmilla Golf Club in Los Cabos, designed by Jack Nicklaus, offer lush landscapes, breathtaking scenery, and challenges at each hole. Consisting of three sets of nine—Arroyo, Mountain, and Ocean—he course sits beautifully in the mountains, its rough areas dotted with 400-year-old cardon cacti, and every hole has a view of the Sea of Cortés.

Two dramatic seaside holes and three outstanding mountain holes are the signature holes of the Cabo Real Resort Golf Course, designed by Robert Trent Jones. Situated midway between Cabo San Lucas and San Jose along the corridor at the Melia Cabo Real Hotel, it features a flower-bedecked rolling green course, in contrast to Nicklaus' desert ones. Staggered tees put the holes within reach of average golfers. Campo de Golf Los Cabos, the original nine-hole local course in San Jose del Cabo, will also offer you a challenging round of play. Further north in Ensenada, the Bajamar resort community boasts two eighteen-hole championship courses, both designed in the classic Scottish links style.

≡FAST FACT

The eighteen-hole Cabo del Sol golf course in Los Cabos features seven oceanside holes, more than any other course in Mexico.

The first resort golf course in Mexico was Club de Golf Cancún Pok-Ta-Pok, a rolling course laid out between the beach and the lagoon on a stretch of flat sand. Cancún also has several new resort courses, including the Hilton Resort's eighteen-hole course, set on landfill next to the lagoon. Fairways are slow due to the special grass needed to cover them. An alligator lives in the water hazard on the fifteenth hole. The Hotel Melia Cancún also offers twenty-seven holes of championship golf.

You'll also find some spectacular courses at the Pacific Coast resorts. Mazatlán offers both an eighteen-hole course at the El Cid Golf and Country Club and a twenty-seven-hole course as a part of its marina development.

Ixtapa's Palma Real course features fairways and greens butting right up against the beach. This course will test your golfing skills with rolling expanses of fairways and greens rimmed with tall coconut palms and dotted with water holes and three lakes with resident alligators. The eighteen-hole Ixtapa Marina Club de Golf, designed by Robert Von Hagge, is a links-style course with a challenging maze of hills and water hazards that will force you to use all your golfing skills.

If you're headed to Puerto Vallarta, the Los Flamingos Golf Club offers a chance to follow through on a movie star or two. This eighteen-hole course is located eight miles north of the airport near some fine hotels. Another resort course crowns the Marina Vallarta development. If you're new to golf, its open undulating fairways offer a wide berth for those wayward shots.

Manzanillo is home to the world-famous La Mantarraya Golf Links at Las Hadas. This lush eighteen-hole course meanders past lagoons, canals, palm trees, and various forms of wildlife. For sheer beauty, as well as difficulty, few courses in Mexico come close to it. *Golf Digest* considers it to be among the best and most scenic in the world.

Acapulco boasts two magnificent courses at the Princess and Pierre Marques Hotels. The first features water on twelve of its eighteen holes, while the second features water on thirteen holes and is extremely well bunkered. You'll also find a good public eighteen-hole course along the main boulevard by the beach in town.

 TRAVEL TIP

If you're going to play golf during the summer, be sure to bring mosquito repellent. The little buggers can be particularly nasty in early evening on most tropical courses.

Ecotourism Activities

Ecotourism has become a popular alternative to traditional tours in Mexico. With diverse terrain and an abundance of natural resources, Mexico is an ideal destination for experiencing nature firsthand. Until recently, only traditional camping and hiking tours were available. Now, however, integrated tours encompassing not only nature but the cultures of Mexico's many indigenous peoples make it possible for you to experience unique adventures.

Horseback Riding

In Mazatlán, Puerto Vallarta, Manzanillo, and San Jose del Cabo, you can feel the thrill of excitement as you ride side by side on horseback through the surf, horses' manes flying in the wind. For $15 to $20 an hour, you can go on one- to two-hour guided trail rides. Or perhaps you'd like to ride through an unspoiled ecological reserve, learning about the trees and animals along the way. Other treks can take you to old mining towns in the foothills of the Sierra Madre.

Hiking

If you like to hike, you'll find plenty of do-it-yourself trails in the national parks of Mexico's central highlands. Hiking through cool pine forests with dramatic vistas will almost make you think you're in the American Rockies. For a real challenge, try hiking the lower trails, or to the summit of two of Mexico's largest volcanoes—Ixtaccíhihuatl (17,159 feet) and Pico de Orizaba (the highest at 18,700 feet). These hikes aren't for the inexperienced, and you'll need to book a guided trip with a local outfitter at least two weeks ahead.

≡ FAST FACT

You can get information and instruction about rock climbing from Asociación de Montañismo y Exploración (UNAM) by writing to Insurgentes Sur, Ciudad Universitaria, Mexico City, D.F.04511 or e-mailing *info@montanismo.org.mx*.

Two other popular hiking destinations are the Barranca del Cobre (Copper Canyon) and the desert and mountain trails of Baja California. If you plan on hiking deep into the canyons, be sure you hire an experienced guide. Local tour operators out of Creel, the largest town at the eastern edge of the canyons, lead week-long treks into the canyons to explore caves and visit remote Tarahumara Indian settlements.

The trails of Baja may be more suited to you if you want to take shorter hikes through untamed wilderness. Trails lead from the desert where cacti reach for the sky to the cool pine forests of nearby mountains. You'll find plenty of established trails in the northern Sierras. However, the further south you travel, the more scarce the trails become.

You'd best bring along your own hiking equipment. Though you can take short hikes with a good pair of casual walking shoes, you'll find the Mexican terrain to be quite rough in most places, so a pair of sturdy hiking boots may be preferable. You'll definitely need them on longer hikes. If you're an inexperienced hiker, stick to older established trails in national parks. If you're planning an overnight hike, be sure to take along all the usual hiking gear—first aid kit, snakebite kit, flashlight with extra batteries, pocket knife, folding rain poncho, compass, and waterproof matches.

TRAVEL TIP

If hiking in the desert, be sure to wear a long-sleeved cotton shirt, long pants, and a light wide-brimmed hat. Sunblock is mandatory. And be sure to carry at least four quarts of water with you for an all-day hike.

Rafting and Kayaking

For white-water rafting, you should head to the state of Veracruz. Rivers like the Rio Pesados offer challenging rides through roaring rapids. If you prefer a quieter ride, then paddling down the Rio Filobobos past Mayan ruins may be more to your liking. The best pleasure rafting is on the Usumacinta River in the state of Chiapas.

You'll discover the best sea kayaking along the Baja coast of the Sea of Cortés, where the waters remain calm. Numerous inlets and coves offer plenty of places to explore, and campsites are readily available.

FAST FACT

One of Mexico's best kayaking destinations—and a great place to learn to kayak—is Bahía Concepción, south of the fishing village of Mulegé, Baja California Norte, along the Sea of Cortés.

If you're visiting Puerto Vallarta, you may want to try kayaking the offshore islands. However, with strong lateral currents and rough surf, you'll need to be an experienced kayaker to do so.

Mountain Biking

Mountain biking is a relatively new sport in Mexico. You can explore the jungles surrounding Puerto Vallarta, visiting small villages and stopping to have lunch and bathe under secluded waterfalls. Or you can bike along remote beaches north of town. The numerous hills and valleys around Mazatlán also provide great terrain for mountain biking. Outfitters provide everything you need—front-suspension mountain bikes, helmets, gloves, and water bottles. From Los Cabos, you can mountain bike to the nearby Sierra Laguna Mountains to look for dinosaur bones in dried-up riverbeds, ancient Indian rock paintings, and unusual plants and wildlife. Along the way, you can stop for a swim in a stream or to relax in a hot spring.

 TRAVEL TIP

For mountain-biking adventures, contact Bike Mex Adventures at Calle Guerrero #361 Puerto Vallarta, Mexico; ✆322-323-1680.

Parasailing

Perhaps you'd like the exhilarating feeling of parasailing. Nothing beats being towed high in a parachute behind a powerful motorboat. At the beaches in Acapulco, Cancún, Mazatlán, Puerto Vallarta, Cabo San Lucas, all you need do is wait your turn. A ten-minute ride costs about $30, and you'll also need lots of nerve.

Cultural Activities

Though you can play golf, go fishing, hiking, diving, or whatever, anywhere, you'll be doing them in Mexico, a different country with its own unique traditions. But make sure you experience the local culture, too, whether it be browsing a market or attending a musical or dance performance. Visit some of the Mexico's excellent museums and be sure to try the local foods.

City/Country Tours/Sightseeing

Tour operators like Tauck Tours offer tours to Mexico, but often they're geared to older travelers. When traveling with a family, it's best to purchase an independent tour package, including air, hotel, and sightseeing tours. You can take a city tour in any of Mexico's major cities to give you an overall view before striking out on your own.

Archaeology/Cultural Activities

Mexico is a veritable open-air museum, with over 11,000 archaeological sites throughout the country. A good starting point for understanding Mexico's past is the National Museum of Anthropology and History in Mexico City. Afterward, you should visit the Templo Mayor downtown. The next most important site is Teotihuacán, thirty miles northwest of the city, where you can climb the 207-foot Great Pyramid of the Sun.

Another must-see archaeological site is Monte Albán, six miles southwest of the city of Oaxaca, where more than 26,000 people lived for centuries on terraced slopes leading up to a flattened mountaintop city . The Zapotec ceremonial center of Mitla isn't far away.

The Mayan ceremonial center of Palenque lies ninety-five miles southeast of Villahermosa in the state of Tabasco. Regarded by many as the most beautiful of Mexico's archaeological sites, its exquisite Mayan temples stand silently amidst dense green jungle. However, the most famous Mayan site is Chichén Itzá. For many centuries sacred ground to the Mayans, its buildings reflect the contrasting architectural styles of the Mayans and the later Toltec civilization. Uxmal, another Mayan ceremonial center lying fifty miles south of Mérida in the state of Yucatan, has beautifully proportioned and lavishly decorated buildings.

 TRAVEL TIP

When visiting archaeological sites, take along a wide-brimmed hat or umbrella to shield you from the sun's heat. Plan your visit for early morning or late afternoon if possible.

Mexico's awesome past comes alive at these and scores of other intriguing sites. Most sites and museums are open year-round, and entry fees are minimal. You'll find text explanations are in English, though you may want to take a guided tour since many sites are complex and mysterious. Accommodations, such as Club Med's Villas Arqueológicas (✆800-258-2633), can be found at most of the major sites, and if you stay over, you'll get an opportunity to see the sound and light shows at either Teotihuácan, Chichén Itzá, or Uxmal.

Shopping

Next to lying in the sun and drinking margaritas, shopping is the favorite pastime for many Mexico vacationers. Mexico is a country rich in handicrafts, offering top-quality goods made of the finest in natural products, fashioned by craftspeople who have the skills of Indian and European designers and who still use old techniques.

Whether selecting handmade products of glass, precious and semi-precious metals, leather, pottery, or fabric, you'll find unique products to take home. While you can purchase many items in stores throughout the country, the markets yield not only the best buys but also the chance to meet and mingle with the craftspeople while bargaining for the best prices. If you're interested in local handicrafts, you should visit regional markets, especially on market days. Mexico City's Bazaar Sabado (Saturday Market) is a good spot to select merchandise from around the country.

≡FAST FACT

San Pedro Tlaquepaque, a small town that is now a part of Guadalajara, Mexico's second-largest city, has some of the best shopping outside Mexico City. Here, you can purchase hand-blown glass, leather, brass, tin, silver, and pottery from 300 merchants. Musical instruments, lacquered wood, and wooden masks are also popular buys.

For silver, head for Taxco, southwest of Mexico City on the way to Acapulco. You'll discover more silversmiths in this colonial town than all over Mexico. You can browse the shops and galleries for days.

Throughout Mexico there's an impressive range of pottery. Some have pre-Hispanic origins, such as those found in Oaxaca and Chiapas. Others have a Spanish influence, such as the Talavera of Puebla and Guanajuato. In most places you can purchase pieces direct from the factories and have them shipped home at a reasonable cost.

Besides handicrafts, some parts of Mexico overflow with folk art. Imaginative figures of papier-mâché are made by a number of artisans for special holidays such as Dia de los Muertos (Day of the Dead) or Semana Santa (Holy Week). Artisans also create piñatas, an important part of fiestas and festive ceremonies, using clay pots decorated with colored cardboard and tissue paper.

If you love metal work, you'll find it in distinctive styles all around Mexico. While Santa Clara del Cobre in the state of Michoacán is especially famous for copper objects, metalsmiths also work in silver in Guadalajara, in copper and brass in San Miguel Allende, and in gold in Puebla.

Some craftspeople specialize in woodwork, producing colonial-style furniture in Mexico City, Cuernavaca, Guadalajara, Colima, and Taxco. In Michoacán, chip-carved pine furniture is popular. You'll find carved ironwood animals along the Pacific Coast. The states of Guerrero, Michoacán, and Chiapas are known for fine lacquer work on gourds, masks, boxes, chests, and trays. Opals, extracted from local mines and cut locally, and in colors like nowhere else, can be found in Querétaro.

Festivals

Mexico's cultural riches and deep historic roots find their most spectacular expression in the more than 4,000 fiestas, festivals, and holidays that are celebrated each year throughout the country. Every town and village has a celebration for its patron saint. Whether the occasion is a small village's fiesta or a national celebration such as

Easter, Fiestas Patrias (Independence Day), Christmas, or the Day of the Dead, Mexico's festivities involve millions of people in the excitement of music, dance, fireworks, and regional cuisine.

Festivals serve to renew and preserve local traditions in the form of food, music, and art. Local traditions and history give each event its own special flavor, yet every celebration has features that make it uniquely Mexican. Three thousand years of civilization converge in song, dance, and processions, where traditional rituals, drawings, and handmade masks help keep alive the heritage of ancient times.

Special festival foods may use ingredients that reflect the local environment, such as prickly pear cactus and tequila from the northern deserts; abundant seafood from coastal areas; tropical crops like mangoes and pineapple; and high-altitude plants such as chocolate and coffee.

Many festivals include *charreadas* (Mexican rodeos) and a special *tianguis,* or traditional marketplace where you can buy local handicrafts and foods. And no Mexican celebration is complete without fireworks. While national holidays and other major events have fixed dates, local celebrations may vary. When traveling in Mexico, check with your hotel or the local tourism office for details.

Bullfights

Bullfights are an integral part of Mexican culture, and although they're not for the faint of heart, you should try to see one if you want to grasp an important part of Mexican culture.

They're held regularly on Sunday afternoons from December through March at the Plaza Mexico in Mexico City, the largest bullring in the world, seating 60,000 people. Amateur bullfights happen the rest of the year. Mexico's second major bullfighting center is in Guadalajara, but the border towns of Tijuana and Ciudad Juarez regularly schedule bullfights as well. To see how the bulls are bred, you should visit the state of Tlaxcala, Mexico's smallest, about ninety minutes east of Mexico City.

Most of the Mexican beach resorts also have a bullring. However, often you'll pay more as a tourist to get in than a local. While most resorts hold their bullfights on Sunday afternoons, Cancún holds theirs on Wednesday afternoons to accommodate passengers from cruise ships in port.

R&R

If you just need some rest and relaxation, then Mexico is the place for you. Just being there and adjusting to the slower pace of life outside Mexico City may be enough to calm your frazzled nerves. But if you want to really relax, you'll need to spend some time lying under a *palapa* (palm-roofed shelter) on a quiet beach or letting all your muscles relax in one of Mexico's new spas.

Beaches

If you're a beach lover, you'll love Mexico. The country abounds with fine beaches spread out along its 6,000 miles of coastline along the Gulf of Mexico and Caribbean Sea to the east and the Sea of Cortés and Pacific Ocean to the west.

The white-powder beaches of the Pacific Coast attract thousands of people each year. Though resorts line many of them, there are some like Pié de la Cuesta, north of Acapulco, that offer quiet seclusion. Unexplored coves, quiet lagoons, and virgin beaches dot the shoreline of the Sea of Cortés.

While the beaches along Mexico's Caribbean coast are soft and white, those along the Gulf Coast are darker. But unlike the Pacific beaches, those along the 1,400 miles of eastern shoreline have strong lateral currents and undertows. Rainy season begins in late April and lasts until mid-December, and between August and November, tropical storms and hurricanes occasionally hit. Though you can enjoy the beaches along the Pacific Coast all year, the ocean temperature drops in winter and the sea can be quite choppy and dangerous at times.

All Mexican beaches are public, so you can sun and swim at any of them, including those in front of luxurious resorts. But if you want privacy, you'll find plenty of untouched beaches to choose from.

Spas

Interest in fitness is on the rise around the world, and Mexico is no exception. Ever since the Aztecs first built a resort in the hills southwest of Mexico City to take advantage of the mineral waters there, visitors have been flocking to Mexico's famous spas. For centuries, Mexico's mineral springs have been recognized for their healing properties and for providing a way to soothe the stresses of everyday living.

Moctezuma II, the Aztec emperor, was one of Mexico's earliest spa enthusiasts. In fact, three of the mineral baths he visited regularly—Tenochtitlán, Oaxtepec, and Ixtapan de la Sal—are still in use today. These springs are heated deep within the earth and, like those at Tequisquiapan, are usually enriched with a host of minerals.

≡FAST FACT

Set atop an underground volcanic spring two hours from Mexico City is the charming Colonial-style spa village of Tequisquiapan, known as "Tequis" to veteran visitors. A dozen small hotels, like the Hotel Relox, offer curative radioactive waters of volcanic origin, which are said to ease the pain of arthritis, cure insomnia, and improve digestion.

A number of Mexican spas, or *balnearios,* are true resorts, with all the amenities. Others, like Ixtapan de la Sal, Tequisquiapan, Uruapan, and Tehuácan, are mainly places to "take the waters," either outside in *balnearios* (natural mineral springs) or inside in spring-fed pools.

Though there are warm water mineral springs throughout the country, today the word "spa" conjures up more than that. Luxurious spas have sprung up in all the beach resorts and many deluxe hotels. Most offer a wide range of health and beauty options, such as facials and massages, body-wraps with herbs and mineral salts, yoga, tai chi, reflexology sessions, hair styling, nail care, vapor and sauna baths, and daily personalized exercise sessions. At some, like Hosteria Las Quintas in Cuernavaca, outdoor sports like horseback riding and nature walks complement the spa treatments.

JUST FOR PARENTS

A good way to find the spa that matches your interests is to look in *The Spa Finder,* an international guide published by Frank van Putten (☎800-255-7727).

Among Mexico's hotel spas are a number of special-interest resorts. These focus on particular activities, like golf, at Hotel Avandaro Golf and Spa Resort in Valle de Bravo, northwest of Mexico City; fitness, at Rancho La Puerta in Tecate, about thirty miles east of Tijuana in Baja California; and beach activities, at Body and Sol at Puerto Aventuras Resort, sixty miles south of Cancún.

CHAPTER 8

Cancún

THE ANCIENT MAYANS NAMED Cancún for the pot of gold at the end of the rainbow. To them, it was a place of unparalleled beauty. Today, it sparkles like a gemstone with more shining facets than you could experience in a lifetime of vacations. Few tropical destinations feature as many vacation diversions. Cancún has become the ultimate package travel destination. In fact, it's the most affordable option for traveling to Mexico.

About Cancún

Cancún was created as a vacation playground, a place where you can indulge in a myriad of activities, all planned around having fun. Beginning as a sleepy fishing village, it has developed into a world-class resort with millions of visitors annually. After a computerized search picked the idyllic barrier island in 1967 as a promising spot for tourism, construction began in 1970, and the first hotel opened two years later.

 **TRAVEL TIP**

To help you orient yourself to Cancún, pick up a free copy of *Cancún Tips*, available at most major hotels, shops, and restaurants.

Action centers upon Paseo Kukulcán, a fourteen-mile land-scaped boulevard that winds its way down the middle of the Zona Hotelera (Hotel Zone). At the northern end stands La Ciudad de Cancún (Cancún City), a city of over 450,000 simply known as Centro. At the other, the beginning of Highway 307 and the beaches of the Riviera Maya. Laguna Nichupté (Nichupté Lagoon) hugs the shore of the inland side of the island, which is shaped like the number 7. Marinas, golf courses, and waterfront restaurants along its shore vie for your attention. The highest concentration of restaurants, shopping malls, and discos exists at the convergence of the arms of the 7, known as Punta Cancún. Here, also, stands the Convention Center.

Best Time to Go

The dry winter months from December through April are the best time to visit Cancún. Spring Breakers arrive from mid-March to mid-April, so you should plan your visit accordingly, unless you want to be disturbed by wild parties and boisterous behavior. Hurricane season, running from August through October, is another risky time, especially in September. Temperatures hover around 80°F year round, but the humidity can be oppressive during the summer rainy season.

Cuisine

Yucatecan food is spicy and flavorful. Though you'll find just about every cuisine known to man in Cancún, it's the regional specialities that stand out. Mayan anchiote paste is a favorite ingredient in grilled foods prepared "a la Yucateca," such as Tikin-xic, fresh fish cooked with anchiote and limes. Cooks bake *pollo* or *cochinita pibil*, tender strips of marinated chicken or pork wrapped in banana leaves, in a *pib*, or barbecue. *Sopa de lima,* chicken soup with tortilla strips and lime juice, is another favorite. But perhaps the most famous Mayan dish is *poc chuc,* grilled strips of pork marinated in sour orange juice.

Cautions and Safety Concerns

Be cautious of the waters on the sea side of Cancún. The beauty of the water hides the strong current lurking underneath, and large swells are common in summer. Only the largest hotels employ lifeguards, so it's safest to swim with someone. Trying to get a fast tan in Cancún can also be dangerous. Be sure to use sunscreen with a high SPF, especially on your children.

Though crime is low, it pays to take precautions with your valuables.

Getting Around Cancún

Cancún makes a great base for exploring. Getting around is easy. Bus service is excellent. You'll find bus stops conveniently sprinkled throughout the Zona Hotelera and Centro. Though air-conditioned buses can be packed during the peak hours, especially when hotel employees are on the move, there's never much of a wait, as buses show up every couple of minutes. Normal fare is about seventy-five cents.

===FAST FACT

Beginning at the edge of town and running through the Hotel Zone, distances along the twenty-seven kilometer Paseo Kukulcán are marked by kilometers (Km) instead of addresses. (NOTE: Km. addresses in this chapter refer to Paseo Kukulcán unless otherwise noted.)

In addition, over 2,000 taxis cruise the streets and boulevards of Cancún. It's cheaper to hail a cab than to hire a parked one. Taxi fares are set and posted by most hotels in their lobbies. Still, you should also check with the driver before getting into the cab.

If you'd rather walk or ride a bicycle, you can take the Ciclopista, a red paved path that winds its way through part of the Zona Hotelera. Pedestrians have the right of way only on designated raised crosswalks.

To get from the airport and back, you can take the public shuttle (☎866-922-6286; *www.cancunshuttle.com*), which can take as long as two hours to reach your hotel. A better idea for families is probably to take a taxi for $35 to $40 or to hire a private car for $45 round-trip. You can also rent a car and drive yourself.

Family-Oriented Hotels

Cancún is leaning more toward families. Today, more hotels cater to kids with water park-like pools and kids programs. Dazzling hotels line Paseo Kukulcán. Large, airy lobbies feature atriums filled with plants and fountains soaring to faceted skylights. Deluxe rooms, fitted with mahogany, brass, marble, and handpainted tile, have private terraces overlooking the sea. Many have lavish interlocking pools, while others are half-hidden under thatched *palapas* (thatched-roof shelters).

 JUST FOR PARENTS

While most major hotels offer baby-sitting services, they're usually extra, even if you've booked your kids into the hotel's Kids' Club.

Club Las Velas (Km. 3.5)

Reservations: ☎800-223-9815 (U.S.), *www.all-inclusives.com*

A 285-room spacious all-inclusive on a lagoon and designed like a Mexican village, with brick-lined streets, a gazebo, and bubbling fountains. Water sports and a children's program make this a great place for families.

El Pueblito Beach Hotel (Km. 17.5)

Reservations: ☎998-881-8800, *www.elpueblitohotels.com*

A deluxe all-inclusive with 350 rooms in twenty-nine colonial villas clustered around flower-bedecked courtyards. Five pools with cascades and three restaurants add to the natural beauty.

Fiesta Americana Coral Beach (Km. 9.5)

Reservations: ☎800-343-7821 (U.S.), ✐*www.fiestaamericana.com*

With 602 split-level suites, this is one of the best hotels in Cancún. Located at Punta Cancún, in the center of the Zona Hotelera, four restaurants, a spa, a free-form pool with water slides, and the kids' club make this a good family choice.

Hilton Cancún Beach and Golf Resort (Km. 17)

Reservations: ☎800-445-8667 (U.S.), ✐*www.hilton.com*

With the largest layout of any hotel in Cancún, this 426-room hotel has commanding views of the Caribbean and the lagoon. It offers several pools, five restaurants, lighted tennis courts, water sports, a golf course, and a kids' program.

Hyatt Regency (Km. 9)

Reservations: ☎800-233-1234 (U.S.), ✐*www.hyatt.com*

This 300-room hotel has a fourteen-story tower rising above a glass atrium and open-air lobby. It has no beach, but its split-level pool with waterfall makes up for it. The hotel has live entertainment evenings and a Camp Hyatt kids' club.

RAINY DAY FUN

Take a tour of the hotels. Each has its own personality and architecture. Who knows? You might find a new place to stay on your next trip.

Meliá Cancún Resort and Spa (Km. 16.5)

Reservations: ☎800-336-3542 (U.S.), ✐*www.solmelia.com*

This huge resort has 492 rooms in a sleek concrete and glass pyramid with a spectacular atrium and lobby on a wide beach, a beachside pool plus one other, five restaurants, lighted tennis courts, golf course, and health club.

Royal Solaris Cancún (Km. 19.5)

Reservations: ☏866-289-8466 (U.S.), ✎*www.clubsolaris.com*

This 500-room family all-inclusive features two towers, one Spanish and one modern, as well as eight restaurants, five snack bars, and a kids' club. Four swimming pools, jacuzzi, and tennis courts offer a variety of activities.

Moon Palace (Km. 36.5)

Reservations: ☏800-868-2802 (U.S.), ✎*www.palace-resorts-cancun.com*

This super-luxurious all-inclusive resort features 2,031 rooms on fifty-five tropical acres, with deluxe jacuzzi suites, three interconnecting pools, and an eighteen-hole golf course.

Villas/Rental Options

Cancún offers more condominiums for rent than full villas. These are especially popular with families that wish to control their food costs and have more home-like accommodations. The following is a list of rental agencies:

- Amigo Paco Real Estate: ☏998-887-1204
- Costa Realty:☏998-885-2016
- Howard Hill & Associates: ☏998-886-2610
- Kan-Kun Sales and Rentals: ☏998-884-450
- Turquesa Real Estate: ☏998-885-2924

Something for Everyone

You can be active twenty-four hours a day or just sit back and let the warm sun wash over you. Many activities center upon the water, from sunning on powdery beaches to fishing and snorkeling, sailing, windsurfing—the list goes on and on. Cancún offers activities for every age and loads of opportunities for your family members to share the fun with one another.

Things to Do

Those who come for a few days often never venture beyond the Zona Hotelera. But to really experience Cancún, you must explore Centro, downtown. Offering great shopping buys and pleasant restaurants with good local food, it's a modern city where your dollars will go further.

 TRAVEL TIP

For a great view of Cancún, ride the rotating tower of La Torre Cancún for $9. (open 9 A.M. to 11 P.M., El Embarcadero Park, ☎998-889-7777.)

To learn about Mexican crafts, visit the Museo de Arte Popular Méicano, showing handicrafts from various regions of Mexico (El Embarcadero, ☎998-849-4848).

If you have an independent streak, you may want to rent a Harley and cruise Cancún on a Fat Boy, Sportster, or Low Rider from Eagle Rider (Paseo Kukulcán, Km. 13, ☎998-885-0988). Or be even more daring and see Cancún by helicopter with Helitours (☎998-849-4222) or with Magic Sea and Sky Tours (☎998-885-1720) for approximately $80 per person.

For the Kids

Take the little ones to the seventeen-acre Parque Nizuc, a Wet 'n' Wild water park south of the Zona Hotelera on the Rio Nizuc at Km. 25 for a day of fun. As with other Wet 'n Wild parks, it includes an aquarium, water slides, and a wave pool. Admission is $33 for adults, $25 for kids aged three to eleven (open 10 A.M. to 5:30 P.M., ☎998-881-3000).

Swimming with dophins has become a popular activity in Cancún. Even though it costs $110 to $135 per person to participate, people are plunking down their dollars to have the experience of a lifetime. This is a particularly rewarding activity for children eight and up. The best place to do this is Dolphin Discovery on Isla Mujeres (☎998-883-0779). A one-hour session, including time for a swim and taking photos, costs $120 dollars per person. Children eight and above can participate. The boat departs Playa Langosta at 9 and 11 A.M. and 1 and 3 P.M. You can also swim with dolphins at Parque Nizuc (see above) for $135 per person, including park admission. The Interactive Aquarium (☎998-883-0436) at the La Isla Shopping Center also has a dolphin swim experience for $110 per person, plus the kids can feed sharks and exotic sea creatures.

 **RAINY DAY**

Just as you would on a rainy day at home, you can take your brood to see a movie at one of four theaters with several screens. The Cinemas Kukulcán (☎998-885-3021) in Plaza Kukulkán and Cinemark (☎998-885-0576) in Forum by the Sea, show first-run American flicks in English.

Younger teens will love to drive their own go-kart at Karting International Cancún (open 10 A.M. to 11 P.M.) south of town. Or take them to play thirty-six holes of miniature golf around pyramids, waterfalls, a river, and a lagoon at the Cancún Palace Resort (Km. 14.5, ☎998-885-0533).

Bullfights

Professional matadors fight six bulls every Wednesday afternoon beginning at 3:30 P.M. at the Plaza de Toros (☎998-884-8372), downtown at Avenidas Sayil and Bonampak. *Charros,* or Mexican cowboys, put on a show of horsemanship and rodeo skills between *corridas,* or bullfights. A folkloric dance program begins at 2:30 P.M. You can buy tickets for $35 through tour desks.

Visiting the Past

Before visiting archaeological sites in the area, you should visit the Museo de Arquelógia, adjacent to the Convention Center (open 9 A.M. to 5 P.M., closed Mondays; ✆998-883-3671). Its exhibits, in English and Spanish, will give you insight into the culture of the Maya.

You should begin your exploration of the Maya at Ruinas del Rey (El Rey Ruins), located within the Hilton Golf and Beach Resort golf course (open 8 A.M. to 5 P.M.). A pyramid, two plazas, and some low platforms showing some remains of Mayan paintings make up the site. When archaeologists uncovered the site, they found a skeleton on top of the pyramid, thus the name of El Rey, the king.

Continue your exploration at Tulum, a Mayan walled city and ceremonial center overlooking the Caribbean, eighty miles south of Cancún. Called Zama, the City of Dawn, by its ancient inhabitants, it's now the most-visited archaeological site in the area. Coba, another site near Tulum, offers a glimpse of Mayan grandeur. Exploring this city of pyramids and buildings along wide avenues set in the dense jungle is like going on your own Indiana Jones adventure. (See Chapter 9.)

If the above whets your appetite, you can take an excursion to Chichén Itzá, less than two hours southwest of Cancún. Climb the 365 steps of the El Castillo to the Temple of the Plumed Serpent. You'll agree that the view is breathtaking. Then explore the ruins—eighteen structures, including the observatory, the warrior temple, the platforms, the jaguar temple—sheltered in a jungle of wild papaya and sapodilla trees. The highlight of this sacred Mayan city is the magnificent Pyramid of Kukulcán, where during the spring and summer equinox you can see the shadow of a serpent, the symbol of Kukulcán, as it moves up the stairs on the pyramid. You can book tours to each of these sites through Mayan Quest Archaeological Tours (✆998-887-2740).

Isla Mujeres

For a change of pace, take the fifteen-minute Rapido ferry from Puerto Juarez to Isla Mujeres for $3. Shaped like a fish and about six miles across from the Bay of Cancún is Isla Mujeres, affectionately known as La Isla, a place that offers a quiet respite from the fast-paced, round-the-clock lifestyle of Cancún. Only five miles long and 1,300 feet wide, people flock here daily to wade in the placid waters, listen to a little afternoon music on one of the many beaches, or snorkel in one of the several reef areas, such as the Manchones, Bandera, and Tavos Reefs, all teeming with colorful parrotfish and angelfish. A good place for neophyte snorkelers is El Garrafón National Park, located a couple of miles out of town. For more daring divers, there's a sixty-eight-foot dive into the renowned Cave of the Sleeping Sharks, said to often hold up to seven sharks at once.

The quaint town at the northern tip of the island is the landing point for ferries arriving from Cancún. Shops selling everything from coral and silver jewelry to hammocks and Mayan figurines line the streets.

Tour boats go to Isla Mujeres daily. Glass-bottomed boats do excursions to undersea gardens or perhaps you'd rather dance while cruising over to the island. Tours cost $30 to $50 per person, including time for shopping and snorkeling, lunch, and open bar. Snorkel gear costs extra.

Here are some suggested tours:

- **Caribbean Funday Tour:** A triple-decker cruise boat (Fat Tuesday Pier, ☎998-884-3760)
- **Dolphin Express:** Best buy, with continental breakfast and buffet lunch (☎998-883-1488)
- **Isla Mujeres Adventure:** A fun cruise boat (Aqua Tour, ☎998-883-0400)
- **Tropical Cruiser Morning Express:** Playa Langosta dock, ☎998-883-3268

Isla Contoy

If you're a bird watcher and nature lover, you shouldn't miss a trip to Isla Contoy, a national wildlife preserve and bird sanctuary, located about an hour from Isla Mujeres.

Flamingos, brown pelicans, cormorants, and frigate birds swoop down on empty stretches of beach. Daily tours from Club Nautico cost about $35 per person (Playa Caracol, ☎998-886-4847).

Festivals, Special Events, Activities

Since the residents of Ciudad Cancún originally emigrated from other parts of Mexico, they don't have the traditions of local festivals that you'll find in other cities in Mexico. However, the resort itself does host a few events that draw large crowds:

- **Cancún Billfishing Tournament:** Held from late April through June.
- **Cancún Jazz Festival:** Held the last week of May.
- **International Yacht Races:** Held on Isla Mujeres at the end of April.
- **Expo-Cancún:** An arts, crafts, and folk dancing festival held at the end of November.

Fun in the Sun

There's probably nowhere else where you can have more fun in the sun than in Cancún. With miles of talcum-powder-soft beaches and warm Caribbean waters, it's the next thing to paradise.

Beach It

Cancún's eleven magnificent beaches are its main attraction. The first six with gentle surf—Playas Las Perlas, Juventud, Linda, Langosta, Tortugas, and Caracol—face the Bahía de Mujeres and are the best for swimming. Those facing the open Caribbean—Gaviota Azul, Chac-Mool, Ballenas, Marlin, and Delfines—have broad sands and stronger surf. You should swim closer to shore to avoid the undertow. Playa Las Perlas is best for families, while Playas Linda and Langosta are departure points for boat tours.

≡FAST FACT

All beaches are free in Mexico—even those fronting posh resort hotels.

Boat It

With so much water surrounding Cancún, it's only natural to want to get out on it. Rent a Sunfish or Hobie Cat and explore the lagoon on your own. Or take a one- or two-person Jet Ski™ or speedboat and tour the mangroves in the lagoon. Mangrove swamps in places along its edge provide shelter for wildlife and birds. If you wish to take someone along, then rent a WaveRunner. The marinas in Cancún offer a variety of activities. Some specialize in diving, offering equipment and excursions to the best diving areas, while others specialize in sailing and waterskiing, and still others are departure points for sightseeing and dinner cruises:

- **Aqua Fun:** Sailing, snorkeling, diving (Omni Hotel, Km. 16.2, ☎998-885-3260)
- **Aqua Rey:** Watersports center (Lorenzillo's Restaurant, ☎998-883-3007)
- **Aqua Tours:** Fishing, waterskiing, snorkeling, lobster dinner cruises (Fat Tuesdays Restaurant, ☎998-883-0400)
- **Aqua World:** Watersports, sportsfishing (Meliá Cancún, Km. 15.2, ☎998-848-8327)
- **Barracuda:** Banana boat rides, WaveRunners, waterskiing (Km. 14, ☎998-885-2444)
- **Club Lagoon:** Jungle speedboat tour (Club Lagoon, ☎998-883-3109)
- **Del Rey:** Waterskiing (☎998-883-1748)
- **Mundo Marina:** Snorkeling and diving (Km. 5.5, ☎998-883-0554)
- **Punte Este:** Watersports, diving, fishing (Km. 10.3, ☎998-883-1210)
- **Royal Yacht Club:** Sailing (Royal Mayan Hotel, ☎998-885-0391)

If you'd rather explore under the sea, you can take floating submarine tours aboard the Nautibus (☎998-883-3552), a double-keeled boat with transparent panels below the water line so you can see the fish and coral without getting wet. The two-hour trip includes all the sodas and beer you can drink for $35 per person.

Or you can take the Sub See Explorer from AquaWorld, a glass-bottomed boat with a deep draft and portholes below the water line that enable you to see marine life underwater, also for $35, including lunch, beer and soft drinks. If you wish, you can combine it with a trip to Paradise Island, a man-made reef platform for swimming and snorkeling for $45 per person.

To dive in an actual submarine, you'll have to climb aboard Destination Atlantis (☎998-883-3021), which shuttles you to Isla Mujeres for a ride aboard the Atlantis Submarine, a passenger submarine for underwater excursions over the reefs. It departs every hour from the Embarcadero at the Playa Linda pier (Km. 8, ☎998-883-4963).

For a super high-speed ride, you'll love the Shotover Jet motorboat rides, a forty-five-minute high-speed tour along Cancún's beaches. The price of $45 per person includes admission to Wet 'n' Wild. Tours depart daily from Parque Nizuc from 11 A.M. to 1 P.M. Children must be at least four feet tall to ride. Be sure to reserve two days in advance (Km. 25, ☎998-881-3000).

After speeding around all day on the lagoon, it's time to take your family on a five-hour Pirate's Night dinner cruise aboard a fake pirate ship, with three-course buffet and live entertainment for $50 per adult, half price for kids under twelve. Dress-up costumes are provided (☎998-883-1488).

Snorkel, Scuba, Fish

If you like to snorkel or dive, Cancún is the place. Snorkeling is best at Playa Tortugas, Punta Nizuc, or Punta Cancún. With a depth of just thirty-three feet and great visibility, Arrecife de Manchones (Manchones Reef), off Isla Mujueres, an island just beyond Cancún, is ideal for learning to snorkel. You can take a family-oriented snorkeling tour with Cancún Mermaid (☎998-843-6517).

Offshore diving is best at Arrecife de Chital or Arrecife de Cuevones, part of El Gran Arrecife, otherwise known as the Great MesoAmerican Reef, the fifth-largest reef in the world. Shallow Arrecife de Chital, with depths to 108 feet, lies north of the Hotel Presidente, and Arrecife de Cuevones, with depths to 146 feet, lies north of Punta Cancún. More experienced divers prefer it because of its series of caves and immense brain and elkhorn coral formations. While Cancún has many dive shops, three of the largest and best equipped are Scuba Cancún (☎998-849-7508, *www.scuba cancun.com.mx*), which conducts novice dive lessons; Blue Water Divers (Km. 15.6, ☎998-883-0327); and AquaWorld (☎998-885-2288, *www.aquaworld.com.mx*)

The waters around Cancún offer some excellent sportsfishing. Whether you'd rather troll for big-game fish like marlin, tuna, dorado, and wahoo, or angle in the lagoon or inlets for snook, tarpon, barracuda, or needlefish, you'll definitely bring home the catch of the day. While April to September offers the best varieties of fish, sailfish run from March to mid-July; bonito and dorado run from May to early July; and wahoo and kingfish from May to September. Barracuda, red snapper, bluefin, grouper, and mackerel are plentiful all year. Fishing charters on a thirty-one-foot boat for up to six fishermen costs about $320 for a half day and $520 for a full day.

 TRAVEL TIP

For a truly unique fishing experience, try the Naviera Asterix party cruise, on which you catch your dinner and the crew cooks it for you for $50 per person, including bait and tackle, departing from Club Nautico (☎998-886-4847).

Parasailing, Waterskiing, Windsurfing

Experience the thrill of being strapped into a colorful parachute and dangling high above the clear waters of the lagoon or sea as you "fly" behind a speedboat for ten minutes, to then be deposited back on the sand. Perhaps you and a son or daughter will want to try the Skyrider Parasail at Marina Aqua Ray, a two-seater attached to the parachute. For a solo flight, reserve through Lorenzillo's Restaurant (998-883-3007) or at your hotel.

If you'd rather fly across the surface of the water, then you shouldn't miss a chance to waterski on the calm waters of Laguna Nichupté. Sailboarding, or windsurfing as it's commonly known, is also a popular sport on the lagoon. You can learn how at the International Windsurfer Sailing School (Playa Tortugas, Km. 7, 998-884-2023).

Horseback Riding and Bicycling

To go horseback riding, try Rancho Loma Bonita (998-887-5465), a bit of a distance down Highway 307. It's the largest ranch around, with 150 horses, and offers rides over 987 acres through jungle and mangrove swamps. Organized trail rides cost $72 per adult, $65 per child (ages six through twelve), including transportation from your hotel, guide, lunch, and instruction.

Cancún is the ideal place to rent a bike and ride the 8.7-mile serpentine bike path that weaves among topiary trees and flowers along Paseo Kukulcán from downtown to Punta Cancún. It's best to do this early in the morning before the heat and humidity get oppressive. You can rent bikes for about $6 an hour from the Cancún Bicycle Club at Plaza Las Glorias or the Radisson Sierra Plaza Hotels. Kiosks along the path rent inline skates for about $7 an hour. There's a discount for multihour rentals.

Golf

Every other hotel seems to be cashing in on the golfing craze, with putting greens and chip-and-putt courses. Three championship eighteen-hole courses, plus two executive par-three courses, at the Meliá Cancún (Km. 16.5, 998-885-1100) and the Oasis Cancún Hotel

(Km. 17, ☎998-885-0867), should provide plenty of play. If you're a serious golfer, you may want to also play some of the courses along the Riviera Maya. (See Chapter 9.)

Time to Relax

With all the luxury resorts in Cancún, you won't have to go far to find a spa. All the major hotels offer the usual spa treatments in plush surroundings. One of the most unusual is the moonlight massage in an outdoor tent on the beach at the Meliá Cancún Resort and Spa (☎998-881-1100).

Shopping

Cancún can be a shop-til-you-drop paradise. It all depends on what you're looking for. You'll find handicrafts from all over Mexico, plus interesting folkart, jewelry, and souvenirs, plus designer clothes, T-shirts, and hammocks of handwoven cotton, silk, nylon, or sisal. From American-style malls and shopping plazas in the Zona Hotelera to more traditional *artesanias* markets downtown, you'll find more than enough to occupy an entire week if you choose. And for the ultimate touch of home, there's always Wal-Mart (Av. Coba, Centro, ☎998-884-1474).

 JUST FOR PARENTS

If you're planning on buying Mexican liqueurs and tequila, you may want to check the supermarkets downtown—Comercial Méxicana or Chedraui—since prices are usually lower there.

Shops open from 10 A.M. to 1 P.M. and open again from 4 P.M. to 10 P.M., but in the Zona Hotelera, they stay open all day. Shop prices are usually in pesos and should be marked "N$" plus the amount. It's a good idea to ask before you buy.

The Coral Negro Mercado de Artesanias is a market with sixty-five shops at Km. 9 on the Paseo Kukulcán. It sells traditional handicrafts and souvenirs at reasonable prices, but you'll find a better selection of Mexican crafts—blankets, black coral necklaces, hammocks, and Panama hats—downtown at the huge outdoor Mercado Ki-Huic, with over 100 vendors. Other handicraft markets include Plaza Mexico, Plaza Bonita, and Plaza Garibaldi, all downtown.

Time to Eat

There are so many restaurants in Cancún that it's hard to know which ones to choose. When it comes to dining out in Cancún, you have your choice of more than 400 restaurants, constituting a real United Nations taste experience. Just about every one of the world's most popular cuisines is represented here, including Italian, French, Japanese, and Chinese, and of course, Mexican. Old stand-bys such as Lorenzillo's are excellent, and new ones such as Iguana Wana (Plaza Caracol, ☎998-883-0829), serving fifty kinds of tequila and twenty-five different beers, are popular with the younger crowd. While Cancún is normally a casual place, some restaurants enforce dress codes. Inquire ahead.

≡FAST FACT

Tropical evening wear includes sport shirts and slacks for men, and a dress or blouse and skirt or pants for women.

As far as luxury eating places go, they've grown the most. At one time the number of three- and four-star restaurants on the island and downtown could be counted on the fingers of one hand. Not so today.

In addition, Cancún has developed into a fast-food Nirvana.

The rowdy restaurant scene, where atmosphere is as important as the menu, includes such places as Carlos 'n' Charlie's (Km. 5.5, ☎998-883-0846) and Señor Frogs (☎998-883-1092). Cancún even has its own Hard Rock Café and Planet Hollywood!

 JUST FOR PARENTS

Take your honey out for a special treat at Hacienda El Mortero (☎998-883-1133), an authentic reproduction of an eighteenth-century hacienda, serving steak and authentic Mexican dishes. Try one or more of their fifteen varieties of tequila while listening to mariachi music. Or dine on Moroccan dishes in a romantic Casablanca-style setting, complete with piano player singing "As Time Goes By," at Bogart's (☎998-848-9800). Both are part of the Krystal Cancún Hotel (Paseo Kukulcán, Km. 9.5)

Local Dining Suggestions

- **Blue Bayou:** Cajun cuisine is served to the accompaniment of New Orleans jazz (Hotel Hyatt Cancún, Km. 10.5, ☎998-883-0044).
- **Casa Rolandi:** Italian specialties are featured here, with a great antipasto bar (Plaza Caracol, Km. 8.5, ☎998-883-2557).
- **El Pescador:** Grilled fish and lobster are the specialties, with pictures of Yucatecan dishes (Av. Tulipanes 28, ☎998-884-2673).
- **La Dolce Vita:** This is Cancún's best Italian eatery, serving fine cuisine in a casually elegant atmosphere overlooking the Lagoon (Km. 14.6, ☎998-885-0150).
- **La Habichuela:** Gourmet Mexican cuisine is served in a candlelit setting in courtyard and dining room. Romantic dining

is available in candlelit gardens with Mayan sculptures (Av. Margaritas 25, Centro, ☎998-884-3158).

- **Lorenzillo's:** One of the first restaurants in Cancún, it's set on a pier over the lagoon. This local favorite serves fresh lobster and seafood (Km 10.5, ☎998-883-1254).
- **Los Almendros:** This is the best Yucatecan eatery in Cancún, serving delicious regional dishes (Av. Bonampak 60, Centro, ☎998-887-1332).
- **Péricos:** At this wild place, waiters dressed as banditos serve barbecued ribs and combination Mexican platters in a room decorated with murals of banditos and movie stars and saddle bar seats.(Yachilan 51, Centro, ☎998-884-3152).
- **Sanborn's:** This restaurant chain features good food and value, serving breakfast twenty-four hours, with free refills of fresh coffee. Mexican dishes are served for lunch and dinner by costumed waitresses. Open twenty-four hours (three locations: Flamingo and Mayfair Plazas, Plaza Las Americas, ☎998-887-5893).

Dining Precautions

Even with so many restaurants and food stands in Cancún, you shouldn't have any problems since those in the Zona Hotelera cater mostly to tourists. However, do be careful when dining downtown. Purified water is available everywhere.

 TRAVEL TIP

Should you have a digestive problem from eating too many rich foods, you can get help at the twenty-four-hour Farmacia Hospital Americano, where the pharmacist speaks English (☎998-884-6133).

Where to Go After Dark

When it comes to nightlife, Cancún rocks with the best. Discos like Dady'O, Tequila Rock, and Up and Down throb with the beat of the latest dance music as tanned bodies churn on the dance floor. Christine's, in the Krystal Cancún Hotel, the oldest, remains a Cancún classic, with a laser light show that is tops. Discos don't start jumping until after 10 p.m. Cover charges range from $10 to $20 per person. Or you may want to end your evening listening to soft jazz in your hotel bar.

JUST FOR PARENTS

Get a sitter for the kids and take a romantic lobster dinner cruise on the Laguna Nichupté on the *Cancún Queen,* a Mississippi-style stern-wheeler bedecked with twinkling lights that cruises for three hours under starry skies while you enjoy a broiled steak or lobster with open bar, plus music and dancing for $60 per person. Departs at 6 P.M. from AquaWorld Marina (☎998-885-2288).

For a fun family night out, cruise over to Isla Mujeres aboard the *Crucero Tropicale* (Tropical Cruiser) on a three-hour Pirate's Night Adventure where you'll feast on a buffet dinner with free drinks while watching a floor show. The boat departs from Playa Langosta.

CHAPTER 9

Riviera Maya

AFTER LIVING IT UP in Cancún, it's time to head south along Highway 307 to the 100-mile stretch of coast known as the Riviera Maya. The road, now a four-lane highway that runs inland and parallel to the coast, winds through dense jungle occasionally marked by spectacular Mayan ruins and dotted with beachside villages and resorts. Here, on crescents of powdery sands washed by the turquoise Caribbean and edged by tropical jungle, you can get away from the hustle and bustle of Cancún.

About the Riviera Maya

While Cancún offers nonstop entertainment, the Riviera Maya offers diversity. Once just a string of secluded beaches, it offers you a variety of activities, from sun worshiping to beachcombing, horseback riding, and water sports. You'll discover why its unique combination of nature (through its ecological reserves), culture (through its archaeological sites), and natural beauty (through its soft palm-fringed beaches), makes the Riviera Maya so popular with families. The region stretches from Puerto Morelos in the north to the Sian Ka'an biosphere in the south, taking in the town of Playa del Carmen and the villages of Puerto Morelos, Akumal, and Tulum.

Puerto Morelos, the first town along the coastal route, offers a peaceful mood combined with easy access to the sea. Known ages ago as the departure point for Mayan women making pilgrimages to Cozumel to worship the goddess Ixchel, shops and restaurants line its streets. Puerto Morelos is also home to one of the nicest diving reefs along the coast, filled with caverns of coral and multicolored marine life.

It used to be that visitors flocked to the town of Playa del Carmen, forty-two miles south of Cancún along the Riviera Maya, only to make the ferry ride to Cozumel. But today, Playa, as it's known locally, has open-air cafés, quaint shops, minimarkets, cantinas, and an ocean-front *malecón* that attract more than just passers by. During the last decade, Playa del Carmen has developed from a quiet fishing village into the main town along the Riviera Maya. Its main street, Avenida la Quinta (Fifth Avenue), running east to west along the waterfront, will provide you with a variety of entertainment and dining options.

JUST FOR PARENTS

While your kids are busy enjoying themselves in the kids' program at the hotel, why not do some shopping along Avenida la Quinta, then loll away the rest of the afternoon sipping a margarita at an open-air café?

One of the newest resort areas in the region is Puerto Aventuras. Located forty-four miles south of Cancún, it offers a 900-acre self-contained resort with a 250-boat marina, private villas, a nine-hole resort golf course, a beach club, dive center, and luxurious hotels. The warm, clear waters of the Caribbean make snorkeling and diving popular pastimes, along with deep-sea fishing and sailing. Your family will enjoy stopping at the CEDAM Underwater Archeology Museum that displays artifacts collected from a sunken Spanish merchant ship.

The next stop below Puerto Aventuras, some sixty-five miles south of Cancún, is Akumal, which means "Land of the Turtles" in Mayan. Here, you'll discover one of the Riviera Maya's more beautiful beaches and a favorite of divers. Or you can explore the subterranean sea caves with over 200 entrances and depths to nearly 500 feet. Once a large coconut plantation, the northern palm-lined area is known as Half Moon Bay, an exceptional snorkeling area lined with villas and condominiums. While some come here for the outstanding diving opportunities, others just stroll the tranquil beaches, combing for shells and catching sight of the ample bird life in the area. There's also a small Mayan community here that offers its wares at informal markets in town.

Best Time to Go

The seasons here are the same as for Cancún, with May through November being the rainy season when it rains a little just about every afternoon. Average annual temperatures range from 77° to 86°F. You should make note that Daylight Savings Time is not observed during the summer months, as it is in the rest of Mexico.

Cuisine

Yucatecan cuisine, particularly Mayan, is the local specialty here. Delicious and varied dishes like *fajitas de pollo* (chicken fajitas), *cochinita pibil* (roast suckling pig), *tacos al pastor* (taco meat slow-roasted vertically), and *pollo pibil* (chicken baked in banana leaves) are popular with locals and visitors alike. Or perhaps you'd like to try *puchero* (stew of pork, chicken, and vegetables). *Huevos moteleños* (scrambled eggs on tortillas smothered in tomato sauce, ham, beans, bacon, and peas) is a popular breakfast dish. Here, Mexican cooks combine Mayan ingredients and techniques with those of Spanish origin.

TRAVEL TIP

Habanero chile peppers, which come in red, green, and yellow, are dangerously hot. Ask your waiter if the dish of salsa on the table contains them before your children eat any.

Getting Around the Riviera Maya

Since the resorts and attractions along the Riviera Maya are spread out, it's a good idea to rent a car if you wish to explore extensively. All the major companies offer rentals here. Taxis are also available, charging a little less than $1 per mile. Call ☎987-873-0032 to order one. A one-hour trip to Cancún from Playa del Carmen, for example, costs about $35. Local bus lines also service points along Highway 307. Cancún International Airport is the closest major airport to the Riviera Maya. Many of the major resorts have pickup services, but you'll also find buses and vans waiting to take you to the major towns along the coast (Grupo Intermar Riviera Maya: ☎984-878-1010, *www.travel2mexico.com*).

Family-Oriented Hotels

The Riviera Maya offers a variety of accommodations—everything from camping grounds and beachside bungalows to luxury hotels and all-inclusive resort villages. In fact, there are more all-inclusive resorts here than anywhere else in Mexico, and many traditional resorts have kids' programs.

Continental Plaza Playacar
Reservations: ☎800-882-6684 (U.S.)
This pink five-story complex, with 188 rooms and sixteen suites, was built around Mayan ruins. Under the shade of the thatched mini-*palapas,* deck chairs line two crystal swimming pools and a nearby bar just off the beach. The air-conditioned rooms have terraces overlooking the Caribbean.

Campout Kai Luum
Reservations: ☎800-538-6802 (U.S.)
In Punta Bete, this rustic camping resort offers guests platform tents with maid service but no electricity. After rising to a sumptuous buffet breakfast cooked by Mayan chefs and served under

a *palapa*-covered beachside restaurant, you can relax in the hammocks strung up under your own *palapa*.

Hotel Club Akumal Caribe

Reservations: ☎800-351-1622 (U.S.), ✎*www.hotelakumalcaribe*
.com

This sixty-one-room resort hotel located on the beach offers a variety of accommodations, ranging from two-bedroom suites to two-bedroom condominiums and bungalows. Activities include diving, kayaking, windsurfing, snorkeling, fishing, tennis, jungle walks, and a private pool.

Caribbean Village Golf and Beach Club

Reservations: ☎800-858-2258 (U.S.)

At this resort catering to golfers, greens fees are included in the nightly rate. Two pools and three tennis courts will keep you relaxed when you're not playing golf.

Bahia Principe Tulum

Reservations: ☎998-875-5020, ✎*www.bahia-principe.com*

This 810-room luxury resort near the ruins at Tulum features spa and jacuzzis, baby-sitting service, and laundry.

Villas/Rental Options

You can rent villas at Akumal, Puerto Aventuras, Playa, and Soliman Bay. Most of the seventy-seven ocean or beachfront villas can accommodate six to eight persons, but there are several that can sleep twenty and that come with a private pool. Prices range from $1,095 to $17,500 per week or an average of $1,500 per night, including a maid/cook (✎*www.locogringo.com*). You can also rent one- and two-bedroom villas from Akumal Vacations (☎800-448-7137, U.S.).

Something for Everyone

Activities range from beachcombing to reef diving to archaeological excursions. Your kids will love visiting a crocodile farm or the aquarium, then going for a swim in the crystal-clear waters of a natural *cenote*.

≡FAST FACT

When acidic rain seeps through the cracks in the Earth's surface and dissolves the limestone underneath, large caverns are formed. The collapsing of the roof of one of these caverns creates a sinkhole called a *cenote*, meaning "sacred well" in Mayan, which is often connected by underground rivers to the sea.

Things to Do

It seems just about everyone has hopped aboard the "eco-green" bandwagon along the Riviera Maya. A number of so-called Eco Parks have sprung up along the coast in the last few years. All seem to be centered upon one or more *cenotes*.

The largest and most expensive of these eco parks, Xcaret, a quiet cove turned tropical waterside theme park, lies about an hour from Cancún and four miles south of Playa del Carmen on Highway 180. An underground river ride, the park's main attraction, winds through jungle surroundings. Wearing a life-jacket and snorkeling gear, you'll swim through cool water currents that flow through mysterious caves and man-made *caletas* (inlets). If you've ever wanted to swim with dolphins, this is the place to do it. There's also an aquarium, zoo, botanical garden, butterfly pavilion, mushroom farm, orchid conservatory, a manatee lagoon, wild bird aviary, horseback riding, and an apiary showing how the Maya cultivated bees, plus some archaeological monuments dating from A.D. 1200 to 1550. Your family will also enjoy the reproduction of a Mayan village where costumed dancers perform daily. The hefty daytime admission charge of $59 per person ($41 for children five to twelve; under four free) includes snorkeling and snuba (an alternative to scuba in which you are attached to air pumps aboard a boat) tours. At night, the entrance fee drops to $42 for adults, $29.50 for children. Add $17.50 per person for round-trip transportation from hotels in Playa (☎998-883-3144, ✐*www.xcaret.com*).

Grutas Aktun Chen, another of these eco parks, lies about two and half miles past Akumal. Its name means "cave with an underground river inside," which is what you'll see in this park spanning 988 acres of low-lying jungle. Here, you can take a walking tour of the largest cave, which shows the usual stalagmites and stalactites found in most other limestone caverns. After touring the cave and walking through the jungle filled with tropical plants, you can stop for a drink and a snack at the small restaurant. (Open daily 9 A.M. to 5 P.M. during winter and 9 A.M. to 7 P.M. during summer, ☎998-892-0662).

Still yet another is Kantun Chi, one mile south of Puerto Aventuras, with freshwater *cenotes* in which you can swim and snorkel. (Open 9 A.M. to 5 P.M. in winter and 9 A.M. to 6 P.M. in summer, ☎984-873-0021, ✐*www.kantunchi.com*.)

RAINY DAY FUN

The CEDAM Shipwreck Museum at the Puerto Aventuras Marina, an interesting as well as educational attraction, features exhibits of artifacts from ships carrying ivory and slaves from Africa. (Open daily 10 A.M. to 1 P.M. and 2 to 6 P.M., donations accepted.)

For the Kids

Kids love reptiles. And nine miles south of Cancún is Croco Cun, a massive breeding station, where your little ones can marvel at an assortment of more than 300 reptiles displayed in walled ponds. Here, they'll learn how American crocodiles and Central American caymans are raised by taking newly laid eggs and placing them in temperature-controlled rooms. (Open from 8 A.M. to 5 P.M., admission about $4 per person)

Another educational activity for kids is a visit to the Xaman Ha Aviary, part of the Playacar development. Here in a simulated jungle habitat, they'll get to observe over sixty species of tropical birds, including flamingos, toucans, macaws, and parrots, along with butterflies, iguanas, and turtles. Admission is about $15 per adult, plus one child per adult admitted free. (Open 9 A.M. to 5 P.M., Paseo Xaman s/n (*sin numero*) Fraccionamiento Playacar.)

A Visit to the Past

The Mayan ceremonial city of Tulum, thirty-nine miles south of Cancún, stands as one of the most visited archaeological sites in Mexico, next to Chichén Itzá (outside Merida) and Teotihuacán (outside Mexico City). Though not vast like many other sites, it sits high on a bluff overlooking the turquoise Caribbean, facing the rising sun. Historically rich, it's the most famous site in the area since it's easily accessible as a tour from Cancún. Reaching its peak between A.D. 1000 and 1500, this walled site centers around a plaza that the Maya used for religious rituals. If you climb to the top of El Castillo, the highest and most impressive structure on the site, you get a commanding view of the coastline and sea. A small site by most standards, it gives thousands of vacationers a chance to learn about the history of the Maya. (Open from 7 A.M. to 5 P.M., admission about $3.50.)

 TRAVEL TIP

If you want to explore Tulum or Coba on your own, arrive early or later in the day, before or after the hoards of tourists debarking from tour buses descend like locusts on the sites.

If you're a fan of the Indiana Jones movies, then you'll love exploring Coba, the remains of a huge Mayan city set within the jungle inland from the main highway about twenty-five miles west of Tulum and thirty-five miles south of Playa del Carmen. With as many as 50,000 inhabitants, it also served as a ceremonial center from A.D. 300 to 1000. Serving as the regional capital of the Northern Lowland

Empire, it features eight *stelae* (tall carved columns that told stories or kept historic records) in the Cucmuc Mul and nine circular altars in Grupo Macanxoc. The Nohoch Mul, the tallest pyramid in the Yucatán at 138 feet, stands as its centerpiece. All are fine examples of the architectural style of the east coast Maya. (Open from 8 A.M. to 6 P.M., admission about $3.50.)

Although the archaeological site and snorkeling park of Xel-Ha have the same name, they're two entirely different though related places. The first refers to the ruins of a Mayan ocean port, trading center, and religious site where the Maya stored food in case of famine. The second refers to a snorkeling park on the inlet of the same name. Both are thirty miles south of Playa del Carmen. From A.D. 100 to 600, Xel-Ha was the largest town along the coast. Its Palace of the Birds, with murals depicting birds and images of the god Tlaloc, shows ties with the culture of Teotihuacán in central Mexico. A half-mile east of the Palace of the Birds stands Jaguar House, showing a painting of a jaguar, which represents the sacred power of the high priests. This and a building decorated with twisted tiles stand next to a *cenote* that's part of a vast system of subterranean rivers that lead to the ocean under the site. (Open 8 A.M. to 5 P.M., admission about $2.50.)

Sian Ka'an

If you have the time, you should visit Sian Ka'an, the world's largest biosphere, also along the coast road. This 1.3 million-acre nature reserve, a UNESCO World Heritage Site since 1987, contains tropical forest, wetlands, and marine habitats, including sixty-nine miles of barrier reef. The name "Ziyan Caán," which the Maya gave to the area that's now the southern part of the state of Quintana Roo, means "Gift of the Sky." As the third-largest protected area in Mexico, it covers 370,500 acres, containing tropical forests, marshes, mangroves, and a large area of the coast with a barrier reef. It's home to over 1,200 species of animals, including 300 types of birds, as well as jaguars, howler monkeys, and crocodiles.

Amigos de Sian Ka'an, a private nonprofit organization that promotes the conservation of the reserve (✆984-884-9583), conducts daily tours (except Sundays and Fridays, lunch included) through Mayan canals in open boats for $50 per person. The trip is fascinating and worth every dollar. The number of daily visitors is limited to eighteen to protect the fragile ecosystem. EcoColors Tours also conducts tours of the biosphere by kayak (☞*www.ecotravelmexico.com*).

Festivals, Special Events, Activities

The following fishing tournaments draw fishing enthusiasts to the Riviera Maya's clear turquoise waters:

- **Copa Faro de Plata:** Held in May from the Puerto Aventuras Marina (☎984-873-5108)
- **Puerto Morelos Tournament:** Held May 1 from the El Cid Marina in Puerto Morelos
- **Flyfishing Tournament:** Held in September at Ascension Bay at Sian Ka'an (☞*www.flyfishingmexico.org*)

Fun in the Sun

The Riviera Maya is all about the sun, sand, and sea. You'll find just about everything you ever wanted to do.

Beach It

Beautiful white powdery beaches are the Riviera Maya's chief attraction. Bathed by warm sunshine and gentle sea breezes, miles of uncrowded talcum-like sandy beaches backed by palm trees await you. Here, you'll find peace and relaxation, along with enough activities to keep your family from becoming bored.

Playa Paamul, Playa Tankah, and Playa Xcalacoco offer gentle sloping sands that the Maya used as embarkation points to nearby islands. All are places to relax in the sun, dive, or snorkel over the nearby reef. From May to July, turtles come ashore at night to lay their eggs. If you like interacting with nature, you just might want to stay in one of the rustic cabins nestled between the turquoise sea and the jungle.

TRAVEL TIP

Due to the whiteness of the sand and the clearness of the water, it's imperative that you use a sunblock that's stronger than you normally use. If you're going to be walking or playing in the sun, be sure to also wear a wide-brimmed hat.

The focus along the Riviera Maya is ecology. While huge resorts have sprung up along the coast in recent years, there seems to be an effort to preserve the beauty of this area, to separate it ideologically from overdeveloped Cancún. Punta Allen makes an ideal place to admire Mother Nature's gifts. Here, you can observe crocodiles in the lagoons or manatees below the water's surface. Herons and other water birds flock to estuaries within the Sian Ka'an Biosphere. Another idyllic spot in the biosphere is Playa Boca Paila. This secluded beach, far from the developed areas, is the best place to fish.

There are several lesser-known beaches in the area that are worth a visit. Powder-soft sand and turquoise sea with swaying palm trees characterize Playa Chemuyil. A reef just offshore brings the waters to a quiet calm by the time they meet the shoreline, making for excellent swimming conditions. The beaches at Xcacel are no less spectacular. Turtles prefer this strand for its calm waters. Any number of privately owned seaside bungalows offer you a place to stay close to nature.

Boat It

Kayak tours of the coastline are a great way to experience the coral reefs. Sailing the calm clear waters is a favorite pastime along the Riviera Maya. You can hop aboard a thirty-six-foot catamaran for a fishing trip or just a sailing excursion with Kantaris Catamaran at the Akumal Dive Shop on the beach in Akumal (☏984-875-9032).

Snorkel, Scuba, Fish

With a *cenote* water temperature of about 76°F and an off-shore water temperature ranging from 78°F in January to 84°F in August, it's no wonder that the coast of Quintana Roo is a favorite of snorkelers and divers alike.

But one place that stands out is Xel-Ha, a natural aquarium just below Akumal, considered to be one of the biggest in the world. Ten acres of stunning lagoons, coves and inlets naturally carved into the area's soft limestone terrain are home to countless species of tropical fish. Xel-Ha offers you a chance to explore underwater caves, *cenotes* (sinkholes), and a partially submerged Mayan ruin. You can rent snorkel gear and underwater cameras. Or you may prefer to motor to the far side of the lagoon by glass-bottomed boat. The park includes a maritime museum and a seafood restaurant. Admission is about $35 per adult and $25 per child. You can rent snorkeling equipment for $10, towels for $3. (Open 8 A.M. to 5 P.M. daily, ✆984-884-9422.)

Although there's good diving up and down the coast, you'll find the best in the clear waters off Akumal, especially drift diving on the reef. *Cenote* and cave diving are also popular. Dive shops in Playa, Puerto Morelos, and Akumal offer a variety of snorkeling and scuba excursions, equipment rental, and PADI instruction. With nearly 100 miles of coastline, the Riviera Maya offers excellent deep-sea fishing, including big-game fish, barracuda, dorado, snook, wahoo, and tuna. Fly fishing, especially for bonefish, is excellent at Ascension Bay. Bonefish and tarpon jump from August through December. Here are some fishing companies that offer full-day tours with pickup at your hotel:

- Community Tours Sian Ka'an (✆984-114-0750, *www.sian kaantours.org*)
- Pesca Maya (✆998-883-4204, *www.pescamaya.com*)
- Cuzan Guest House, Punta Allen (983-834-0358, *www.fly fishmx.com*)

Jungle Tours

Experience the jungle riding an ATV at Punta Venado Eco Park just outside Playa del Carmen (☎998-898-1331, ✐*www.puntavenado.com*). If you'd rather ride a more traditional mount, you can ride through the-jungle on horseback with Rancho Loma Bonita (☎998-887-5423).

Golf

If you like to golf while on vacation, you'll currently find five courses along the Riviera Maya to test your skills, with more to come. Each is a different design by a top designer, so you'll find challenges on every green:

- **Iberostar Playa Paraiso Golf Club:** An eighteen-hole course, located thirty minutes south of Cancún. Facilities include clubhouse with changing rooms and showers, putting green, lighted driving range, nine-hole chip-and-putt course for families, and full-service pro shop where you can rent equipment (☎984-877-2800, ✐*www.iberostar.com.mx*).
- **El Camaleon Mayakobá Golf Club:** Located forty miles south of Cancún within the luxury resort development of Mayakobá, this eighteen-hole course includes a driving range and full-service clubhouse and pro shop with all amenities (✐*www.cancun.com/Tours/Golf_Camaleon_Mayakoba*).
- **Mayan Palace Riviera Maya Golf Club:** This challenging eighteen-hole course features a putting green, driving range, and clubhouse with pro shop and equipment rental (☎984-206-4043 or ☎800-506-8171 (U.S.), ✐*www.mayanresortsgolf.com*).
- **Playacar Golf Club:** A magnificent eighteen-hole championship course, includes a putting green and driving range, plus a full service clubhouse and pro shop (☎984-873-0624, ✐*www.palaceresorts.com/PlayaCarGolf/index.asp*)
- **Puerto Aventuras Resort Golf Club:** This nine-hole resort course is perfect if you're a golfing novice. Facilities include a putting green (☎984-473-5109, ✐*www.puertoaventuras.com*).

Time to Relax

If Cancún is the Yucatán's mass market destination, then the Riviera Maya is its deluxe and family destination. As such, you'll find more luxury spas at resorts along the coast than at most other beach resorts in Mexico. Most offer a variety of treatments, including Swedish, Ayurveda, deep tissue, and Shiatsu massages, crystal therapy, Reiki, body cleansing scrubs, facials, and more. The following is a selection of some of the best spas:

- **Alhambra:** Holistic massage and yoga a specialty (☎877-642-4235 (U.S.), ✍*www.alhambra-hotel.net*).
- **Cabanas Copal:** Holistic spa with hatha yoga, *temazcalli* (Mayan steam house), Mayan clay massage, and flotation tank. (☎877-532-6737 (U.S.), ✍*www.cabanascopal.com*)
- **Ceiba del Mar Hotel and Spa:** Marine mud tonification, Nitke massage, Mayan Balsamico, corporal exfoliation (☎877-545-6221 (U.S.), ✍*www.ceibadelmar.com*)
- **Itza Spa:** Day spa with water healing and Mayan therapies, body waxing, and dry sauna (☎984-803-2588, ✍*www.spaitza.com*)
- **Temazcal:** Mayan *sobada* massage, Mayan sauna, including special spa packages (☎998-887-5470, ✍*www.anayjose.com*)
- **Royal Hideaway Resort and Spa:** Synchronized four hands massage, balneotherapy (hydrotherapy), hot stone massage, and seaweed wrap (☎800-999-9182 (U.S.) ✍*www.royalhideaway.com*)
- **Secrets Capri:** Riviera Maya's newest spa, with over thirty different treatments, including aromatherapy saltglow (☎866-467-3273 (U.S.), ✍*www.secretsresorts.com*)

Shopping

Shopping in Playa del Carmen centers upon Avenida la Quinta, a pedestrian thoroughfare and the main street of town. Over the years, the number and variety of shops has greatly improved. The town even has two shopping malls where you can find everything from batik beach wraps with Mayan motifs to hand-tied hammocks to handmade cigars. You'll also find the usual Mexican silver jewelry and handicrafts. Most shops are open from 10 A.M. to 10 P.M., but close from 2 to 4 P.M. for lunch.

Time to Eat

While you'll find good restaurants in your hotel, most good independent ones are in Playa del Carmen. Substantial distances between some hotels and Playa del Carmen have encouraged the growth of all-inclusive resorts along the Riviera Maya.

JUST FOR PARENTS

If you like tequila, then head for El Tukan Maya in Playa for samplings from over eighty different varieties.

Local Dining Suggestions

- **Restaurante Don Emilione:** Italian and Mexican food is served either indoors with live jazz or outdoors under an umbrella on the patio. Seafood is a specialty. (Avenida la Quinta between Avenida Juárez and Calle 2, Playa, ☎984-873-2074).
- **Da Gabia:** This fine Italian restaurant serves freshly cooked seafood and brick-oven pizzas, as well as Mexican dishes, in a quiet romantic atmosphere under a giant *palapa* (Calle 12 and First Avenue North, Playa, ☎984-873-0048).
- **YAXCHE:** Authentic Mayan cuisine is served in a traditional-Mayan built and decorated house (Calle 8 between Avenida la Quinta and Tenth Avenue, Playa, ☎984-873-2502).
- **Hola Asia:** Excellent Chinese, Japanese, and Thai food is served with a view of the Caribbean. Rooftop bar and take-out. (On the *zócalo* in Puerto Morelos, ☎998-871-0679.)

- **Lol-Ha on Akumal Bay:** This beachfront landmark serves local dishes and pizza. The *palapa*-style beach bar is a favorite with divers (Hotel Villas Maya Akumal Caribe, ✆984-875-9011).
- **Máscaras:** This long-standing favorite serves Italian pastas and pizza indoors and out (Avenida Juárez at the zócalo, Playa, ✆984-873-1053).
- **Limones:** International and French dishes are served in a romantic candlelit environment. The bar features live music nightly (Fifth Avenue at Calle 6, ✆984-873-0848).
- **La Parilla:** This popular spot serves a variety of Mexican dishes and great margaritas (Avenida la Quinta at Calle 8, ✆984-873-0687).

Dining Precautions

Restaurants in tourist areas are clean and safe. You'll find bottled water for sale everywhere. For best meals, stick to fresh seafood and Yucatecan specialties.

Where to Go After Dark

While the Riviera Maya can be a relaxing place, you have a choice of staying at your hotel and having a late dinner or going out for the evening. Avenida la Quinta lights up after dark with an assortment of cafés, cantinas, and restaurants. Begin at the Blue Parrot, where you can hop in a swing at the beach bar and listen to Golden Oldies, salsa, and reggae. If you're looking for more action, drop into discos like the Mambo Café or Moon. *The* nightclub in Playa is Capitán Tutix, with the best live bands in town, then continue at La Santanera, upstairs. For a truly alternative experience, try Deseo, a cool lounge-bar where you can lie on big mattresses and watch silent old movies while listening to music played by a DJ. All open around 9 P.M. and close at 4 A.M. If you'd rather not stay out that late, there's always Mannee's Biergarten. If you'd like to cap off the night with an espresso or cappucino, try Segafredo Zanetti Espresso Bar along Avenida la Quinta.

CHAPTER 10

Cozumel

JUST A SHORT FERRY hop from Playa del Carmen south of Cancún, the island of Cozumel reveals its underwater beauty as you approach. Strands of aqua blue, green, and yellow sea squiggle around the shore—the locals call it *las siete colores de azul* (the seven colors of blue)—to wash over a reef that has made Cozumel Mexico's premier diving spot. But the island's real treasure is its natural beauty.

About Cozumel

Mexico's largest island, Cozumel lies less than twelve miles off the east coast of the Yucatan Peninsula and forty miles south of Cancún. Only ten miles wide and thirty miles long, it was here the Spanish first visited Mexico. During Mayan times, Cozumel was a sanctuary to Ixchel, the goddess of fertility and the moon, and a destination of pilgrims who came to worship and offer sacrifices to her. According to Mayan legend, the goddess sent swallows, her favorite birds, in thanks for the temples built to honor her. The birds still inhabit the island today.

Famed oceanographer Jacques Cousteau, drawn by stories of magnificent undersea vistas from Navy frogmen who trained there, visited Cozumel in 1961 to film a television documentary. He explored Arrecife de Palancar (Palancar Reef) and called it one of the finest dive sites in the world. Afterward, cruise lines began to call at the island, and it became a world-class diving destination.

≣FAST FACT

Cozumel derives its name from the Mayan words *cuzam* (swallow) and *lumil* (land of), which joined together as *Cuzamil* means "Land of the Swallows." In 1527, Spanish captain Don Francisco de Montejo arrived on the island and changed its name to San Miguel de Cozumel.

Known for its crystal clear water and for its proximity to Palancar Reef, the second-longest reef in the world, Cozumel now attracts divers from around the world. Palancar, with visibility to 200 feet, is actually a series of reefs. It offers beginners a spectacular introduction to the wonders of the sea, while advanced divers can explore the magnificent undersea canyons. As many as 250 different species of fish live in the warm waters surrounding the island. Plus, you'll find some of the largest sponge formations in the world—some spanning twelve feet. You'll also enjoy not only easy access to the reefs but water temperatures that fluctuate from 77 to 82°F.

TRAVEL TIP

If you wish to go over to Playa del Carmen on the mainland, take the air-conditioned water jet ferry, which departs Cozumel twelve times daily, beginning at 5 A.M. The one-way fare is $9 and there's no need for reservations. Contact Cruceros Marítimos del Caribe (☎987-872-1588, ✎*www.crucerosmaritimos.com.mx*).

Today, you'll find Cozumel has a laid-back atmosphere. You'll experience real Mexican culture and hospitality here.

Best Time to Go

Due to its location in the tropics, Cozumel is hot and humid. Although there's a rainy and a dry season, the abundant rainfall year round seems to make very little difference between them. The temperature hovers around 80°F most of the year, but in July and August it can climb into the low 90s. In December and January, it can dip to the mid-70s. Price-wise, December through August is high season, and September through November is low season.

Cuisine

Local cuisine on Cozumel is Yucatecan or Mayan. Dishes such as *cerviche* (raw fish marinated in lime juice with coriander, onion, and tomato) or *pollo pibil* (chicken baked in banana leaves) are popular.

Cautions and Safety Concerns

Cozumel is safe. The streets are well lit and violent crime is rare, so it's an ideal place to bring children. However, use common sense, keep your valuables concealed, and only take as much money with you as you think you'll need. More of an annoyance are the mosquitoes and sand flies. Use bug repellent and wear long-sleeved shirts and pants when walking in jungle areas. You should also bring along a wide-brimmed hat, plenty of sunscreen, and sports sandals since the best snorkeling lies near rocks.

═══FAST FACT

If you arrive by cruise ship, check the time as there's often a difference between ship time and island time.

Getting Around Cozumel

Except for taxis, there's no public transportation on Cozumel. It's important to negotiate fares for taxis before you get in. The average one-way fare between the hotel zone and San Miguel is $6, but you could pay as much as $8 for hotels farther out. If you arrive by plane, it will cost $5 to $6 to take a van to your hotel. To see the island's color and have some fun, too, why not rent a car or a moped for $25 to $30 a day from Marlin Cars and Scooters (✆987-872-0433).

If you want more exercise, rent a bicycle along the waterfront or by the cruise ship pier. A new *ciclopista* (bike path) will take you from town to Parque Laguna Chankanaab (Chankanaab Lagoon Park). You can rent a bike for about $15 dollars a day or weekly for $65, including gloves, map, lock, pump and repair kit, rack, and helmet from Isla Bicycleta (*cozumelbikes@gocozumel.com*).

Family-Oriented Hotels

Cozumel has a surprising number of wonderful hotels, most of which are smaller but just as luxurious as those in Cancún. You'll find spacious rooms, pools set in gardens, and great restaurants.

Coral Princess Hotel and Resort

Reservations: ✆800-253-2702 (U.S.), ✐*www.coralprincess.com*.

Ten minutes from town on the island's north side, this five-story, 253-room hotel features one- to three-bedroom suites with kitchenettes, making it the most modern and luxurious on the island.

El Cozumeleño Bounty Beach Resort

Reservations: ✆800-437-3923 (U.S.), ✐*www.elcozumeleno.com*.

A 252-room, six-story all-inclusive family resort with many activities and a kid's pool on a white sandy beach on the north side of the island, five minutes from town. Balconies have superb views and a golf course is across the road.

Hotel Cozumel & Resort

Reservations: ✆987-872 2900, ✐*www.hotelcozumel.com.mx*.

Located on the coastal road within walking distance of town, this self-contained resort has 180 rooms in three buildings, along with a beach club, dive shop, and the largest pool on Cozumel. A kids' program will keep little ones busy.

Fiesta Americana Cozumel Dive Resort

Reservations: ✆800-343-7821 (U.S.), ✍*www.fiestaamericana.com*

Located close to Palancar Reef and adjacent to Chankanaab Park, this seven-story, 224-room hotel offers a full range of water sports, including full dive services.

Meliá Cozumel Golf & Beach Resort

Reservations ✆800-336-3542 (U.S.), ✍*www.solmelia.com*

This impressive 147-room resort features all amenities and is directly across from the island's only golf course. You'll find several restaurants, two swimming pools, and a daytime entertainment program with cooking, dance, and bartending lessons, plus a Flintstone kids' program.

Occidental Grand Cozumel Hotel

Reservations: ✆800-858-2258 (U.S.), ✍*www.grandcozumel.com*

This 251-room luxury all-inclusive resort stands on Playa San Francisco in the southwest part of Cozumel. Eleven colonial-style buildings have twenty-four rooms each with all amenities, including a small refrigerator and coffee machine. The all-inclusive price includes a kids' club.

Villas/Rental Options

If you'd rather rent a villa, Cozumel has more than ninety to choose from, ranging in price from $435 for two people to $8,750 for up to thirty people for a week. Most accommodate two to six persons and come with one to five or more bedrooms, as well as a swimming pool and maid. You can hire reliable baby-sitters inexpensively (✍*www.cozu melvillas.com*).

Something for Everyone

Cozumel is made for families. There are things for everyone to do together.

Things to Do

To soak up local culture, explore San Miguel de Cozumel, the island's only town, which lies on the northwest side of the island near the hotel zone. Tropical cafés and boutiques line the busy twelve-block *malecón,* Avenida Rafael Melgar. The center of activity, especially on Sunday evenings, is the Plaza del Sol, San Miguel's *zócalo,* where the strains of salsa music flow from the outdoor cafés and locals gather to listen and dance.

Why not step into the cool depths of the Museo de la Isla de Cozumel (Cozumel Island Museum) on the waterfront near the main pier in San Miguel on a hot afternoon? Here you can view displays of underwater treasures and Mayan relics . Exhibits focus on the origin and history of the island, including pre-Columbian artifacts and colonial-era cannons and swords. You can also learn about the island's plant and animal life and topography, including an excellent exhibit on the Palancar Reef. Afterward, sip a cool fruit drink in Del Museo, its rooftop restaurant, and enjoy the spectacular harbor view. Later, pay a visit to San Miguel's old cemetery to see brightly decorated family mausoleums and shrines.

 JUST FOR PARENTS

> Get a sitter for the kids and take a boat from Cozumel's north shore for a Robinson Crusoe trip to Isla Pasión, which offers some blissful isolation for the two of you to enjoy.

About six miles south of town, you'll come to a snorkeler's paradise, Parque Laguna Chancanab. If you're a beginner snorkeler, you'll find the area of Laguna Chankanaab, which means "Small Sea" in Mayan, an ideal spot to break in your mask and flippers. Just steps away from Cozumel's beachfront hotels, the marine park blossoms with brilliant life in just a few feet of crystalline water. The lagoon bustles with barracuda, parrotfish, octopus, and sergeant majors.

The nearby ocean causes the formation of petrified coral in the lagoon. Fish move between the ocean and the lagoon through two underground caves. An archaeological park contains sixty replicas of Mayan art set in a lush botanical garden with over 700 species of plants and resident iguanas. Snorkeling shops provide everything you'll need to explore the coral of the lagoon. You can swim or lie under a *palapa* on the beach after having lunch in the one of the restaurants. Entrance fee is $12 for adults, $6 for kids ages three to eleven, and those under three enter free.

The 247-acre Punta Sur National Ecological Park, located at the southern tip of the island, is home to birds, reptiles, and fish that inhabit Columbia Lagoon and adjacent mangrove swamps. A tiny snail-like Mayan temple, called Tumba de Caracol, dates to A.D. 1200. You also can visit the park's museum in the late nineteenth-century lighthouse at Punta Celerain, which focuses on the history of navigation around the island. Afterward, you can go for a swim or on a guided jungle walk, then stop for a bite or a cool drink at the snack bar or restaurant. Plan on a minimum of five hours to see it all. Admission is $12 per person; children eight and under get in free. Shuttles make stops throughout the park every fifteen minutes, taking you from point to point.

📋 TRAVEL TIP

Take a four-hour jungle and coastal tour, driving your own fully-equipped Honda ATV, for $95 for adults and $52 for kids six and up. Follow your guide through the jungle to see ruins and deserted beaches, then stop to kayak and snorkel. A two-hour tour to Ruinas La Palmar costs $70 for adults, $39 for kids. Drivers must be at least sixteen.

Though nothing compared to archaeological sites on the mainland, it's worthwhile to visit the ancient Mayan ruins of San Gervasio, the island's most interesting and accessible site. The Maya erected its small temples, built between A.D. 300 and 1500, to honor the goddess Ixchel. It's said that many Mayan women made at least one pilgrimage to these temples to present offerings to this goddess of fertility. You can take a guided tour in English of the four groups of buildings.

Day tours to the Mayan archaeological sites of Tulum, Coba, and Chichén Itzá on the Yucatán Peninsula are available at hotel desks and from local travel agencies.

For Kids

Cozumel is made for kids. Begin with Playamia Grand Beach Park (formerly Playa Sol Beach Adventure Park) (✆987-872-9030, ✑*www.playamia.com.mx*), located fifteen minutes south of San Miguel. Here, you'll find a playground and waterpark for adults and kids, where you can use WaveRunners, kayaks, and a water trampoline or slide down a water mountain; go water skiing and parasailing; ride in paddleboats, sailboats, and banana boats; go snorkeling and diving; play volleyball; shop for Mexican handicrafts; visit a small zoo with regional animals. After all that, you can sit under a large *palapa* or relax in a floating lounge chair sipping your favorite drink. You have a choice of three packages: Basic, which includes use of all equipment and facilities, for $12 per person; Fiesta, which includes the basic package plus an unlimited open bar for $35 per person; and Premium, which includes the Fiesta package plus snorkel gear, a towel, and a Mexican buffet, for $42 per person.

Also, you may not want your kids to miss a chance to swim with the dolphins at Dolphin Discovery (✆987-872-9702, ✑*www.dolphin discovery.com*) within Chankanaab National Park. After watching a video and working with trainers for twenty minutes to learn how to interact with the dolphins, you get to "play" with the friendly creatures for ten minutes. Children must be at least eight years old to participate. The cost is a rather steep $125 per person for children and adults. The price for just a dolphin encounter is $99 per person. Nonswimmers can also play with the dolphins. A session for nonswimmers is $75 for adults and $70 for children under twelve. If you want to dive with the dolphins, the price is $165 for adults only.

Chankanaab also has a large, shallow children's pool sheltered from the ocean, where small fish can come in with the gentle waves. Teens will enjoy the better snorkeling at nearby Dzul Ha Beach Club.

Fun in the Sun

Nowhere in Mexico can you have as much fun on or under the sea as on Cozumel. Soft white sandy beaches will bring out the hedonist in you, and the wonders under the calm, clear waters will enthrall you. And though Cozumel is known for its fine diving and snorkeling, there are lots of other activities for you to do, including horseback riding, playing tennis on lighted courts, and playing a round on the island's relatively new golf course. If you're a nature lover, you'll discover an amazing variety of flora and fauna as you hike through the island's diverse landscapes.

Beach It

What's a tropical island without beaches? And Cozumel has some beauties. The tranquil west coast offers long stretches of golden sand overlooking the calm sea—great if you have small children. The rugged eastern shore offers a mix of white powder beaches and rock-strewn coast, with seas producing strong waves and currents.

The busiest and most family-friendly beach on Cozumel is Playa San Juan. Lined with hotels, it offers shade trees under which you can sit and watch windsurfers skim the waves. If you want to join them, sailboards are for rent. Its soft waves are perfect for children.

Playa Maya, on the other hand, is a quiet beach backed by low-lying jungle and dotted with palapa umbrellas and plastic reclining seats. Mixed in with the sand are broken conch shells and coral. Swimming is excellent. Here, you can relax.

≡FAST FACT

Playa Chen Rio, a crescent beach with shallow, close-to-shore tide pools to play in, is the best beach on Cozumel for little kids. But powerful undercurrents and riptides make swimming dangerous farther out.

Cozumel's main beach, Playa San Francisco, has two parts. The largest section, to the south, offers a woods with shaded picnic tables and large *palapas*. The smaller section to the north sits between two groups of shade trees fronting a calm sea. Both have gentle waves. Rent snorkel gear to explore the undersea world in front of you.

 **TRAVEL TIP**

Rent a horse from Rancho Palmitas (☎987-800-2778) for approximately $25 an hour and go horseback riding along the beach early in the morning.

Boat It

If you'd rather not snorkel or dive, you can take a two-hour trip on the Atlantis Submarine through Laguna Chankanaab. The forty-eight-passenger, battery-powered vessel dives to a depth of 100 feet, where you can view marine life through oversized portholes in air-conditioned comfort. Tours run from 9 A.M. to 5 P.M. daily for about $79 per adult and $45 for children (☎888-732-5782, *www.atlantis adventures.com*).

Those afraid to go underwater can take a glass-bottomed boat tour with Palapa Marina (☎987-462-0539) for $15 per person. Or you can hop aboard the Fury Catamaran for a four- to five-hour snorkeling boat tour with lunch, for $55 for adults; kids six and up are half price, and those five and under go free.

For a wilder ride, take a water tour by speed boat with Hideaway Power-Boat and Beach Escape for $79 for adults, $59 for kids. You get to drive your own boat while following a guide to a secluded beach for a Mexican grilled buffet.

Snorkel, Scuba, Fish

You can snorkel along the shore in several areas, but be careful of the boat traffic. In town, you can snorkel near the Lobster Cove; they have a man-made beach area with lounge chairs and tables. Cold drinks and food can be served along the ocean. You can also snorkel from the Plaza Las Glorias Hotel. Other areas include Playa Corona south of town and Parque Chankanaab, but it's best to go when there aren't many cruise ships in. Laguna Chankanaab offers sixty species of tropical fish, crustaceans, and corals. Besides trees of black coral, you'll discover large yellow sponges, anemones, and gorgonian fans hanging from the lagoon's wall. You can also snorkel just north of the marina, which is located before the Presidente Hotel. Snorkeling is also quite good near Villa Blanca and La Ceiba Hotels. Most ocean-front villas and condos have good snorkeling right along the shore.

≡FAST FACT

Everyone pays an additional $2 Mexican Marine Park fee on all snorkeling and diving trips.

An alternative to scuba is snuba—you're attached to air pumps aboard a boat while you go on a guided exploration down to a depth of twenty feet (children must be eight and above). Sea Trek, or helmet diving, allows you to walk on the sea floor at a depth of twenty to twenty-five feet and breathe at the same time, using a space-age helmet. You'll find Sea Trek and Snuba Cozumel within the park. Rates are $52 per hour for either.

Or you can go on a half-day snorkeling boat tour for about $20 to $35, including equipment. Otherwise, mask and flippers rent for about $5 to $8 a day.

If you're into scuba diving, you can choose from thirty-seven dive sites where you can observe moray eels, red hinds, queen angels, hermit crabs, parrot fish, giant sponges and anemones, and multicolored globes of brain coral, cactus coral, and galon on the more than thirty reefs, which range in depth from fifteen to ninety feet.

The most famous of the island's dive sites, Arrecife de Palancar, is also a national underwater park. Here, you'll find dramatic canyons and terraces from twenty-five to 200 feet in depth.

Sea turtles and stingrays inhabit the San Francisco Wall, which begins at a depth of forty feet and slopes into a black abyss, while moray eels and great groupers swim around the sand bank known as Tormentos.

Arrecife Punta Sur is one of the deepest and most impressive dives on Cozumel. You can see the famous Garganta del Diablo (Devil's trota) where you enter the mouth of an undersea cave at fifty feet and exit into an abyss at 130 feet. If you're planning to dive into any of the deep coral canyons, make sure you hire a local guide to lead you to hard-to-find dive sites.

≡FAST FACT

The more than fifty members of the Cozumel Watersport Association (ANOAAT) offer half- and full-day diving excursions for $60 to $65 to the most popular sites as well as three-hour Discover Scuba classes with PADI-certified instructors (✆987-872-5955).

Cozumel is *the* place in Mexico to learn scuba diving or win the certification that entitles you to sign up for the more advanced diving adventures. An introductory scuba course from Blue Angel Dive Shop (✆987-872-1631) or Dive Cozumel (✆987-872-4567) costs about $60, while a full certification course costs about $300. Many hotels on Cozumel also offer dive packages.

Golf

The challenging eighteen-hole course at the Cozumel Country Club (✑www.cozumelcountryclub.com.mx), designed by Jack Nicklaus, offers an alternative to diving. Cut away from coral rock, it spreads over expansive wetlands with tall mangroves, coral canyons, and cool lagoons with crocodiles. Water hazards and marshy areas will challenge your skills. You'll pay $150 in greens fees and can rent carts and equipment.

Shopping

Shopping is great in San Miguel. Stroll along the *malecón,* browsing the boutiques in search of onyx sculptures and coral jewelry. Avoid the "coral factories" and stick to the specialty shops that sell fine jewelry and sculptures made from black coral, the island specialty. You'll find not only shops along the waterfront but also on side streets, offering everything from silver jewelry to brass animals to ceramics and leather. There are more shops at La Ceiba Plaza, next to the cruise-ship pier. Do your shopping in the morning or early evening since the shops get crowded with cruise passengers who are in town for just a few hours.

RAINY DAY FUN

If you're looking for Mexican handicrafts, browse the Mercado Artesinias on the *zócalo.* Shops are open Monday through Saturday from 9 A.M. to 1 P.M. and 5 to 9 P.M. If you're looking for local color and foods, visit the El Mercado, Cozumel's oldest market, located five blocks back from the *malecón* on Avenida 25.

Besides the indigenous handicrafts and coral items, handwoven hammocks make a great souvenir. They're also a comfortable way to remember your vacation and something the whole family can enjoy. Some vendors also sell reproduction Mayan pottery. And because Cozumel is a busy cruise port, you can purchase watches, perfume, fine jewelry, and liquor at duty-free prices. For a taste of Cozumel, look for Xtabentum, a local liqueur, and Xnepec, a local hot sauce.

Time to Eat

Dining in Cozumel is a dream, with over ninety restaurants serving a variety of cuisines from pure Mexican to Caribbean, Italian, Mediterranean, and even Tex-Mex. But fresh seafood tops most restaurant menus. Choose an informal place like El Portal or Las Palmeras along the seaside promenade and watch the world go by. Or wind down after an active day with a drink or coffee at one of the outdoor cafés that line the *zócalo*. Most stay open late. If you hunger for American fast food, there are a few options. And the Lone Star Café has the best and only Tex-Mex chili and country music in town. Restaurants fill up by 8 P.M., so it pays to go early.

Local Dining Suggestions

- **Carlos 'n' Charlies:** A party hangout, serving Mexican food at reasonable prices. Noisy and fun, and great if you have teens along (Punta Langosta Mall, ☎987-869-1646).
- **Morgan's:** Casually elegant restaurant in the former customs house named after the infamous pirate with a decor to match on the north side of the *zócalo*, serving continental and Mexican food (Av. Juárez, ☎987-872-0584).
- **Pepe's Grill:** Moderately priced, busy long-time local favorite, serving steaks, lobster, and shrimp with salad bar by candlelight from a second-story dining room with nautical decor (Av. Melgar and A.R. Salas, ☎987-872-0213).
- **El Acuario:** Seafood by the seaside, where tables are set among tropical fish tanks. Orange shrimp or live lobster a specialty (Av. Melgar and Av. 11, ☎987-872-1097).
- **La Cabaña del Pescador:** A restaurant north of town, specializing in lobster. You get to choose your own (Km. 4 Northern Coastal Rd., ☎987-872-3917).
- **La Choza:** A family-owned Mexican kitchen that's popular with locals and visitors. Traditional Yucatecan dishes served in a down-home atmosphere (Corner of Av. 10 Sur and Adolfo Rosado Salas, ☎987-872-0958).

Dining Precautions

Restaurants on Cozumel are clean and friendly. Bottled water is available everywhere.

Where to Go After Dark

Even though Cozumel is quieter than Cancún, the island has its night spots that offer a mix of Mexican and Caribbean flavor. Sports bars, like Viva Mexico, and karaoke bars are popular. And pulsating discos like Neptuno empty out by midnight. Tony Roma's Bar and Restaurant, a casual place serving savory ribs and pasta, has live entertainment nightly. And many of the hotels have live entertainment showcasing Mexican music and dance.

CHAPTER 11

Los Cabos

LOS CABOS (THE CAPES) is a place like no other, where the mountains lining the coast loom like lunar peaks, surrounded by a silent, desert landscape that falls into the sea. Set at the tip of the Baja Peninsula where waves pound the craggy cliffs, Los Cabos is a three-in-one wonderland, comprised of the towns of San José del Cabo, Cabo San Lucas, and El Corredor, the eighteen-mile stretch that links them—the perfect place for a family vacation.

About Los Cabos

Today, Cabo is fast becoming the "Palm Springs of Mexico," with ultra-luxurious hotels and more holes of golf than any other Mexican beach resort.

The two towns, just twenty miles apart, are very different. Cabo San Lucas, originally a stop for Spanish galleons on their way to Manila from Acapulco, now caters to the well-heeled, with high-priced boutiques in American-style malls, sleek hotels, gourmet restaurants, dozens of T-shirt shops, and a thriving nightlife. San José del Cabo, on the other hand, with its central plaza and tree-lined boulevard, remains the quiet town it has been since the Jesuits founded it in 1730. In between the two, along a ribbon of highway called El Corredor, sit lavish hotels and golf resorts that have made the desert landscape green once again.

Best Time to Go

With over 300 days of sunshine and low humidity all year, there really isn't a bad time to come to Cabo. However, it can reach 100 degrees in summer, staying in the upper 70s and low 80s even after the sun sets. The coldest months are December and January, with an average temperature of 50 to 80°F during the day and the 60s at night. The rainy season—what little there is of it—runs from July to October.

Cuisine

Seafood dishes get top billing on most Baja menus, but as Cabo has grown, so have the offerings. And while you'll find Mexican food served here, most restaurants cater to American tastes.

Cautions and Safety Concerns

Though Cabo is a safe place, don't let your guard down and take it for granted. Secure your valuables. If you're driving, be cautious of cows wandering along the roads, especially at night.

The Pacific Ocean produces strong undertow. Be extra cautious, and stay above the tide line when walking. And if the water is rough, stay out as there are no lifeguards.

Getting Around Los Cabos

Transpeninsular Highway One travels eighteen miles from Cabo San Lucas to San José del Cabo. That's a daunting distance when you want to get around. Though taxis are plentiful, rates can be expensive—a whopping $27 from one town to the other. If that's too high for your budget, you can take the bus.

Public buses run between Cabo San Lucas and San José daily, beginning at 5:00 A.M. and running until 10:00 P.M. Even though there are bus stops, you can flag down a bus from almost anywhere by waving your arms. You'll pay only about $1.50—about 15 pesos in exact change—between the two towns, compared to the exorbitant taxi fare.

Family-Oriented Hotels

Magnificent resorts, perched on the rocky bays, are what Cabo is all about. Large upscale estate-like palaces, with rates ranging from $300 to $800 per night—the most expensive in Mexico—line El Corredor. However, there are less expensive places to stay in either town.

Hotel Meliá Cabo Real

Reservations: ☏800-336-3542 (U.S.), ✎*www.meliacaboreal.sol melia.com*

This sprawling, family-oriented all-inclusive beachside resort combines Mexican flavor with Continental service and offers 292 rooms, a water-sports center, pool, restaurants, two bars with entertainment, a kids' club, two lighted tennis courts, health center, and a golf course.

Presidente InterContinental Los Cabos

Reservations: ☏800-327-0200 (U.S.), ✎*www.loscabos.interconti.com*

This family all-inclusive resort, next to the Estero San José, offers a pool, fitness center, several restaurants, ATV rental, and a full kids' activities program.

The Westin Resort & Spa

Reservations: ☏800-228-3000 (U.S.), ✎*www.westin.com/loscabos*

This dramatic 305-room luxury resort, set on a bluff with spectacular views of the coastline, offers four restaurants, two bars, three oceanside pools, kids club, Jacuzzi, tennis courts, fitness center, and spa.

Villas/Rental Options

An alternative to staying in a hotel room is to rent a condo for $75 to $180 per night. In this relatively expensive resort, this may be the best solution for a family. The following companies arrange condo rentals:

- **Baja Properties:** ☎624-142-0988
- **Dynasty Real Estate:** ☎624-142-0523
- **Los Cabos Properties:** ☎624-143-1164

Something for Everyone

Los Cabos offers something for everyone, from sun-drenched sands to desert golf to day-long shopping. Surrounded by two seas, it offers a full menu of water sports as well. By day, it's an outdoor paradise with a full range of sporting activities. But even if you're just a sun worshiper, you'll find hidden coves made for sunbathing or snorkeling. You'll never run out of things to do here.

Things to Do

The emphasis in Cabo is on sports. There isn't much authentic Mexican culture here. The closest thing to the real Mexico is San José del Cabo, an agricultural and cattle-raising community surrounded by fields of mango, avocado, and orange trees. It has a Casa de la Cultura (House of Culture) with a small museum and a library. You'll enjoy strolling along the Paseo Mijares, with its stone arches and white cottages full of flowers. The Iglesia de San José, built in 1940 on the site of the original Jesuit mission, looks out over Plaza Mijares. Sit on one of the benches. You'll feel as if you stepped into a pastel-colored time capsule.

If you love cactus, you'll enjoy a visit to Cacti Mundo, Cabo's Jardín Botanico (Botanical Garden), a unique collection of cacti in San José. Get to know what all those cacti are on the hillsides.

 TRAVEL TIP

For a bird's-eye view of Cabo, take an ultralight glider tour over Cabo San Lucas with Cabo Sky Tours. You'll be strapped into an ultralight airplane with no cabin, so there's nothing between you and the desert air. Ten- and twenty-minute tours cost $65 to $150 (☎624-143-8837).

Completely opposite to the tranquility of San José del Cabo is the zaniness of Cabo San Lucas, where you'll find most of the action along Bulévar Marina. Its marina makes the town look like a glittering Mediterranean village, although most of it is new. Fishing boats depart in a scurry in the early morning, and glass-bottomed boats carrying tourists on sightseeing excursions come and go all day long.

For the Kids

Though swimming with dolphins began along the Riviera Maya, the activity has spread to other resorts in Mexico. Cabo now has its own facility, Cabo Dolphin, claiming to be one of the most exclusive in the world. That's probably because it costs $165 for thirty minutes to swim with a group of Pacific bottlenose dolphins. The minimum age is five, and kids under twelve must be accompanied by a paying adult. You can experience a swim with the dolphins weekdays at 10 A.M., noon, 3 P.M., and 5 P.M. On weekends, you can only do it at 10 A.M. and noon (☎888-303-2653, U.S.).

Visit Todos Santos

Down narrow winding desert Highway 19, an hour past the last golf course in Cabo San Lucas, lies the quiet art colony of Todos Santos, a Mexican hamlet with just over 3,000 residents, on the Pacific side of southern Baja California.

Today, a small group of American artists call Todos Santos home. The museum in the Casa de la Cultura, with its exhibits of local building techniques and photographs from the Mexican Revolution, offers you a chance to see what life was like before the tourists—before Los Cabos and its golf courses.

Fun in the Sun

Cabo's striking desert landscape surrounded by azure blue seas invites you to play in the sun. Here, sports are king—at least any that you can play on sand and in the water. That's what put Cabo on the map, and that's what makes it so successful as a resort.

Beach It

You'll find Cabo's beaches in five different areas: in Cabo San Lucas and San José, along the Pacific, along El Corredor, and on the East Cape. They offer lots of variety, from those fronting the Sea of Cortés to the windswept ones along the Pacific. However, only a few are good for swimming.

Of all of them, Playa El Médano (Dune Beach) in Cabo San Lucas is the most popular and has the most water-sports facilities. Just beyond town is Playa del Amor (Love Beach), next to El Arco (the Arch)—the only one in the world with two opposing shores—the other side of which is often called Playa del Divorcio (Divorce Beach). Playa Santa Maria along El Corredor is one of Cabo's best swimming and snorkeling beaches.

 TRAVEL TIP

> Few of Cabo's beaches have any shade, fresh water, or restroom facilities. Be sure to pack plenty of water, sunscreen, a beach umbrella, toilet paper, a plastic bag for garbage, and insect repellent during the rainy season.

Most of Cabo's good surfing beaches—Playas Costa Azul, Monumento, and El Tule—lie along El Corredor, but they're more for advanced surfers. If you're just beginning, you can try Playa Acapulquito in San José or Playa Los Cerritos, near Todos Santos. You can take lessons from Costa Azul Surf Shop (✆624-142-2771).

Boat It

Take a boat ride to El Arco, where the Sea of Cortés and the Pacific waters merge in a swirling spectacle of sea and foam. The magnificent rock formation has become Los Cabos' trademark. Sea lions live happily on nearby Rocas de los Frailes (The Friars'

Rocks) on the surrounding rocks. Pelicans roost on the smaller Roca Pelicanos (Pelican Rock). El Faro de Cabo Falso, a lighthouse from 1890, stands on the rocky headland. One of the best ways to see all this is aboard a *fondo de dristales* (glass-bottomed boat) tour. The forty-five-minute trip takes in Pelican Rock, the sea lion colony, and the arch, and you can be dropped off and picked up at Playa del Amor.

Two-hour sunset cruises aboard the fifty-foot *La Princesa* catamaran or the forty-two-foot *Pez Gato* catamaran (☎624-143-2252) head out first to Land's End, bringing you close in for a bird's-eye view of El Arco, bathed in orange light at the end of the day. Some head out to the open Pacific for a panoramic view of Los Cabos, then sail up to Cabo Falso. If you prefer a smaller boat, carrying only ten passengers, try the thirty-foot *Tlaloc* (☎624-112-2349). Cruises depart an hour before sunset. Be sure to bring along a jacket. The cost includes onboard drinks. If you'd rather not go on a booze cruise, ask before you book your cruise.

If you prefer a dinner cruise, sail the *Sunrider,* an elegant yacht with full open bar and an all-you-can-eat Mexican buffet for slightly more than the regular cruises (☎624-143-3929).

Snorkel, Scuba, Fish

If you prefer to explore under the water rather than on top, you'll find good snorkeling and diving year round in Cabo. Three major ocean currents collide here and bring with them large amounts of plankton, attracting over 800 species of marine life.

 TRAVEL TIP

Pick up a water-taxi at the Cabo San Lucas Marina and ask the boatman to take you to Playa del Amor where you can snorkel, dive, or watch the sea lions.

Guided two-hour snorkeling tours to Land's End, with a stop to view the sea lion colony, cost $25 per person. You can also rent snorkeling equipment for $10 per day from dive shops around the marina and head out on your own. Most snorkel tours also leave from Playa El Médano.

Cabo's coastline offers innumerable lagoons that offer great diving. Because its waters are a temperate 72°F, this area lacks the bright tropical coral of the Caribbean. What you'll enjoy about diving here is the opportunity to swim with such large creatures as whales, sea lions, dolphins, manta rays, and groupers.

One of the best diving sites is halfway along El Corredor at Bahía Santa María and Bahía Chileno. You'll find a dive shop at Bahía Chileno. Be sure not to miss the Blowhole, a 40- to 100-foot dive down the backside of a rock wall covered with *gorgonians* (sea fans), as well as eels, various rays, guitarfish, and small nurse sharks.

Diving on the bay side of El Arco is excellent, with visibility from 30 to 60 feet down in winter and 80 to 90 feet down from July to November. If you're less experienced, try Roca Pelicanos, Dedo de Neptuno (Neptune's Finger), and the sea lion colony. If more advanced, you'll enjoy diving the challenging El Abismo (The Abyss) or the Sandfalls, a ninety-foot dive documented by Jacques Cousteau, which begins at Roca Pelicanos then drops to an incredible 1,200 feet. Playa Cabo Pulmo, containing the largest living coral reef on the west coast of North America, is another. Dive trips, including equipment, start at $40. Of the many dive shops in Cabo, the following are some of the best:

- **Amigos del Mar:** 642-143-0505, *www.amigosdelmar.com*
- **Baja Dive:** 642-143-3830
- **Cabo Vacationers Contact (Cabovc):** 624-144-3419
- **Deep Blue Diving Club:** 642-143-7668, *www.cabodeepblue.com*
- **Land's End Divers:** 642-143-2200
- **Manta SCUBA Diving:** 624-144-3871

During the 1950s, Cabo became known as the Marlin Capital of the World. In fact, it's still not unusual to hook one on your first trip. Fishing in Cabo used to be the sport of the rich and famous. Now, if you have the money, you can have the experience of a lifetime. You can hire a twenty-two foot panga for $165 to $198 or a thirty-six-foot cruiser for $300 for six hours, or $650 for eight hours. Larger boats can run as high as $1,300 for eight hours. Chartering a yacht can set you back as much as $3,500. Here are a few options:

- **Cabo Magic Sportfishing:** ✆888-475-5337 (U.S.)
- **Cabo Sport Fishing Charters:** ✆624-119-1603
- **Gaviota Sportfishing Fleet:** ✆800-932-5599 (U.S.), ✐*www* *.grupobahia.com*
- **Pisces Sportfishing Fleet:** ✆642-143-1288, ✐*www.pisces* *sportfishing.com*
- **Solmar Sportfishing Fleet:** ✆800-344-3349 (U.S.), ✐*www* *.solmar.com*

PWC Rentals, Kayaks, Parasailing

The only limits in Cabo are your energy level and budget. You can rent Jet Skis, Sea Doos, and Waverunners for $40 an hour all along Playa El Médano. For self-propelled waves, try boogie or paddle boarding. On windier days, Hobie Cats and small sailboats are easy to maneuver around the faster vessels in the bay. If the wind's up, you can rent a windsurfer for $15 an hour, or, if you prefer not to get quite that wet, hire a Hobie Cat for $40 an hour. Arrange a ride from JT Water Sports (✆642-144- 4566, ✐*www* *.jtwatersports.com*).

Kayaking has really caught on in Cabo. Lightweight sit-on-top kayaks are efficient, streamlined, and easy to launch in the gentle surf at Playa El Médano. Try kayaking over to Playa del Amor across the bay. Or try kayaking in Bahéa Chileno in El Corredor.

To get the best view of Cabo, and an exciting thrill, try parasailing, where you'll dangle from an enormous, colored parachute, soaring into the air while attached to a 600-foot rope being towed by a speedboat. You'll pay from $30 to $40 for ten minutes.

Ecotourism

Cabo is a great place to get back to nature. If you love birds, you'll find the palm-fringed Estero San José (San José Estuary) teeming with 150 species of tropical varieties. Rent a canoe and see the birds from water level, or stroll along the Paseo del Estero, following the estuary.

Whether you're a beginner or an accomplished climber, you'll find rapelling and climbing on the rocks of Playa del Amor exhilarating. RipTip Climbing offers a variety of guided rapelling and rock climbing tours, including instruction and climbing or rapelling gear, under the trained eye of its expert guides.

You can also rent mountain bikes for $5 an hour or $20 a day at Tio Sports in Cabo San Lucas and at Desert Park, Cabo Real's ecological reserve. Ride over the desert or over to El Faros at Cabo Falso. Be sure to take plenty of water and a map with you. Do not cycle alone in remote areas or on the busy streets of Cabo San Lucas.

 TRAVEL TIP

For the wackiest adventure of them all, try being harnessed inside a Zorb, a large plastic ball with windows, then being sent head over heels down a hill. A cushion of air protects you from harm (✆624-105-9196, ✐*www.zorb.com*).

The landscape around Cabo is made for ATVs. In Cabo San Lucas, guided tours to the Pacific Coast and into the desert run mornings and late afternoons. Take the twenty-five-mile trek through Cabo Real Resort's network of connecting trails along *arroyos* (dry riverbeds), narrow canyons, and rugged hillsides with Desert Park ATV

Tours. You'll ride at low speeds with many stops so you can enjoy views of the Sea of Cortés. You'll find this is a great way to experience the desert. Fees start at $50 per person (✆624-144-0127).

Rather not ride yourself? Take your family along on a Baja outback adventure, cruising in the air-conditioned comfort of a HumV with Baja Outback Adventures (✆624-142-9200). Or take a backcountry Jeep tour for $95 to $125 per person with Baja Wild (✆624-142-5300, ✑*www.bajawild.com*). And not to be outdone by other resorts, Cabo offers its own version of a canopy tour. Instead of flying along through the treetops, you ride high above Costa Azul Canyon, suspended safely in a harness. Tours depart at 9 and 11 A.M. and 1 and 3 P.M. (✆624-115-4112).

≡ FAST FACT

ATVs weaken Cabo's fragile ecosystem and are illegal on its beaches.

If you prefer to see the scenery the old-fashioned way, go on a guided horseback trail ride for $25 to $40 per person along the surf or on a backcountry trail with any of the following:

- **Cuadra Equestrian Center:** ✆624-144-0160
- **Rancho Collins:** ✆624-143-3652.
- **Red Rose Riding Stables:** ✆624-143-4826, ✑*www.los caboshorses.com.*

Whale Watching

Marine biologists regard the Sea of Cortés, separating the Baja Peninsula from mainland Mexico, as the richest marine habitat on earth. It's home to numerous species of *ballenas* (whales), including the gray whales that make their well-known 6,000-mile migration from the Bering Sea in early spring to calve in the buoyant shallow lagoons north of Cabo. Ranging from forty to fifty feet long and weighing up to 73,000 pounds, shore-loving gray whales are the only ones to bottom feed.

On a whale-watching excursion, you'll see *ballenas* spouting, sounding (or showing their flukes), and, most dramatic of all, breaching, when a whale leaps out of the water and falls back with a large splash. Cabo Expeditions's whale-watching tours from January to March will bring you as close as possible for $30 to $50 per person (☎624-143-2700).

Tennis

Most of the major resort hotels have one or two tennis courts. The Mayan Palace golf course in San José has six lighted ones (☎624-142-4166).

Golf

Golf is Cabo's passion. And if it's your passion, you'll be in paradise. As Mexico's premier golf destination, Cabo offers enough holes of challenging golf to fill your entire vacation. You'll need a reservation for a tee time from October through April. Here are a few courses to choose from:

- **Cabo Real Resort Golf Course:** Two dramatic seaside holes and three outstanding mountain holes are the signature holes of this Robert Trent Jones course. Situated midway between Cabo San Lucas and San José at the Meliá Cabo Real Hotel (☎624-144-0040).
- **Cabo del Sol:** Two separate eighteen-hole courses, one a desert layout, provide what designer Jack Nicklaus calls the "the two best finishing holes in the world" (☎624-145-8200).
- **Mayan Palace Golf Los Cabos:** Originally Cabo's nine-hole public course, it's now part of the Mayan Palace Hotel and has been restructured to double greens for each hole, so you can play eighteen (☎624-142-2090).
- **Club de Golf El Dorado:** At this eighteen-hole resort course, designed by Jack Nicklaus, accuracy is prime (☎624-144-5451).

- **Palmilla Golf Club** Jack Nicklaus' first Latin American course, and the one that put Cabo on the world golf map, this twenty-seven-hole target-style desert layout was the best course in Mexico when it opened in 1992. And even though others have come along since then, it's still one of the most challenging (☎624-144-5250).
- **Raven Golf Club:** Designed by Roy Dye, this eighteen-hole course, formerly the Cabo San Lucas Country Club, offers splendid views of Land's End and a junior golf program for kids aged six to fourteen (☎624-143-4653).

Time to Relax

Luxury spas abound in Los Cabos. The sheer number of swank resorts makes choosing a spa a delightful experience. Of the following spas, all but two are European. All offer massage, stress control, weight reduction, and skin and beauty care. Many incorporate local desert ingredients such as clay, aloe, and desert flowers. Here are some of the best:

- **Fiesta Americana Grand:** Yoga, weight training, spa cuisine (☎624-145-6287)
- **Meliá Cabo Real Resort:** Aerobics, hydrotherapy, fitness trainer (☎624-144-0277)
- **Pueblo Bonito Rosé:** Aerobics, yoga, hydrotherapy (☎624-143-5500)
- **Rosewood Ventanas al Paraiso:** Outdoor spa, hydrotherapy (☎624-144-0300)
- **Villa del Palmar:** All of the above, with the most features of any spa (☎624-143-2694)
- **Westin Regina Resort:** Aerobics, weight and cardiovascular programs, hydrotherapy (☎624-142-9000)

Shopping

Shopping vies with golf and fishing as a favorite pastime for visitors to Los Cabos. Uncover hidden treasures in the shops that line the colonial streets of San José del Cabo. Popular items include resort wear, original art, silver jewelry, blown glass, and an assortment of crafts from around Mexico. You'll find most shops in Cabo San Lucas conveniently located along Marina Boulevard or at one of the several small shopping plazas around town. Hand-painted pottery and tableware, pewter frames, and carved furniture are some other items you'll find.

You'll find most of the shopping opportunities in San José around the *zócalo*, on Calle Zaragoza, and on Bulévar Mijares. Perhaps you'll want to buy carved wood animals from Oaxaca, masks from the state of Guerrero, or black coral jewelry.

Time to Eat

There are enough restaurants to allow you to dine in a different place every evening and still have some left over. You'll find everything from Tex-Mex to Italian to Japanese, as well as good old Mexican served with a Cabo flare. Some of the outdoor eateries along El Corredor have become famous for their tasty food.

Local Dining Suggestions

- **Casa Rafael's:** Overlooking Playa El Médano, this elegant and romantic dining spot features exquisite international cuisine, live dinner music, and an excellent selection of wines (Playa El Médano, ✆624-143-0739).
- **Damiana:** The best restaurant in San José, it serves a varied menu, including charbroiled lobster and other seafood specialties in achiote sauce and imperial shrimp and steak (Mujares 8, San José, ✆624-142-0499).
- **Da Giorgio II:** For Italian food, this outdoor eatery can't be beat. Homemade pasta, an inviting salad bar, plus brick oven pizza are all served with outstanding views and accompanied

by strolling violins (El Corredor three miles east of Cabo San Lucas, ✆624-143-3988).

- **Mi Casa:** Noted for its fine Mexican cuisine, this favored dining spot glows with candlelight against the backdrop of the main square in Cabo San Lucas (Av. Cabo San Lucas, ✆624-143-1933).
- **The Shrimp Factory:** Top-quality shrimp and lobster are served by the kilo boiled or by the plate any style (Marina Boulevard, Cabo San Lucas, ✆624-143-5066).

Dining Precautions

Due to the high volume of *norteamericanos* that visit Cabo each year, you'll find all the restaurants to be as good as those back home. In fact, because Cabo is a "created" resort, purified water is available not only in its hotels but in most of its restaurants.

Where to Go After Dark

While you may take part in sporting activities all day, when the sun goes down you'll want to party, and Cabo San Lucas has plenty of watering holes where you can do just that. You can revel until the wee hours in bars like the Giggling Marlin and discos like Cabo Wabo, where the beat goes on until it's time to go fishing again.

JUST FOR PARENTS

Spend a romantic evening alone in the formal elegance of Pitahayas, dining on exotic Chinese, Thai, and Polynesian dishes while looking out over the beach (Km. 10, El Corredor at Cabo del Sol, ✆624-145-6126).

Walking down Bulévar Marina in either direction, you'll also find Squid Roe, Planet Hollywood, and the Hard Rock Café. And, of course, there's always Carlos 'n' Charlies. Or you may want to attend the fiesta, held on Saturday evenings during the winter season, in San José.

CHAPTER 12

Mazatlán

ONE OF THE OLDEST resorts on the Pacific Coast, Mazatlán, known as the "Pearl of the Pacific," has earned the reputation as one of Mexico's most popular and active beach communities. It's a bustling commercial port—Mexico's largest—renowned for its fine sport fishing, clean beaches, sunny climate, excellent dining, and nightlife. It's also known for its billfishing tournaments and for its succulent shrimp—and, of course, for the best Carnaval in Mexico, after Veracruz.

About Mazatlán

Mazatlán, a vibrant city, where *mariachis* will strike up the band in a parking lot and people will start to dance on the beach, sits at the foot of the Sierra Madre Mountains. It doesn't need tourism to survive, so the atmosphere remains laid-back and less touristy than other Mexican beach resorts.

With its natural bay and sheltered harbor, Mazatlán covers much of a fifteen-mile peninsula in the state of Sinaloa. The original settlement and port area, called Mazatlán Viejo (Old Mazatlán), stands at its southern tip. A small *zócalo* and a cathedral highlight El Centro, Mazatlán's downtown area. To the north lies La Zona Dorada (The Golden Zone), stretching from Punta Camarón (Shrimp Point) north to the Costa de Oro (Gold Coast), visited by more than a million tourists a year. A palm-lined *malécon* (beachfront promenade), the longest in Mexico, connects the two areas.

Once the home of the Totorames Indians, Mazatlán, based on the Nahuatl word *Mazatl*, which means "Place of the Deer," goes back thousands of years.

☰FAST FACT

Mazatlán was the second city in the world after Tripoli, Libya, to experience aerial bombardment. During the 1910 Revolution, General Venustinano Carranza ordered a biplane to drop primitive bombs on the El Cerro de la Nevaría (Icebox Hill), but it missed its target and hit the city.

Today, this city of 600,000 supports the largest shrimp-fishing fleet in Latin America, shipping tons of frozen shrimp to the United States daily.

Best Time to Go

Mazatlán, unfortunately, has developed a reputation as the Spring Break Capital of the West. During March and April, thousands of students descend upon the city, so it's best to avoid it during those times. Otherwise, Mazatlán's warm tropical climate, with high temperatures in the low 80s in January and the low 90s in August, keeps the resort refreshingly comfortable most of the year. While it does get hot in the summer, the temperature and humidity aren't nearly as bad as at spots further south. It does rain on summer afternoons, but afterwards the humidity drops.

Cuisine

Fresh seafood tops the list of good things to eat in Mazatlán. Succulent *camarón* (shrimp), Mazatlán's specialty, comes anyway you like it, followed by *langosta* (lobster) and *caracól* (conch). Or perhaps you'd prefer *sierra* (mackerel) prepared *zarandeado* (split in half and charcoal-grilled). Or maybe fresh *ostiónes* (oysters), piled high on a street cart. And don't forget to try *tacos de mariscos* (seafood tacos), filled with marlin, shrimp, or oysters, often served *capeados* (deep fried). You can satisfy your sweet tooth with a *churro*, a foot-long doughnut covered with cinnamon sugar. And as the home of the Pacifico Brewery, you'll enjoy Mexico's best *cervezas* (beers)—Pacifico, Corona, Modelo, and Negro Modelo—served ice cold.

Cautions and Safety Concerns

Mazatlán is safe if you stay in the major tourist areas and along the *malécon* downtown. In spring and summer, abundant jellyfish on beaches north of the Zona Dorada can be especially annoying.

Getting Around Mazatlán

Mazatlán's downtown connects to its beach areas to the north by a curving twelve-mile oceanside avenue, El Malécon (The Seawall), which changes names several times along its length. Beginning as Venustiano Carranza, it changes to Paseo Centenario, followed by Avenida Olas Altas, then Paseo Claussen through the downtown area, and finally becomes Avenida del Mar at Playa Norte (North Beach), and north to Avenidas Camarón-Sábalo and Sábalo-Cerritos.

While nearly 400 regular buses ply routes throughout Mazatlán, special green tourist buses travel up and down Avenida del Mar for a flat fee of seventy-five cents. Regular buses charge about forty cents, and there are no transfers. You can flag down a bus anywhere along its route, or you can wait for one at the *paradas de camiones* (bus stops).

Mazatlán is a great place to walk, whether you stroll around El Centro or along the avenue in the Zona Dorada. If you tire of walking, you can take a *pulmonia*, an open-air taxi holding two or three passengers that's unique to the city. Your ride will cost about $3 to $4 in the city and more for further out. As with taxis, which cost double the amount, agree on the price before you get in.

Family-Oriented Hotels

An increasingly popular tourist destination, Mazatlán has thousands of hotel rooms in more than 140 hotels. You'll find excellent family accommodations to fit your budget along the Zona Dorada, Mazatlán's tourist center. Here, everyone caters to tourists like you.

Hotel El Cid Megaresort
Reservations: ☎888-733-1308 (U.S.), ✐*www.elcid.com*

The largest privately owned resort in Mexico, with 1,200 rooms spread over 900 acres, it consists of three hotels—the villas of the Granada Country Club; the El Moro Beach Hotel, with luxury suites; and the Castilla Beach Hotel, with more luxury rooms. All have five-star restaurants, bars, and pools. There's also a kids' club, disco, golf course, and seventeen tennis courts.

Pueblo Bonito Hotel
Reservations: ☎800-442-5300 (U.S.), ✐*www.pueblobonito.com*

With 250 suites with kitchenettes and balconies overlooking the luxurious pool and the sea, this hotel is ideal for families that want a more upscale accommodation.

Playa Mazatlán
Reservations: ☎800-762-5816 (U.S.), ✐*www.hotelplayamazatlan .com*

This 408-room hotel, the first one built in the Zona Dorada, is the center of the action. Larger one-bedroom suites are great for families. Facilities include a beachside *palapa* restaurant, pool and jacuzzi, and a bar with live music nightly.

Fiesta Inn
Reservations: ☎800-343-7821, ✐*www.fiestainn.com*

This comfortable, 117-room hotel has a workout room, pool, and a reasonably priced restaurant.

Villas/Rental Options

If you'd rather have your family stay in a home or condo, Mazatlán has some that rent at reasonable rates. To see what's available, check the classified section of the *Pacific Pearl,* Mazatlán's tourist newspaper (✐*www.pacificpearl.com*) or contact any of the following:

- **Bernal Real Estate:** ✆669-914-1753, ✐*www.pacificpearl .com/bernalre*
- **Century 21 El Cid:** ✆669-916-4141, ✐*www.elcid.com*
- **Walfre Real Estate:** ✆669-983-0011, ✐*www.mazatlanre alty.com*

Something for Everyone

Beach fun competes directly with the attractions of Mazatlán's historic center, offering you a variety of activities to fill every day of your vacation.

Things to Do

The best way to get a feel for Mazatlán Viejo is to walk its winding streets. The historic area conveys an authentic image of the city's glorious history between 1830 and 1913. Restored buildings, museums, shops, and cafés all bring the flavor of the past to the present.

 TRAVEL TIP

Join an organized walking tour of Mazatlán Viejo every Wednesday at 10 A.M. (✆669-982-4447).

Mazatlán Viejo is still the civic, religious, and commercial center of the city. Its beautiful nineteenth-century, double-spired La Basílica de la Immaculada Concepción (The Basilica of the Immaculate Conception) stands on the Plaza de la República, Mazatlán's *zócalo*. Begun in 1855, it wasn't elevated to cathedral status until 1937. On Sundays, the air rings with the melodic strains of church bells and band concerts from the ornate Victorian wrought-iron gazebo in the *zócalo's* center, to entertain those sitting under the neatly pruned trees.

A few blocks over, a neighborhood with 479 national historic landmarks awakens as centuries-old buildings have been restored, including the historic Teatro Ángela Peralta (Angela Peralta Theater), just off the corner of the Plaza Machado, site of a weekend crafts and antiques bazaar. Named after Juan Machado, a Filipino immigrant merchant, the little plaza remains a gentle oasis of culture in this bustling resort city.

═══FAST FACT

Built in 1865 by Manuel Rubio as the Teátro Rubio, and later severely damaged by a hurricane, the Teatro Ángela Peralta now stands fully restored. Angela Peralta, famous nineteenth-century opera star, died of yellow fever in the Hotel Iturbides, next door to the theater after giving her only Mazatlán performance. You can tour it daily from 9 A.M. to 6 P.M.

After your tour, you may want to sit under a sidewalk umbrella table on the north side of the square and sip delicious cinnamon coffee at the Altazor Café or perhaps down an ice-cold bottle of Pacifico Beer at the Café Pacifico nearby before strolling the streets off the square.

At the end opposite the theater stands the Portales de Canobbio (Canobbio Arcade), a colonnade which originally served as a market called Porta de la Lonja. But Luis Canobbio, an Italian pharmacist, bought the building, added a second floor and changed its name to Portales de Canobbio after himself. Today, it's known as Museo Casa Machado. Stepping into the past, to imagine how people lived in turn-of-the-century Mazatlán, is as easy as walking through a door and up a flight of stairs. The house's upper-floor rooms, decorated with nineteenth-century antiques, reveal much about life back then.

From the plaza to the southwest, historical treasures abound. Along most streets between Plaza Machado and Bahía Olas Altas, fuschia bougainvillea smothers faded lavender and cobalt walls. Flaming orange trumpet vines entwine the iron railings of gates and fanciful balconies. Cast-iron fans and rows of iron bars guard windows and doors. In fact, you'll notice the use of iron for every possible effect, testimony to the Fundicion de Sinaloa, the nineteenth-century iron foundry where ornamentation reigned.

The Museo de Arqueológia (Museum of Archaeology) (Open Tuesday through Sunday 10 A.M. to 7 P.M., ✆669-981-1455), a few blocks toward the sea, chronicles Mazatlán's rich heritage. Objects on display include hundreds of pre-Columbian relics, such as burial ornaments and the distinctive black-and-red polychrome pottery left behind by the Totorames. The rocks standing outside the museum are Aztec route markers found in Sinaloa. The museum provides a good basic pre-Columbian exhibition if you haven't seen others. Be sure to see the shrunken heads in the corner of the back room.

 TRAVEL TIP

Pick up a free copy of *Viejo Mazatlán*, a bilingual newspaper, or the *Pacific Pearl*, the tourist newspaper, to find out what's going on in Mazatlán.

Standing in the center of the old café-lined resort strip north of Playa Olas Altas is the city's most famous landmark, the Monumento al Venado (Monument of the Deer). An old Spanish fort, Fuerte Venustiano Carranza, just west of downtown adjacent to Playa Los Pinos (The Pines Beach), is where Mazatlán defended itself from French invaders in the 1860s. At the southern end of the peninsula atop El Cerro del Crestón (Crest Hill) stands El Faro, the old lighthouse, the second-tallest in the world after Gibraltar's. Climb to the top for a magnificent view of the coast. Or take a *pulmonia* to El Cerro del Vigía (Lookout Hill), a former observation point where colonial soldiers scanned the horizon for pirates, for a panoramic view of downtown and the port.

At the famous diver's cliff, Punta de Clavadistas (Diver's Point), on Paseo Claussen near the Monumento Mujer de Mazalteca (Monument to the Women of Mazatlán), your heart will race as you watch daring locals plunge into forty-five feet of turbulent water surrounded by rocks. The dive requires expert timing because without a high wave, the waters are only six feet deep.

 TRAVEL TIP

Thirty minutes from Mazatlán, an old tequila distillery has been converted into Rancho Las Moras, a charming hacienda hotel. Original buildings have been restored. You can visit the ranch for lunch and take a horseback ride into the mountains with advance reservations (✍*www.lasmoras.com*).

On most Sundays, in neighboring villages of Mazatlán, such as Llanito, you can see the ancient ball game *ulama*, which dates back to the dawn of Mesoamerican civilization, being played. Today, this game only survives in the state of Sinaloa around Mazatlán, where it has been passed down for generations.

But the favorite pastime of Mazalteco families is strolling along the *malécon* in the evenings. It offers a front row seat for some of the best people-watching, second only to some of the best sunsets you'll ever see.

For the Kids

You'll find plenty for your kids to do in Mazatlán. Begin by visiting the Acuario Mazatlán (Mazatlán Aquarium), the largest in Mexico and home to more than 300 species of fish, including sharks, eels and seahorses. Kids love the seal shows. Outside, there's a playground and small zoo that sits amid the trees in a botanical garden. Admission is $5 for adults, $2.50 for kids. (Open 10 A.M. to 6 P.M., ✆669-981-7815.)

For daytime play, there's Parc Mazagua on Playa Cerritos (open 10 A.M. to 6 P.M., ✆669-988-0041), a water park with giant slides, wave pool, and a miniature golf course. Admission is $8 for everyone over three. And for those kids who play baseball, there are batting cages and a chance to see the city's Mexican Pacific Coast Baseball League team, Los Venados (The Deer), play at the Estadio Teodoro Mariscal.

RAINY DAY FUN

With movies costing only $3, the theatre is a good place to spend a couple of afternoon hours out of the rain. Mazatlán has five theaters, showing movies in English with Spanish subtitles. Cinemas Gaviotas features six screens (✆669-983-7545).

California sea lions winter on Isla Tortuga (Turtle Island), a small rocky island a half mile from town. Your kids will enjoy seeing these "trained seals" of the circus in their natural habitat, sunning themselves on the rocks.

Visit Concordia and Copala

Unlike other resort areas, there's lots to see in the countryside. For about $50 per adult and $35 per child eleven and under, the "country tour" offered by most hotels includes a stop at Concordia, twenty-eight miles east of Mazatlán. This picturesque former mining town is known for its fine hand-crafted furniture, especially its rocking chairs. Copala, twenty-seven miles northeast of Concordia, is another old mining town founded in 1565.

On Sundays, local families from Mazatlán travel Concordia's cobblestoned streets to enjoy a day in the country. You can picnic or stop into Daniel's Restaurant for lunch. The restaurant serves an excellent banana coconut cream pie. Daniel's also runs private van tours to Copala (✆669-916-5736).

Concordia's Church of San Sebastian, at 350 years old, is the oldest in the state of Sinaloa. This is mango country, and you'll see fresh ones for sale along the road. A huge rocking chair stands in the *zócalo*, a symbol of the town's furniture industry.

Bullfights

On Sundays from Christmas through Easter, you can take in a bullfight at Mazatlán's Plaza de Toros La Monumental.

Fun in the Sun

Fun and sun go hand-in-hand in Mazatlán. With miles of glorious beaches and warm waters, you're sure to find plenty to keep you busy during your stay.

Beach It

Mazatlán offers fifteen miles of clean, expansive beaches, with better surfing than other Pacific resorts. In fact, it's one of the only resorts in Mexico that permits surfing on town beaches. You'll find the waves best at Playas Cerritos (Hills Beach) and Bruja (Witch Beach), north of the Marina El Cid. Playa Los Pinos, north of the fort, known in surfing circles as "The Cannon," is also good. Local surfers seem to favor the high rollers at Playas Los Sábalos (Shad Beach) and Olas Altas (High Waves). The water temperature hovers between 65 and 75°F year round. Boogie boards rent for $4 per hour on Playa Los Sábalos.

While other resorts may have more miles of beach, Mazatlán's beaches are probably the most active—a reason why it's so popular with students during Spring Break. Beaches in the Zona Dorada begin at Punta Camarón, where the beach widens into the silky smooth sands of Playa Los Sábalos, followed by Playa Gaviotas (Seagulls

Beach), the focus of the action. Here, gentler waves make for good swimming.

TRAVEL TIP

While other Mexican beach resorts have banned beach vendors, Mazatlán has not. To avoid being harassed, sit closer to the surf or go to one of the less touristy beaches to the north of the Zona Dorada.

Beyond Punta Sábalo, you'll come upon Playa Bruja, a glorious wild stretch of beach with grass-topped dunes and a shore littered with shells and driftwood, named for the shaman women who used to perform rituals there. The beach boulevard ends at Playa Cerritos, probably the best inshore fishing and shell-hunting spot in Mazatlán.

Boat It

You can take boat rides to Tres Islas (three islands) off Punta Camarón from the El Cid Marina. While the quiet seclusion of Isla de los Venados (Deer Island) and Isla de los Chivos (Goat Island) may suit you, others prefer to go bird-watching on Isla de los Pajaros (Bird Island), where hundreds of species nest.

For about $30, you can also head south aboard either the tour-boat *Renegado* (☎669-982-14-3130) or the *Catamarán Brisas del Mar* (☎669-916-7870) to Isla de la Piedra (Stone Island) for its tropical palm-lined beaches and South Seas atmosphere. Actually a peninsula, it has the third-largest coconut grove in Mexico. Or you can opt for a sunset dinner cruise to Isla de la Piedra aboard the Yate *Costalegre* (☎669-916-5747) for about $42. The peninsula's giant *palapas* shade seafood restaurants where the aroma of grilled shrimp is hard to pass up. If you came to Mazatlán to lie in the sun, drink from a coconut, and eat shrimp, this is the place. It's also a favorite Sunday gathering place for Mexican families.

▐ TRAVEL TIP

Daily overnight car and passenger ferries leave from Mazatlán for La Paz in Baja California Sur, and vice versa. (✆669-981-0643)

If you want to see the sites of Mazatlán's harbor, you can take your family on a three-hour cruise aboard the Yate *Fiesta* (✆669-981-7154) for about $15 per person.

Snorkel, Scuba, Fish

Scuba diving and snorkeling are best at Isla Los Venados, just off Playa Los Gaviotas. You can rent snorkeling equipment for $8 dollars per person.

There are places to scuba dive in Mazatlán, but there are better places to dive in Mexico.

Mazatlán is the deep-sea fishing capital of Mexico and has been for a long time. The waters teem with tuna, marlin, sailfish, dorado, bonita, yellowtail, and sea bass. Charter boats moored in the Marinas Mazatlán and El Cid, and in Marina del Crestón by the lighthouse, head out for marlin all year except December, for swordfish in the spring, for sailfish in the spring and early summer, and for tuna and bonita year-round. If you prefer catch-and-release fishing, just ask your captain. The port hosts numerous large sport-fishing fleets, many with more than thirty years' experience. You'll pay about $80 to $100 per person per day to join a group, or from $200 to $450 to charter a boat for your family from the following fleets:

- **Aries Fleet Marina El Cid:** ✆669-916-3468, ✎*www.elcid.com*
- **Escualo Fleet Marina Mazatlán:** ✆669-918-1173
- **Star Fleet Marina del Crestón:** ✆669-982-2665, ✎*www .starfleet.com.mx*
- **Viking's Fleet:** ✆669-986-3484

If you prefer fishing for Spanish mackerel, black snook, grouper, red snapper, and roosterfish closer to the shore, hire a *panga* for $50 (including bait and equipment) from one of the fishermen on Playa Norte. And if you'd like to try fishing for large-mouth bass, go to Lago El Salto, ninety minutes from Mazatlán. You can either rent equipment or bring your own.

PWC Rentals, Kayaks, Parasailing

Mazatlán's beaches overflow with Hobie Cats, WaveRunners, and banana boats. Any water sport you can imagine is just steps away from your resort hotel in the Zona Dorada. Beaches bustle with concessionaires just waiting to provide you with thrills by the half hour. Jet Skis rent by the half hour for $54 for a one-seater and $63 for a two-seater. Or fly over the waves on a banana boat for a half hour for $8 per person. You can rent sea kayaks for $10 an hour for a one-person, $20 for a two-person, and paddle over to Isla de los Venados. Or if you prefer to sail, rent a *velero* (sailboat) for $30.

You'll see people floating high above Playas Costa de Oro, Los Sábalos, and Gaviotas, where you can go parasailing for $25 for ten minutes.

Ecotourism

Unlike other Pacific resorts, you won't find horseback riding on Mazatlán's beaches. However, you can rent horses on Isla de la Piedra from Stuart's Ghostriders (✆669-985-4618) from 8 A.M. to 3 P.M. or from Ginger's Bilingual Horses (✆669-922-2026) on Playa Bruja north of the Zona Dorada. Ginger's also offers burro cart rides for your kids.

Tennis

Playing tennis with a view of ocean may not make your game any better, but being able to practice on some of Mazatlán's many courts will. Courts rent for $10 an hour. While most major hotels have public courts, the following offer fine facilities and lessons ($20 an hour) to the public:

- **El Cid Golf and Country Club:** Seventeen courts (☎669-913-5611)
- **Playa Real Hotel:** Two courts on a bluff with a view of the sea (☎669-913-1111)
- **Racquet Club Las Gaviotas:** three clay and four hard courts (☎669-913-5939)
- **Sports World Kaoz:** three hard courts, squash courts, and pool (☎669-983-3922)

Golf

Golf took a back seat to fishing in Mazatlán until recently. With the addition of a magnificent course on Isla de la Piedra, you'll get hours of enjoyment and a chance to improve your skills:

- **Club de Golf El Cid:** This twenty-seven-hole beauty is only open to the public during off season (El Cid Mega Resort, ☎669-913-5611).
- **Club de Golf Estrella del Mar:** A public eighteen-hole course, designed by Robert Trent Jones Jr., this one skirts the ocean south of town on Stone Island (Camino Isla de la Piedra, ☎669-982-3300).
- **Club Campestre:** An older nine-hole course, twenty minutes from town near the airport, that needs some work (Camino Internaciónal al Sur, Km. 1195, ☎669-980-1570).

Time to Relax

Take time out and pamper yourself with a massage, facial, sauna, or steam bath at one of the spas below:

- **El Cid Megaresort:** ☎669-913-3333, ✉*www.elcid.com*
- **Los Sábalos Resort Hotel:** ☎669-983-5333, ✉*www.lossaba los.com*
- **Olas Altas Inn:** ☎669-981-3192, ✉*www.olasaltasinn.com.mx*

Shopping

Because Mazatlán existed as a city before becoming a resort town, modern malls—there are three—were slow to appear here. Instead, you'll find a more Mexican feel to the shops, many of which are open-air. The usual handicrafts pack the local shops, including custom-made leather clothing, serapes, rugs, and works of art. Beach vendors ply the sands with an unbelievable assortment of goods. The iron-wood bird and animal sculptures are the best you'll find anywhere and at reasonable prices. One of the more bizarre stores is Sea Shell City (✆669-913-1301), which sells an amazing variety of shells and ornaments made from them. Meanwhile, the Mazatlán Arts and Crafts Center (✆669-913-5022) offers an array of Mexican handicrafts.

 **TRAVEL TIP**

When shopping in the local market or buying from street vendors, try to get at least a 30 percent discount.

For a true Mexican experience, visit the lively downtown Mercado José María Pino Suarez, otherwise known as El Mercado Central, an art nouveau steel masterpiece built in 1899, which sells everything from *huarache* sandals to suet and from painted gourds to garbanzo beans. The diversity of merchandise will astound you.

Time to Eat

You won't have to go far to satisfy your hunger in Mazatlán. Seafood tops most restaurant menus. But restaurants also serve a staggering variety of cuisines, from Italian to Asian to good old American and Mexican. You'll find enough restaurants in the Zona Dorada to provide you with a diverse selection, including some fine hotel eateries. If you want more Mexican atmosphere with your meal, head for Mazatlán Viejo. Cafés line Plaza Machado.

JUST FOR PARENTS

For a special night out, dine by candlelight at Señor Pepper, where tuxedoed waiters serve Sonoran steak, shrimp, and lobster dinners on crisp linen-covered tables (Camarón Sábalo, ☎669-914-0101).

Open-air seafood restaurants line the beaches of the Zona Dorada. While some don't look like much, their food is often delicious. If your palette desires fast food, there's more than enough of the usual fare to satisfy you.

Local Dining Suggestions

- **El Shrimp Bucket:** This local institution serves shrimp any way you like it in a party atmosphere, with live marimba music with dinner (Hotel La Siesta, Avenida Olas Altas 11, ☎669-981-6350).
- **Mamucas:** Known as the "King of Seafood," this downtown eatery serves up delicious grilled treats from the sea (Bolivar Poniente West, ☎669-981-3490).
- **Pancho's:** One of Mazatlán's best traditional Mexican eateries, it also overlooks the beach (Playa Goviatas, ☎669-914-0911).
- **Pedro y Lola:** Offering an extensive menu of Mexican and international dishes, here's where you'll also find great desserts, plus live music Wednesday through Saturday nights (Plaza Machado, ☎669-982-2589).
- **El Parador Español:** Good Spanish and Portuguese food is featured here, especially paella and a long list of tapas, served to the accompaniment of a flamenco show on weekends in the winter season (Camarón Sábalo, ☎669-913-0767).

Dining Precautions

Generally, food served in restaurants in the Zona Dorada is safe, and they also use purified water in ice cubes, but use caution with food served from small stands and street carts. Plus, bottled water is available everywhere.

Where to Go After Dark

Fiesta Land, a large Moorish complex and Mazatlán landmark on Punta Sábalo is your headquarters for a fun time in Mazatlán. Whether you start or end your merriment here, you'll find a variety of clubs and discos to suit your mood. The city's nightlife concentrates in the Zona Dorada, so you can easily club-crawl without taking a taxi. Discos like Valentino's and El Caracol in the El Cid Resort, with $20 cover charges, don't open until 9 or 10 P.M., and the beat pounds until 4 or 5 A.M. If that's not your thing, spend a couple of hours at a piano bar like Mikinos next to Valentino's. Or listen to the sonorous sounds of a *tambora* band at El Toro Bravo. And for the hottest in Latin rhythms, head to Avenida Rudolfo Loaiza where you'll find Joe's Oyster Bar, Gringo Lingo, and Mangos.

On Tuesday, Friday, and Saturday nights, the Playa Mazatlán Hotel offers a Fiesta Mexicana, which includes a free buffet and drinks, folkloric dancing, live music, and *charro* exhibitions (✆669-989-0555). The Hotel El Cid holds its Mexican fiesta on Wednesday evenings (✆669-913-3333). Either costs $30 per adult, half price for kids. Or enjoy a ballet, opera, or other performance at the Ángela Peralta Theater (✆669-982-4447).

CHAPTER 13

Puerto Vallarta

LOCALS CALL IT VALLARTA. Visitors call it PV. Either way, it hasn't been the same since Richard Burton and Elizabeth Taylor scorched its streets with a torrid romance in 1964 during the filming of Tennessee Williams's *Night of the Iguana.* If you're expecting the backwater lunacy of John Huston's film, you'll be pleasantly surprised. No resort better exemplifies the palm-fringed beaches, thick jungle, and posh resort hotels of the Mexican Riviera than Puerto Vallarta. From its sleepy seaside village roots, it has grown into one of Mexico's slickest and most loved destinations.

About Puerto Vallarta

Once a remote and nearly forgotten fishing village, Puerto Vallarta has blossomed into one of Mexico's most popular resorts with over 350,000 residents that attracts nearly 2 million visitors a year.

Puerto Vallarta combines the slow-paced ambiance of yesterday with the sophisticated accommodations of today. Nestled at the foot of Bahía de Banderas amid lush tropical foliage and the rugged coastal mountains of the state of Jalisco, it still retains the charm of a Mexican seaside village.

It's perhaps the cleanest beach resort in all of Mexico. This is the most striking aspect of downtown. Cobblestone streets wind past the jumbled collection of white stucco buildings with red tile roofs and wrought iron balconies overflowing with colorful bougainvillea vines, giving it an air of Old Mexico at every turn.

Now a city of 350,000 with a decided California flavor, Puerto Vallarta has spread out to include four areas—Viejo Vallarta (Old Town), along the Río Cuale, the Zona Hotelera (Hotel Zone) Marina Vallarta, a hotel and condo development north of town, and Conchas Chinas, along the road south of town.

Best Time to Go

Though Puerto Vallarta generally has mild tropical weather, the temperature can get up into the low 90s in the summer when there are afternoon rain showers, beginning in June and lasting into late fall. As at other places on the Mexican Riviera, the rain only lasts for a few hours. The best time to visit is from January to April when the temperature only reaches the mid-80s during the day and low 60s at night. However, the ocean can be rough and cold.

Cuisine

Besides the usual Italian, French, American, and Asian foods served in vacation resorts, Puerto Vallarta offers delicious Mexican fast food that is served at food booths throughout town. Each booth serves one type of food, from tacos to *tortas* (tarts) to grilled seafood, starting at noon each day. Or, if you prefer to sit down, sample the delicious homemade soups, *moles* (chicken and meats served with spicy chocolate sauce), and *chiles rellenos* (stuffed peppers) at a *fonda* (food stall) in the Mercado Municipal.

Cautions and Safety Concerns

Puerto Vallarta's town fathers are proud that their city has the cleanest water in Mexico. The water here isn't only treated and purified, it has been certified by the Mexican government's Health and Public Works Department to be clean and safe for five consecutive years; Puerto Vallarta is the only tourist resort in Mexico to receive the certification. However, the town continues to rebuild its water-main system, so, unless you're staying in a large hotel, it's still advisable to drink bottled water.

 TRAVEL TIP

Beware of timeshare salespersons offering freebies in exchange for their pitch on a Puerto Vallarta timeshare. Some set themselves up in false "Tourist Information" booths on the street. If you need information, visit the local tourist office at Avenida Juarez and Independencia (☎322- 221-0242).

Puerto Vallarta doesn't have many lifeguards. The ocean can be rough in the winter and have large swells in the summer, even inside the bay. Be sure to swim with someone for safety.

If you do encounter a problem or need to ask a question, you can seek out special tourist police, dressed in white safari uniforms and helmets, found in the major tourist areas.

Getting Around Puerto Vallarta

Though Puerto Vallarta has grown immensely, you can still get around easily. You may opt to rent a car. The main road, which parallels the sea, runs south through town from Nueva Vallarta to the north (in the state of Nayarit), changing names several times along the way. The multilane section going north to the airport is called Búlevar Francisco Medina Ascencio, more commonly known as Carretera Aeropuerto (Airport Highway). The ten-block cobbled section along the *malecón* is Paseo Díaz Odraz, and finally, as it passes through town, the road is called Avenida Morelos. A new *libramiento* (bypass) helps you avoid the congested city traffic if you're driving. But for forty cents you can hop on a bus to take you anywhere along this route. To go north, look for buses marked "Ixtapa." To go south, look for those marked "Mismaloya."

TRAVEL TIP

After collecting your luggage at the airport, head to the front of the terminal to catch a *collectivo* (taxi van) to the Zona Hotelera. These fill up fast and charge about $4 per person. Otherwise, you may have to take a private, Aeromovil taxi, for $20 for up to four persons.

Taxis are plentiful, but you'll pay more in Puerto Vallarta because of the longer distances, as fares are calculated by zones. It can cost as much as $10 to ride from your hotel to town. Though hotels post fares, always ask before getting into a cab.

Family-Oriented Hotels

You can opt for lodging in the heart of the action or tucked away in a remote tropical villa. Most family-oriented resorts lie along the Zona Hotelera, north of Old Town.

Dreams Puerto Vallarta Resort & Spa

Reservations: ☎866-237-3267 (U.S.), ✍*www.dreamresorts.com*
This luxurious all-inclusive resort has 250 rooms in a high-rise tower and an additional 150 rooms with jacuzzis. Meals, drinks, and water sports, plus a supervised kids' club, are included. Kids accompanying parents stay for half price.

La Jolla de Mismaloya Hotel and Spa

Reservations: ☎800-322-2344 (U.S.), ✍*www.lajollademis maloya.com*
Located fifteen minutes south of town with a spectacular view of the ocean and a nice beach, this deluxe resort features five restaurants, four bars, water sports, spa, and a kids' club for children aged five to eleven.

Hotel Canto del Sol

Reservations: ☎322-226-0123, ✐*www.cantodelsol.com*

This 434-room high-rise offers balconied rooms overlooking a large pool and palm-shaded patio. Both room-only and all-inclusive rates are available. Features include a kids' club, exercise room, jacuzzi, and tennis at the adjacent John Newcombe Tennis Center.

NH Krystal Vallarta Hotel

Reservations: ☎800-231-9860 (U.S.), ✐*www.nh-hoteles.com*

A low-rise resort with 460 rooms, suites, and villas spread through landscaped gardens has a great atmosphere designed especially for Mexican families. Deluxe garden villas open onto private pools. Facilities include a huge pool with a colonial aqueduct spilling water into it and several restaurants.

Hotel Qualton Club and Spa

Reservations: ☎800-327-1847 (U.S.), ✐*www.qualton.com*

This busy, friendly 320-room all-inclusive resort, features continuous food, drinks, and entertainment from morning to night. Buffet theme dinners, a children's program, two pools, a complete gym and spa, day and night tennis, all water sports, yoga, aerobics, stress therapy, and more will keep you busy throughout your stay.

Villas/Rental Options

If you prefer not to stay in a hotel and want the freedom of an apartment or villa, you'll find Puerto Vallarta has the most reasonable rentals of any beach resort in Mexico. Winter season rates range from about $500 per month for studios to $1,000 for three-bedroom villas. Contact any of the following for possibilities:

- **Bayside Properties:** ☎322-223-0898, ✐*www.baysideprop ertiespv.com*
- **Casas & Condos:** ☎322-224-4200

- **MexiRent Vallarta:** ☎800-656-5555 (U.S.), ✐*www.mexirent.com*
- **Rent 'n Vallarta:** ☎322-222-1606
- **Vacation Condominiums International:** ☎322-221-2490

Something for Everyone

Whether you prefer to just sit back and let the world go by or take a more active role, your family will find enough to do in Puerto Vallarta to fill a month of vacations.

Things to Do

Old Town, with its cobblestone streets and bougainvillea-draped walls, bisected by the Río Cuale River, remains recognizably Mexican. A morning stroll might take you along the *malecón* to watch the fishermen and the pelicans, then to the crown-topped church, passing a train of burros while on your way to the *catédral*.

 TRAVEL TIP

For a free walking tour map filled with historical facts about Viejo Vallarta, stop into the tourism office on the north side of Plaza Juárez. While you're there, also pick up a free copy of *Vallarta Today*.

Located in the center of town, La Iglesia de Nuestra Señora de Guadalupe (Church of Our Lady of Guadalupe), Puerto Vallarta's cathedral and most visible landmark. Built as a small church in 1892, it took thirty-three years, from 1918 to 1951, to convert it into the cathedral. Angels holding hands decorate its exterior. And topping its steeple is an enormous replica of the crown supposedly worn by Carlota, Empress of Mexico in the 1860s.

Spend a languid afternoon in the cool shade of the Isla Río Cuale, a long narrow five-acre island, exploring the small free archaeological museum, Museo Río Cuale, and afterward sipping a cool margarita in one of its cozy bistros. Artisan shops offering everything from *huipiles* (embroidered blouses) to *huaraches* (leather sandals) to handicrafts dot its meandering walkways canopied with lush tropical foliage. At one end of the island stands a statue of the late film director, John Huston, the man who put Puerto Vallarta on the map. And if you look up, you'll see a hill above Old Town known affectionately as Gringo Gulch, the neighborhood made famous by Burton and Taylor's steamy romance, and home to many wealthy Americans.

Sunday evenings bring out both the local families and tourists along PV's *malecón*. If you'd rather sit than stroll, you can relax in one of the cafés overlooking PV's famed bronze sculpture, *Caballito de Mar* (Boy on a Sea Horse), by Rafael Zamarripa. Often, there are public art exhibits set up along the walkway. Here, you'll also find restaurants specializing in fresh seafood, with second-floor balconies from which you can watch the sunset.

Another popular pastime is gallery hopping around town. Because of its artistic heritage, Puerto Vallarta boasts more galleries than any other Mexican beach resort. Biweekly Old Town art walks guide you to the best shows.

For a Tarzan-like experience, try a three-hour jungle trip by Jeep through the mountains to swim in beautiful coves. Or see Puerto Vallarta from the air in a hot-air balloon at sunrise or sunset with Puerto Vallarta Balloon Tours (✆322-323-2002).

If you want to learn how tequila is made, visit El Pitillal, a tequila micro-distillery. Take the tour, then sample $100-a-bottle pure heaven (✆322-324-9674).

For the Kids

Swimming with dolphins, a popular activity in other Mexican beach resorts, has come to Puerto Vallarta. But you'll have to travel to the Nuevo Vallarta Marina in the neighboring state of Nayarit to do so (✆329-297-1212). The waterpark in Marina Vallarta also offers a day of fun.

If you're in Puerto Vallarta from December to April, take the kids on a whale-watching excursion with Vallarta Adventures (✆322-297-1212). Boats follow the humpback whales, which migrate down from Alaska. There's nothing more unforgettable than seeing a whale breach out of the water. Some come right up to the boat. Or at night from June to September, kids can help release baby turtles into the sea through programs sponsored by Puerto Vallarta hotels.

RAINY DAY FUN

During those afternoon summer rains, take the kids to a movie in one of Puerto Vallarta's malls. Films, shown in English with Spanish subtitles, change every Friday.

Kids eight and above will enjoy swinging through the trees like Tarzan or Jane at several jungle locations around Puerto Vallarta. Mexico's newest thrill ride sends them hurtling at speeds of up to thirty-five miles an hour over the treetops while safely wrapped in a nylon harness.

If your kids like to race, take them to Super Go Karts, north of the airport (✆322-321-2293) where they can race around a 3,250-foot track in a high-tech go-kart.

Bullfights

Like Cancún, Puerto Vallarta holds bullfights on Wednesday afternoons at 5 P.M. from November to June at Plaza de Toros La Paloma. Tickets cost around $25.

Fun in the Sun

Seemingly limitless year-round sunshine, coupled with twenty-five miles of silky soft beaches surrounded by tropical mountains make Puerto Vallarta a paradise if you prefer an active vacation in the sun.

Swimming, golf, tennis, sailing, fishing, and horseback riding are among the most popular sports.

Beach It

Beyond Old Town, three miles of sun-drenched beaches stretch out along Bahía de Banderas, Mexico's largest bay, north to Marina Vallarta. Beginning with Playa Camorones, the golden-sand beaches form a continuous strand through Playas Las Glorias, Los Tules, and de Oro. Here, you can swim in the gentle waves without the huge crowds of the beaches south of town. And your kids will delight in hunting for tropical shells along the shore. Since resort hotels line these beaches, renting water-sports equipment isn't a problem. Surf fishing is popular.

Playa Los Muertos, also known as Playa Olas Altas and Playa del Sol, just south of the Río Cuale, is one of the most popular beaches. Little undertow makes it a perfect family bathing beach. Sundays, when locals come to have fun with their families, it gets particularly crowded. Mariachis play while little boys hawk "fish on a stick" to tourists. You can even fish off the rocks at its southern end.

To the south of Playa Los Muertos lies Playa Conchas Chinas (Chinese Shells Beach), a series of sandy coves interspersed with rocky outcroppings. Snorkeling and fishing off the rocks is popular here, also.

While seemingly overdeveloped with condos and a huge resort hotel, Playa Mismaloya offers excellent swimming and snorkeling. Colorful fishing *lanchas* (launches) lie in the sun along its length in front of *palapa* restaurants where you can sample grilled seafood. Also, the view of algae-dappled Los Arcos is spectacular.

Boat It

Some of Mexico's prettiest coves and inlets lie along the shores of Bahía de Banderas. You can reach most only by boat, all of which depart from the *muelle* (town pier)or Terminal Maritima, north of town near the airport. Two excursion boats, the *Princesa Yelapa* and the *Princesa Vallarta* (✆322-224-4777, ✐*www.cruserosprincesa.com.mx*), depart around 9 A.M. for Yelapa, a palm-lined village with several beach-front restaurants serving fresh seafood and cold beer. The former, for $40 per person, stops at Los Arcos, a grouping of three huge rock formations, for snorkeling and then at Yelapa, and includes continental breakfast, lunch, and open bar. You can reach a 150-foot waterfall, Cola de Caballo (Horsetail Falls), surrounded by jungle, by a twenty-minute walk inland.

TRAVEL TIP

Have your child's photo taken with an iguana for a dollar on the beach at Yelapa. It will be a memory to treasure and something to use for show-and-tell.

Or you can take a sunset cruise aboard the smaller *Princesa Vallarta* from 6 to 9 P.M., including open bar, snacks, live music, and dancing, also for $40 per person. Cruceros Princesa also operates the *Serape,* a sailboat holding thirty people. Sailing first to Los Arcos for snorkeling, it then continues on down the coast to Playa Las Animas and Quimixto for a horseback ride. Included are lunch, two drinks, and music for about $40 per person. In all cases, you'll have to board a motor launch to go ashore.

If you'd prefer the serenity of a sailboat, several companies offer sailing options:

- **Sail Vallarta:** Sunset cruises, three-day sailing cruise, day sailing, and sailing lessons (☎322- 221-0096)
- **Bora-Bora:** Daily coastal trimaran trips (☎322- 224-3680)
- **Neptune Charters:** Charter sailings for swimming and snorkeling, plus sunset cruises (☎322-223-1065)
- **Marigalante Cruises:** Sunset cruise aboard a pirate ship (☎322-323-0309)

Snorkel, Scuba, Fish

The craggy coves of Puerto Vallarta offer the perfect opportunity for snorkeling and scuba diving. You'll find the best snorkeling at Los Arcos and the surrounding national marine park where tunnels and caverns overflow with goat, angel, butterfly, and parrot fish. Local operators can take you for a full day of snorkeling, including equipment, for about $30.

Pacific Scuba (☎322- 222-4741) offers PADI instruction, or they'll arrange a custom trip for you if you're more experienced. Or you can take a guided dive with Chico's Dive Shop (☎322-222-1895, ✍*www .chicosdiveshop.com*) to Los Arcos or Quimixto for $65 for one tank and $80 for two, including equipment. Trips to the Islas Marietas (Marietas Islands), Puerto Vallarta's best dive site, cost $100 for two dives, with lunch and nonalcholic drinks. Beginner lessons start at $20.

Though Puerto Vallarta isn't known for its sportfishing, you'll find it adequate for your needs. November through April is the best time for marlin. Dorado run from May to November, wahoo from October to March, and yellowfin tuna from June to February. Sailfish, while plentiful year round, are best between November and April. Larger cabin cruisers can be chartered for $100 per person or for $300 to $500 for the entire boat for the day, or you can hire a smaller pangas on any beach for $25 an hour. Here are a selection of fishing charter companies:

- **Chefero's Fleet:** Captain and English-speaking crew (☎322-222-6899)
- **Fishing with George:** Provides shuttle service and will cook your catch (☎322-224-5676)
- **Vallarta Five-Star Fishing Charters:** Sport-fishing yacht with fish finders and radar (☎322- 221-0037)

PWC Rentals, Kayaks, and Parasailing

You can rent Hobie Cats and WaveRunners on the beaches north of town at the larger hotels for $50 per half hour. Or you can go water skiing for $75 an hour. You can also rent kayaks and explore Puerto

Vallarta's rivers and estuaries. A ten-minute parasailing ride will set you back $25—and provide lots of white-knuckling sweat.

Ecotourism

Mountain biking has come to Puerto Vallarta. Participate in an escorted mountain bike tour to the villages of San Sebastian, Yelapa, or Mascota, arranged by Bike Mex Adventures (✆322-223-1680, ✍*www.bikemex.com*), including bikes, gloves, helmet, and bottled water, plus an English-speaking or bilingual guide, all for about $30.

You may prefer to go horseback riding into the jungle. You can rent horses at several stables in Puerto Vallarta for about $10 an hour, including Rancho El Charro (✆322-224-0114), Rancho Ojo de Agua (✆322-324-0607), or Rancho Palma Real (✆322-321-2120). Join the group or canter along the beach. You can ride for as little as three hours along the beach or join a guided leisurely excursion into the foothills of the Sierra Madre through picturesque villages and spectacular scenery, stopping for lunch along the way. If you're in Puerto Vallarta for a longer time, perhaps you might want to join a three-day horse camping trek to the historic silver mining town of San Sebastian, founded in 1604.

Tennis

Considered one of the best tennis destinations in Mexico, you'll find dozens of tennis courts at area resorts, like the Sheraton and NH Krystal, as well as Puerto Vallarta's several fine tennis centers, including these:

- **The John Newcombe Tennis Center:** Play at four indoor and four outdoor courts for $16 an hour. Or take lessons for $35 an hour. Afterward take a steam bath or get a massage (Hotel Canto del Sol, ✆322-226-0123).
- **Los Tules Tennis Center:** Six courts (Adjacent to Fiesta Americana Hotel, ✆322-224-4560)
- **Las Iguanas Racquet Club:** Two covered courts (Marina Vallarta, ✆322-221-0683)

Golf

Though Puerto Vallarta can't compare to Los Cabos and the Riviera Maya when it comes to golf, you'll find several good courses that will provide hours of playing pleasure:

- **Vista Vallarta Club de Golf:** Two eighteen-hole courses, one designed by Jack Nicklaus, the other by Tom Weiskopf, provide a challenging round each time (✆322-221-0402, ✑*www. vistavallartagolf.com*).
- **Club de Golf Marina Vallarta:** An eighteen-hole course, designed by Joe Finger with the vacationer in mind; within the Marina Vallarta development (✆322-221-0545, ✑*www .foremexico.com*)
- **Los Flamingos Club de Golf:** An older easy-play eighteen holes, designed by Percy Clifford, twenty-five minutes from Puerto Vallarta (329-226-0404)

Time to Relax

Indulge yourself in ultimate relaxation provided by sophisticated indoor and outdoor spas with treatments that address your senses and complement days of extreme activity. Choose from full-body massages to aromatherapy and facials. One of the most unusual is Terra Noble, an outdoor spa featuring a *termascal,* or pre-Hispanic sweat lodge. Here are some others to consider:

- **Dreams Puerto Vallarta Resort & Spa:** Playa de las Estacas, ✆866-237-3267 (U.S.), ✑*www.dreamresorts.com*
- **Hacienda Hotel and Spa:** Near Terminal Maritima, ✆322-226-6667
- **La Jolla de Mismaloya Beach Resort & Spa:** Playa Mismaloya, ✆322-228-0660
- **Qualton Club & Spa:** ✆322-224-4446

Shopping

Puerto Vallarta has some of the finest shops in Mexico. The quality of the goods is superb and the variety surprisingly good. You'll find a wide selection of shops offering everything from fine art and exquisite folk art to furniture, designer clothing, and jewelry. As you walk the town's streets, you'll see artists working in their studios and workshops.

You can spend hours browsing the shops and boutiques of Isla del Río Cuale, along the *malecón*, downtown along Juarez and Morelos streets, and at the numerous American-style shopping malls. For traditional handicrafts, try the outdoor flea market at the Marina or Mercado Municipal Río Cuale (Municipal Market) along the banks of the river. Puerto Vallarta's four malls—Plaza Caracol, Plaza Genovesa, Plaza Iguana, and Marina Plaza—and shops stay open from 9 A.M. until 8 P.M. However, shops in Old Town often close between 2 and 4 P.M. for lunch.

For something really different, seek out the artwork of the Huicholes, the indigenous people of Nayarit, at galleries in Old Town. Their colorful yarn paintings and exquisite bead-encrusted sculptures of animals inspired during spiritual rituals while under the influence of hallucinogenic *paote* are treasures to behold. Frogs, iguanas, jaguars, turtles, and eggs join the more traditional snakes, wolves, scorpions, and deer. Sculptures start at $200 and can go for as much as $10,000.

🌂 RAINY DAY FUN

To learn more about Huichol Indian art, visit Arte Magico Huichol, which displays a large collection of beadwork, jewelry, masks, and tapestries made by the Huichol.

If you're an art lover, you'll be in heaven. Fine-art galleries showing the works of famous Mexican and international artists seem to be on just about every street in town. A new exhibit opens every Friday night during the winter season.

Time to Eat

Your tastebuds will get a workout in Puerto Vallarta. Over 250 restaurants offer everything from fast-food McDonald's to sushi and Asian stir fries, Italian, French, and, oh yes, Mexican. Whether you choose to dine in cozy intimate bistros or in family restaurants, you'll find so many good restaurants here that you'll want to do nothing but eat. You can eat on a budget or spend extravagantly on gourmet delicacies. The aromas of freshly baked breads and pastries waft through the air in the morning. And ice cream shops serve up cool, refreshing dips on hot afternoons. You'll find a great selection of restaurants downtown along Basilio Badillo, Puerto Vallarta's *Calle de Cafés* (Restaurant Row), and in Puerto Vallarta's many hotels. You'll need a reservation for dinner at even modest eateries during winter season.

 **TRAVEL TIP**

> Dine on succulent seafood in quaint jungle-hidden hideaways like Chico's or Chino's Paradise, or El Edén, the setting of the film *Predator,* in the jungles south of town. While you're munching on mouthwatering shrimp and lobster under a huge thatched-roof *palapa*, you can converse with the parrots that inhabit the places.

Aching for a cappuccino or a latte? In keeping with its trendy ambiance, Puerto Vallarta now sports coffeehouses serving these caffeinated concoctions, all made from locally grown beans. Stop into Café San Cristobal on Calle Corona, just off the *malecón*, Café Sierra and Fiascos Bar on Calle Insurgentes, or the local favorite, Mundo de Café on Olas Altas. All serve *cafecito,* the specially brewed Mexican espresso. Even though you probably will have breakfast included at your hotel, just once stop in at La Casa de Los Hot Cakes (The House of Pancakes), on Basilio Badillo and indulge in a variety of pancakes or a full American and Mexican breakfast, accompanied by a bottomless cup of rich Mexican-grown coffee.

Local Dining Suggestions

- **Las Palomas:** This busy eatery on the *malecón* serves freshly caught seafood. On a warm evening, to the strains of marimba music, their cold gazpacho Anduluz hits the spot. Breakfasts are especially good (Gustavo Diaz Ordaz and Aldama, ☎322-322-3675).
- **Café des Artistes:** Nouvelle French cuisine, prepared by an award-winning chef, is served in a romantic atmosphere of candlelight, ceiling fans, and soft music. It's a good place to splurge. Piano bar and great Sunday brunch (Guadalupe Sanchez 740, ☎322-322-3228).
- **Café de Olla:** Here you'll find reasonably priced traditional Mexican food, served as *plato tipico* Mexicano, with a selection of enchiladas and *chiles rellenos*, or a platter of *antojitos* with tostadas (toasted sandwiches) and tacos, in a café environment (Basilio Badillo 168, ☎322-223-1626).
- **Cuiza:** This trendy cantina, decorated with handpainted tiles and complete with live music, serves California-style light dishes and fruit-infused drinks at reasonable prices (Isla Cuale, ☎322-222-5646).
- **La Dolce Vita:** Here you'll find Italian dishes and wood-fired oven pizza, with a romantic view of the ocean while you eat(Paseo Díaz Ordáz, ☎322-222-3853).

 JUST FOR PARENTS

For a romantic night out, begin with a cocktail at Puerto Vallarta's primo viewing spot, the lobby bar of the La Jolla Mismaloya Resort and Spa, then head up to the ruins of the former set for *Night of the Iguana*, now the restaurant El Set, for a candlelight dinner overlooking the ocean (☎322-221-5341).

Dining Precautions

With so many Americans coming to Puerto Vallarta, restaurants practice good hygiene. The city itself has purified water, so you shouldn't have any problems. Beach restaurants generally are also clean and safe.

Where to Go After Dark

Puerto Vallarta offers a diverse mix of nighttime entertainment, with more live music clubs per square block than any other Mexican seaside resort town, featuring everything from blues to Cuban and Peruvian to jazz, and, naturally, *mariachi*. Though you can dance the night away at chic discos like Christine's, The Zoo, and Friday Lopez, you may choose instead to spend a relaxing evening at one of the new dinner clubs like River Café or Cuates y Cuetes, listening to Latin jazz.

Don't miss one of the Fiesta Mexicana nights held at either the NH Krystal Hotel on Tuesdays, the Sheraton Hotel on Thursdays, or the Restaurant Iguana (☎322-222-0105) south of the Río Cuale on Tuesdays and Thursdays at 7 P.M. For about $45 per person, you'll have your choice of Mexican dishes from a sumptuous buffet, followed by folkloric music, dancing, *charro* exhibitions, and fireworks. Make reservations at your hotel's tour desk.

CHAPTER 14

Manzanillo

SURROUNDED BY LUXURIANT JUNGLE, tropical fruit plantations, and deserted beaches, Manzanillo, in the state of Colima offers families sophisticated comfort in a setting of breathtaking natural beauty. Located along the Pacific Coast in an area known as the Mexican Riviera, between Ixtapa and Puerto Vallarta, Manzanillo isn't a homogenous resort complex. Instead, it's a port city that features a number of hotels strung along two five-mile-long bays that are separated by the Santiago Península.

About Manzanillo

The city of Manzanillo is home to the largest Mexican seaport on the Pacific Coast. Farther northwest, at the end of Bahía de Manzanillo, rises the Península de Santiago, a majestic natural seaside wonderland of rock and battered trees that juts up sharply from the deep azure-blue sea and is dotted with luxurious homes of the wealthy. The centerpiece of Mexico's jungle-clad coastline, the city is set between two magnificent bays—Manzanillo and Santiago—and was named after a tree used for shipbuilding. Tropical fruit plantations filled with coconut, mango, and avocado trees, and lush jungle line its beaches, dotted with coves. Two towns, Salagua and Santiago, plus the city of Manzanillo stand on the shores.

What really put Manzanillo on the map was the filming of the movie *10*, starring Bo Derek and Dudley Moore in the 1980s. Shot on the grounds of Las Hadas (The Fairies), an Arabian-Nights-style resort built by Bolivian tin magnate Antonio Patiño, and on the beaches of Manzanillo, the film brought many others to these shores seeking romance.

Best Time to Go

The weather is always excellent. Manzanillo is on the same latitude as Hawaii, with January, February, and March the months of lowest humidity. However, summer months can be sweltering, though tempered by ocean breezes. Temperatures average 78 to 84°F.

Cuisine

The waters off Manzanillo offer a delicious array of fresh seafood. So it's no wonder that you could eat some type of it for every meal if you wanted. Most of the time, you'll see seafood grilled over charcoal, but cooks also prepare it *sarandeado* style (flame-roasted), in shellfish soup, by marinating sailfish or dorado in lime juice for *ceviche*, or raw in the case of clams and oysters. If you like seafood, you can get your fill of it here.

≡FAST FACT

A popular dish in the state of Colima is the *sopito* (little sope), made by topping a small tortilla with meat in a spicy tomato sauce. You can also add lettuce, crumbled cheese, onions, and so on. Normally, you get five or six to an order.

Cautions and Safety Concerns

The beaches along the shore of Bahía de Manzanillo are steep, creating a strong undertow. It's safer to swim at Playa de Miramar, along Bahía de Santiago.

Getting Around Manzanillo

When you arrive in Manzanillo, you'll have to take one of the airport vans operated by Transportes Turísticos Benito Juárez—$22 to $29 for private, *taxi especial* service or $9 to $11 per person for sharing in an orange *collectivo*. Many hotels also provide shuttle service. Most of the major car rental firms provide service in Manzanillo.

You'll have no trouble getting a taxi in Manzanillo. Fares are fixed. Charges from the Zona Hotelera out near the Península de Santiago to town are about $5. Always agree on the price before you get into the taxi. You can also hop on local buses, which come by every ten minutes and go to a number of destinations for fifty cents. If headed to one of the major beaches, look for the beach name on the front of the bus—Miramar, Brisas, Audiencia. If headed to town, look for buses marked "Mercado," and in the other direction, "Commercial" or "Com. Mexicana."

Family-Oriented Hotels

Most of the family-oriented hotels are located in the Zona Hotelera, a four-mile-long beachfront section called Boulevard Miguel de la Madrid adorned with benches and potted plants, shade trees, and sidewalks, three miles north of town.

Club Maeva

Reservations: 314-331-0800, *www.clubmaeva.com*

With 550 rooms and suites, Club Maeva was Manzanillo's first all-inclusive resort. Today, it caters to American and Canadian families in the winter and Mexican families in summer. Kids under eighteen stay at reduced rates. The all-inclusive package includes all meals and drinks, as well as all water sports, horseback riding, entertainment, and even Spanish lessons. In addition to kids' playgrounds and the largest pool in Latin America, there are seventeen tennis courts and an on-site water park. It also features a kids' club for ages four to seven.

Hotel Gran Costa Real

Reservations: ☎800-543-7556 (U.S.), ✐*www.realresorts.com.mx*

Located on the Península de Santiago, this 332-room, nineteen-story all-inclusive hotel has a great restaurant, pool with swim-up bar and lots of activities, tennis courts, spa, and live entertainment. Rates include all water sports, golf, and tennis. Children under seven stay free, with a kids' club and child care available.

Karmina Palace

Reservations: ☎800-234-6222, *www.karminapalace.com*

This 324-suite, deluxe all-inclusive resort rises above the northern end of Playa Azul. With interconnected pools, nightly shows, several restaurants, and a kids' club for ages four to twelve, as well as game room, and waterslide, it's the perfect family hotel.

Hotel Villas La Audiencia

Reservations: ☎314-333-0861

A good family value, this villa hotel offers one-, two-, and three-bedroom layouts, each complete with kitchen and air-conditioning. There's also a pool and restaurant.

Palma Real Hotel & Villas

Reservations: ☎314-335-0000, ✐*www.palmareal.com.mx*

This timeshare hotel on Playa La Boquita offers luxurious accommodations ranging from one-bedroom junior suites to three-bedroom, three-bath apartments with full kitchen, the latter perfect for large families. Facilities include a minimart, laundry, pool, and restaurant.

Days Inn Hotel Fiesta Mexicana

Reservations: ☎314-333-1100

Located on the main road between downtown Manzanillo and the Península de Santiago, this 200-room hotel, decorated in traditional Mexican style, offers comfortable accommodations at reasonable rates and is a favorite of Mexican families.

Villas/Rental Options

If you'd rather stay in your own apartment or villa rather than a hotel, go to ✍*www.manzanillopacificrealestate.com.*

Something for Everyone

Beach fun is the number-one activity in Manzanillo, whether it be lying under an umbrella, building sand castles, or peeking into the watery depths. But the city is developing some unique attractions to round out your days.

Things to Do

Manzanillo, with its population of just 130,000, used to have little in the way of sights to see. Except for the immediate downtown area and some magnificent views of the beaches from high up on the coastal cliffs, most of the attractions were some distance away. In recent years, the town fathers have invested heavily in building a new harborside boardwalk, upgrading the downtown area, and opening a new archaeological museum.

A large rock formation splits Old Manzanillo in two—on one side the harborfront, with the Jardin de Obregón, the main square, and on the other the shopping area. Spend some time strolling around the plaza, with its twin fountains, large blue sailfish sculpture by artist Sebastian, and Victorian bandstand. Busts of Benito Juárez and Father Hidalgo stare at each other from across the park. Perhaps stop and have your shoes shined or buy a colorful animal balloon for your child. Next, step into the cool depths of the Parroquia Nuestra Senora de Guadalupe (The Church of Our Lady of Guadalupe) to see the story of Juan Diego and the miracle of the Virgin of Guadalupe told in four stunning stained glass panels on either side of the altar. Wander through the colorful stalls of El Mercado, the city market, about ten blocks away. Though there's not much specific to see, you can absorb lots of local color. And don't forget to visit the boat-filled harbor and shipyards across from the plaza. Manzanillo is one of the largest ports on the Mexican Pacific Coast and one of the bases for the Mexican navy.

RAINY DAY FUN

To understand about Manzanillo's pre-Columbian past, visit the Museo Universitario de Arqueología, on the waterfront boulevard northeast of town, where you'll see exhibits of ceramic vessels and figurines, plus ancient shell jewelry. Admission is $1. (Open 10 A.M. to 2 P.M. and 5 to 8 P.M., ✆314-332-2256.)

For a great view of the city, port, and surrounding area, climb to the top of Cerro Vigía Chico, Manzanillo's highest hill. Continue further to the top of Cerro Cruz and see an even better view. Make sure you do either or both climbs in the early morning or evening, wear a hat, and take plenty of water with you. The view is particularly spectacular at sunset.

But it's when you head for the hills of New Manzanillo that you witness true splendor—verdant hillsides tumbling down to an azure sea, with miles of beachfront. North of Old Manzanillo lies the Península de Santiago, separating the Bahía de Manzanillo from the Bahía Santiago.

Some visitors choose to rent a Jeep and go on an excursion past orchards of lime and mango trees and fields of chili peppers to idyllic Barre de Navidad, a quaint beach resort with excellent rustic beachside seafood restaurants, terrific fishing, and a Bohemian atmosphere, and neighboring San Patricio on Melanque Bay, a short thirty-five-mile drive west from Manzanillo. Here, you can take a boat taxi across the deep blue lagoon to an outdoor seafood restaurant, where the biggest decision you'll have to make is whether the tiny sweet oysters from the lagoon are tastier than the big ones from the bay.

≡FAST FACT

In 1541, Viceroy Antonio de Mendoza arrived on the shores of a barrier island which he christened Barre de Navidad, after the Spanish word for Christmas.

For the Kids

Take the kids on an excursion to the Centro Ecológico de Cuyutlán "El Tortugario" (Turtle Sanctuary) in Cuyutlán, an old beach resort about thirty miles south of Manzanillo. Whether you drive yourself or take a van tour, you'll ride through miles of coconut and banana plantations to the thirty-one-mile-long Laguna de Cuyutlán. Here, your kids will enjoy seeing baby turtles being raised in pools until they're old enough to be released into the ocean. You can even have the kids pose for pictures with the sanctuary's resident alligator. Admission is $2 for adults, $1.50 for children under twelve. (Open 8:30 A.M. to 5:30 P.M., ✍313-328-8676.)

TRAVEL TIP

If you want your children to participate in the releasing of the baby turtles daily at 4:30 P.M., August through October, you must make an appointment.

Afterwards, take a $5 guided boat ride on the lagoon to see all sorts of birds and wildlife. And don't forget to visit the Museo de la Sal (Salt Museum), an old wooden salt warehouse filled with exhibits on Cuyutlán's salt industry. Your child can even buy a small bag of sea salt to take home for show-and-tell at school. (Open 10 A.M. to 6 P.M., ✆313-322-1687.)

Visit Colima

The main attraction to visit is Colima, the state capital, with a population of 90,000. A two-hour drive to the northeast, you can easily visit it in a day. This colonial city was founded in 1523 on the former site of Cajitlán, meaning "where pottery is made." It's an attractive, slow-paced town of simple architecture and lush gardens that stands at the foot of twin volcanoes, snow-capped Nevado de Colima and Volcán de Fuego. The former, an extinct volcano also called Zapetépetl or "mountain of the sapodilla trees," is the sixth-highest peak in Mexico at 14,222 feet. The latter, at 12,992 feet, erupted in 1991, and still fumes and smokes. Both look down on a forested valley and quiet lagoon. Because of the city's proximity to the volcanoes and a severe earthquake in 1941, not many colonial buildings remain.

Be sure to visit the Museo de Culturas del Occidente (Museum of Western Cultures), which is open 10 A.M. to 6:30 P.M., Tuesday through Saturday (✆314-312-3155). Five galleries are filled with over 700 archaeological artifacts, including exhibits of *ixcunclis,* or "Colima dogs," terra-cotta sculptures in varying poses, which the Indians believed accompanied the souls of the dead. And don't miss the collection of over 350 antique automobiles, dating from 1884 to 1950.

North of Colima in the shadow of Volcán de Fuego stands La Campana (The Lookout), the archaeological remains of the former capital city of Coliman. Archaeologists believe the platforms, pyramids, and ceremonial plazas date from about A.D. 800. They also believe the Aztec-speaking inhabitants abandoned the site before the conquest due to earthquakes from the volcanoes. Though it covers approximately 120 acres, only a small portion has been unearthed. (Open 9 A.M. to 5 P.M., ✆312-313-4946.)

Festivals and Special Events

On Sunday evenings, you can join the locals as they relax, socialize, and listen to band music while eating ice cream on the *zócalo* in downtown Manzanillo. The El Coloma or Salagua bullrings play host to occasional bullfights during the winter. Ask at your hotel.

Fun in the Sun

Manzanillo is another great place to have fun in the sun. Its golden sandy beaches and warm waters are perfect for sunning and water sports.

Beach It

Beyond these resort enclaves, miles upon miles of palm trees line the land just inside the coastal shores. Jungle-covered mountains plunge into the Pacific or fall short to reveal golden sandy beaches, begging to be discovered and walked upon by tired feet. Ten miles of white- and black-sand beaches attract ocean lovers.

Alongside the five-mile-long Playa Azul (Blue Beach) stand open-air seafood restaurants within a stone's throw of the Pacific Ocean. The aroma of grilled shrimp fills the air as huge waves pound the shore along the length of Bahía de Manzanillo. The surf is calmer from December through May.

 TRAVEL TIP

Stop at an open-air restaurant for a tropical seafood lunch of ceviche, fresh oysters and clams, shrimp, filet of dorado, red snapper, or lobster, all caught that morning by local fishermen. Strolling musicians play while you drink ice cold Mexican beer under the shady palapas.

At the southeastern end of Playa Azul lies Playa Las Brisas, one of the cleanest and safest in Manzanillo. From here, you can watch the ocean-going ships as they enter or leave the harbor. South of town, you'll find spectacular Playa Las Ventanas (Windows Beach) where you can experience the spouting *bufadora* (blowhole), with its vertical column of spray and terrific roar. Stand back, you might get a shower! Beyond this lies Playa de Campos de Coco (Coconut Plantation Beach).

The better beaches lie further north on Bahía de Santiago. Playa Santiago comes first, followed by Playa Olas Altas (High Wave Beach), the top surfing spot in the area, and Playa Miramar (Seaview Beach), which is good for body surfing. Here, you can rent boogie boards and inner tubes, or perhaps an umbrella for $3 a day to provide some shade from the midday sun.

For seclusion, wild Playa de Oro (Beach of Gold), windswept, with fine grey sand, can't be beat. It weaves for miles backed by dramatic cliffs and rock formations and low dunes. It got its name not from the color of its sand but rather from the wreck of the *Golden Gate,* a steamship that sailed from San Francisco loaded with $1.4 million in gold and 337 passengers, in July of 1862. Only eighty of the passengers survived, and the gold was lost. In the 1960s, an American expatriate recovered much of it, but who knows what treasures lie just offshore. If you prefer to feel the thrill of excitement as you ride horseback through the surf, manes flying in the wind, you'll love the dark sand of Playa Santiago.

Beyond Playa de Oro lies Playa La Boquita (The Little Mouth Beach), appropriately named as it's located at the mouth of the Laguna de Juluapan, a wildlife-filled lagoon. Here, little seafood *ramadas* (thatched palapa food stands)—selling fresh oysters and clams, grilled shrimp, and lobster—and fishing boats cluster on the sand. With its mild surf, it's perfect for families with small children. Plus you can choose from a variety of activities, including boogie-boarding, banana boat rides, snorkeling, diving, and horseback riding. And between activities, you can relax under your own personal *sombrilla* (palm-thatched umbrella) while drinking a *coco,* a coconut with its top hacked off. First you drink the milk of the coconut, after which you can eat the meat with hot sauce, salt, and lime.

About thirty minutes south of Manzanillo lies Playa Cuyutlán, the best black-sand beach in Mexico. This long beach faces open sea and the town of Cuyutlán, home of the amazing La Ola Verde (Green Wave). During the full moon in April or May, monstrous thirty-footers, full of phosphorescent colors, roll in. A giant sixty-five-foot tsunami destroyed the town in 1932.

≡ FAST FACT

Cortés's first lieutenant, Gonzalo de Sandoval, is said to have met with a local Indian chief in 1522 on Playa Audiencia, thus its name.

The best beach for swimming is Playa Audiencia (Audience Beach), a gold-and-gray sand arc nestled in a protective inlet between two rocky outcroppings on the north side of the Península de Santiago. It was here that Dudley Moore wooed Bo Derek on the beach in the movie *10*. The waves are gentler here than elsewhere. Because of this, it's a favorite destination of excursion boats. You can rent lounge chairs, tables, and umbrellas right on the beach. If the women or girls in your family want to get *trensitas* (minibraids), they should check the vendors at the beach's entrance. You can also climb the El Faro (lighthouse) for a panoramic view.

Boat It

Take a *crucero de atardecer* (sunset cruise) on the *Explorer*, departing at 4:15 P.M. on Mondays, Thursdays, and Saturdays from the marina at Las Hadas Resort. For $36 per person, you'll get drinks and snacks and a front row seat for a fantastic Manzanillo sunset, while viewing dramatic rock formations with names like the Three Kings, the Elephant, and the Rhinoceros (☎314-331-0101, ext. 3210).

Snorkel, Scuba, Fish

Water sports—windsurfing, waterskiing, sailing, diving, and snorkeling—are king in Manzanillo.

With its beautiful bays and coves teeming with fish and coral, Manzanillo is a natural if you love to snorkel. The rocky shores of

Playa La Boquita and Playa Las Brisas, plus the shoals on either side of Playa Audiencia, offer the best snorkeling.

Although Manzanillo isn't known for diving, you'll find several sites to interest you. Because of Manzanillo's volcanic origin, you'll discover archways to swim through, crevices and cracks, visible lava flows, and fissures. You can either explore the remains of a cargo ship that sank in 1959 off Playa La Boquita or feed octopuses and eels off Playa Audiencia. Visibility ranges from thirty to fifty feet close to shore and up to over eighty feet south of Elephant Rock, with water temperatures ranging from 76 to 86°F. A two-tank dive will cost you about $80 dollars, including equipment. You can also purchase special two- or three-day dive packages for $70 to $80 per day. Underworld Scuba offers beginners classes in their pool, followed by an hour's dive in a quiet cove. They also offer a Bubblemaker program for kids ages eight to eleven for $35. This teaches youngsters to breathe underwater using a series of games (Plaza Pacifico on Av. Audiencia, Península de Santiago, ☎314-333-0642, ✑www.dive manzanillo.com).

Considered one of the best deep-sea fishing spots in the world, the waters of Manzanillo are teeming with marlin and tuna from November to March. You can also catch snapper, sea bass, dolphin, and yellowtail in abundance during the same time period. Sailfish and dorado, however, are plentiful year round. The largest fleet of charter boats belongs to Flota Amarilla (Yellow Fleet) of the Sociedad Cooperativa de Prestación de Servicios Turísticos Manzanillo (☎314-332-1031). Charters, departing from the La Perlita (Little Pearl) pier and near the harbor, cost about $300 per day for up to eight persons and with three fishing lines. Larger boats for up to a dozen persons and six fishing lines cost about $400. Even if you don't catch any fish, which is doubtful, you'll see plenty of seabirds and perhaps even some whales from January to March.

Kayak and PWC rentals

The calm waters off Playa Audiencia offer the best opportunity for kayaking. You can rent kayaks for $16 dollars per hour, and also boogie boards, banana boats, and sailboards on Playas Audiencia, Miramar, and Olas Altas.

Surfing

Of all of Mexico's beach resorts, Manzanillo is the best for surfing. Powerful rollers crash onto Playas Olas Altas and Miramar. You can rent a board at Miramar.

Ecotourism

If you love adventure, then you'll want to take a volcano trek through the tropical forest to explore lava-tube caves, perhaps visit a coffee plantation, and swim under a waterfall. Or if you're even more adventurous, you can hike the slopes of Volcán de Fuego. For an even more breath-taking adventure, try rapelling down volcanic cliffs (Asociación de Guias de Manzanillo, ✆314-332-1185).

You could also take a thrilling three-hour ride on an ATV to Montaña de la Voca (La Voca Mountain) and along the uninhabited expanse of Playa Peña Blanca (White Rock Beach) further up the coast. You can rent equipment from Rancho Peña Blanca. Be aware that the beach may be closed during September and October when sea turtles come ashore to lay their eggs.

You can also ride horseback along a trail by Laguna de Juluapan to see iguanas and exotic birds and then make your way back to Playa La Boquita. Or you can see the lagoon from a kayak. Rentals are available from Trinidad Torres at Marina Punta Santiago (✆314-334-1313).

If you would rather do your exploring on two wheels, you can rent a mountain bike from Bicicletas Norco (✆314-333-2067) and travel a variety of routes from the beach inland to the ecological park at Sierra Manantlán.

Tennis

The only hotel that rents tennis courts to nonguests is the Hotel Gran Costa Real. You play on one of six courts in the early morning or evening for $8 per hour during the day and $10 at night (☎314-333-2000). Or you can play on the courts of Club de Golf Santiago for $6 per hour (☎314-335-0370).

Golf

Two championship courses and one resort course will provide you with endless rounds of challenging golf:

- **Club Las Hadas:** An eighteen-hole championship course, designed by Roy Dye, renowned as one of the most scenic and challenging courses in the world and rated as one of the top five courses in Mexico (☎314-331-0101, ext. 3703)
- **Club de Golf Santiago:** A good nine-hole course with palm-lined fairways that's good for a quick round (☎314-335-0370)
- **Club de Golf Isla de Navidad:** A championship twenty-seven hole course, designed by Robert Von Hagge, made up of three sets of nine—lagoon, mountain, and ocean layouts, with brick cart paths (☎314-341-8283)

Time to Relax

Both the Karmina Palace and the Hotel Gran Costa Real have full spa facilities. Though both are all-inclusives, spa treatments aren't included. If you're staying elsewhere, you can make an appointment for a traditional massage or an entire day of pampering at either hotel.

Shopping

Shopping is concentrated in several small plazas along Highway 200, as well as downtown around the Jardín and for eight blocks along Avenida Mexico. You can bargain for typical souvenirs at El Mercado downtown on Avenida Cinco de Mayo. The best place to buy handicrafts—leatherwork, pottery, blown glass, and papier-mâché figures, fruit and birds—is Centro Artesanal Las Primaveras on Av. Juárez in the village of Santiago.

 TRAVEL TIP

Mercado and *tianguis* (street markets) vendors expect you to bargain for a better price. Start by asking for half the price and work your way up. If you can get 40 percent off, you've got a deal. Don't appear too desperate for the item.

If you collect shells, then you don't want to miss the magnificent collection of conches, corals, and snails at El Palacio de las Conchas y Caracoles (The Palace of Conches and Snails) nearby. Plaza Manzanillo, an American-style mall near the Península de Santiago, has many shops selling a variety of clothing, jewelry, and pottery.

Time to Eat

If you choose to venture out from your idyllic resort, you'll find some fine restaurants serving Italian, French, American, and Argentinian, as well as traditional Mexican cuisine. However, with many hotels offering all-inclusive packages, there aren't as many to choose from as in other Mexican beach resorts.

Local Dining Suggestions

- **El Vaquero:** A great family place, this replica of a circa-1900 cantina serves mesquite-broiled steaks and hearty chili and beans with all the fixins' (Crucero Las Brísas, ✆314-333-1654).
- **Restaurant L'Recif:** Enjoy a romantic dinner of traditional dishes at sunset at this elegant hideaway with a spectacular

view of Bahía de Manzanillo from high on a hill. Reservations required (Av. Cerro de Cenicero on Península Juluapan, ✆314-335-0900).

- **El Fogón:** Taste the hearty meat dishes of *norteño* cooking while dining in the atmosphere of an old-fashioned Rancho Grande (Highway 200, Km. 9.5, ✆314-333-1654).
- **La Pergola:** Handmade pasta and freshly baked bread accompany German dishes and steaks at this patio-style restaurant set under the palms (Near Plaza Manzanillo, ✆314-333-2265).
- **Juanito's:** This popular eatery, owned by an American expatriate and his Mexican wife, serves up delicious burgers, milkshakes, and ribs, plus great breakfasts. You can even read an American newspaper or surf the Internet while you wait for your order (Highway 200, Km. 13.5, Santiago, ✆314-333-1388).

Dining Precautions

Most restaurants in the Zona Hotelera are clean. Bottled water is available everywhere. However, be cautious of buffets served outdoors in the intense summer heat.

Where to Go After Dark

Nightlife centers upon the hotels and restaurants around Península de Santiago. For a family fun night, head to the Colima Bay Café on Playa Azul where you can sit at oceanfront tables while eating giant shrimp and barbecued ribs. If the booming sound of disco beckons you, stop in at Club Maeva's Disco Boom Boom (where the name says it all). And chivalry isn't dead here. The cover charge is less for ladies. Or you may want to try Disco Vog, a disco on the highway at Playa Azul or Disco Solaris in the Hotel Playa de Oro. Cover charges range from $6 to $10.

JUST FOR PARENTS

For a unique experience, visit a local *botanero* (beer hall), a Colima specialty. Locals come to listen to mariachi music and watch stage shows while eating *botanas* (snacks)—plates of refried beans, guacamole, and ceviche—and drinking beer. You can even play the *rifas* (raffle). Some, like El Caporal, are only open from mid-afternoon to early evening.

You can also take in a Fiesta Méxicana at Club Maeva from 8:00 to 11:30 P.M. on Saturday nights for about $35 per person, including a full buffet and open bar. Kids pay half price (☎333-331-0800). Or you can try a similar all-you-can-eat feast at Manos Morenos Restaurant on Thursday nights during the winter season (☎314-333-0323).

CHAPTER 15

Ixtapa/
Zihuatanejo

IXTAPA/ZIHUATANEJO IS REALLY TWO destinations in one—the lobster-and-champagne Zona Hotelera of Ixtapa and the clams-and-beer, laid-back village of Zihuatanejo. As Mexico's second "computer resort," it's set on twenty-four miles of palm-lined beaches and coves, with rolling surf and pounding breakers. There's not much to do but soak up the sun, play golf, and get away from it all. Here, after a couple of days, you'll sigh as you sip from the salted rim of a chilled margarita—*"Ahhh, Ixtapa!"*

About Ixtapa/Zihuatanejo

Ixtapa is a modern development of a dozen high-rise hotels that loom over Playa El Palmar, a mile-and-a-half-long arc of fine sand that curves like a smile around the Bahía del Palmar. A three-mile landscaped boulevard, Bulevar Ixtapa, with speed bumps every few feet to ease you into the pace of paradise, runs between them and the Club de Golf Palma Real Ixtapa. Located on the stretch of Pacific Coastline known as the Mexican Riviera, the resort is set against the lush green backdrop of the Sierra Madre del Sur mountains.

Ixtapa, however, maintains its sense of space and communion with nature. Developed in the 1970s, Ixtapa's ecology-sensitive master plan allots half the land on the site to ecological reserves. Hotels and residential structures, both limited in size, have been built to be proportionate to their land area. The resort has its own international airport and a water purification and treatment facility.

Ixtapa, which means "the white place" because of its white sand, is geared to natural pleasures—the enjoyment of spectacular scenery, sports, and sheer relaxation. The water is warm, the beach lit for nighttime strolls.

≡FAST FACT

More than sixty cruise ships visit the port of Zihuatanejo annually. It was also a port-of-call for TV's *Love Boat*.

Four miles down the road from Ixtapa, you'll find Zihuatanejo, a sleepy fishing village wrapped around the pristine Bahía de Zihuatanejo (Zihuatanejo Bay). Known locally as "Zihuat," the centuries-old town offers cobblestone streets lined with shops and cafés where a frosty beer and a dozen oysters is still a traditional breakfast.

By the 1930s, tourists seeking adventure were driving fifteen hours from Acapulco to Zihuatanejo and staying in private homes. Eventually, residents began building small hotels. Originally the Mexican government wanted to build a new resort in Zihuatanejo, but the residents protested. So it expropriated a large coconut plantation north of the village to develop into Ixtapa, and tourism development began.

Best Time to Go

The average annual temperature is a comfortable 78°F with a high of 96°F and a low of 50°F, and the area averages 340 days of sunshine a year. While any time of year is a good time to be in Ixtapa/Zihuatanejo, the heat and humidity of mid-summer can be oppressive. Also, afternoon thundershowers happen almost daily from June through September, with the latter being the rainiest month.

Cuisine

Since the waters off the Pacific Coast are renowned for superb fishing, it's only natural that fresh seafood, from lobster to oysters to red clams to octopus and shrimp, is a main ingredient in local cuisine. Locals prefer eating *huachinango* (red snapper) and dorado, locally referred to as dolphin fish, while watching the sunset. *Tiritas*, thin fish strips marinaded with onions and hot peppers, are a specialty in Zihuatanejo. Fresh *ceviche*, raw fish marinated in lime juice, and shrimp and fish tacos are also local favorites.

Cautions and Safety Concerns

Both Ixtapa and Zihuatanejo are clean and well kept. With fewer tourists, the resort has fewer problems. Since the hotels in Ixtapa front an open-ocean beach, flags indicate swimming conditions—green means it's safe to swim, yellow means to take precautions, and red means to be careful of strong waves or currents.

Getting Around Ixtapa/Zihuatanejo

To get from the airport to the hotels in Ixtapa or Zihuatanejo, you have to use the official airport transportation service. A van with up to eight persons costs about $40, while a car holding up to four persons is about $22. If you share a van, it will cost you $6 a person. You must purchase tickets at the ground transportation counter upon leaving the terminal.

 **TRAVEL TIP**

If you're in Ixtapa/Zihuatanejo during high season and are planning to use an ATM, be sure to do so as early as possible—the ATMs often run out of cash because of heavy use.

Beach names, rather than street names, are often used for directions. Taxi rates are fixed. Within Ixtapa, you'll pay between $2.50 and $5. To go from Ixtapa to Zihuatanejo costs about $4.50. From midnight to 6 A.M., you'll pay 50 percent more. And during the summer months, taxis with air conditioning often charge 40 percent more. Between Ixtapa and Zihuatanejo, buses called *peseras* shuttle back and forth constantly for anywhere from $4 to $6.50 one way. Good van service is available to and from the international airport for about $9.

There's also bus service every twenty minutes from 6 A.M. to 11 P.M. between Ixtapa and Zihuatanejo for about 35 cents. Buses stop at designated stops in front of each hotel along the boulevard in Ixtapa. Be sure to watch out for buses that say "Ixtapa" or "Bulevar Ixtapa."

FAST FACT

Ixtapa has been the setting for several popular films, including *The Shawshank Redemption* and *When a Man Loves a Woman*.

If you wish to be more independent, you may want to rent a golf cart that holds up to five persons for about $15 an hour or, for individual family members, motor scooters that rent for $10 an hour. You can also rent either one by the day at a substantial discount.

A *ciclopista* (bicycle path) runs the entire length of Bulevar Ixtapa to Playa Linda. You can rent a bike for $10 an hour from several places along the way.

Family-Oriented Hotels

Ixtapa/Zihuatanejo offers a variety of lodging choices. Ixtapa's major hotels are modern, high-rise beach resorts lining the two-mile-long Playa del Palmar, while those in Zihuatanejo are more traditional and not necessarily on the beach. The latter offer lower rates but cater more to singles and couples than families.

Barceló Ixtapa Beach Resort

Reservations: ☎877-214-5154 (U.S.), ✉*www.barceloixtapa.com.mx*

This large 332-room beachfront resort features all types of sports, including several swimming pools, an exercise gym, and water sports. There are also several restaurants and bars with nightly dancing. With all first-class services, this resort operates on both all-inclusive and room-only plans. Kids under twelve stay free.

Best Western Hotel Posada Real

Reservations: ☎800-528-1234 (U.S.), ✉*www.posadareal.com.mx*

Though the hotel's 110 rooms are relatively compact, kids under twelve stay free with a parent here. This low-rise hotel offers two pools and a beachside restaurant, but not much else.

Club Med

Reservations: ☎800-258-2633 (U.S.), ✉*www.clubmed.com*

Of all the Club Meds in Mexico, this is the only one that caters specifically to families. Kids from ten months to eleven years can participate in the kids' club, plus parents and their children can take part in the circus workshop in which participants learn to fly on the trapeze, the basics of clowning, and acrobatics. At the end of the week, everyone puts on a circus show. The all-inclusive price includes all sports, workshops, meals, and drinks.

Hotel NH Krystal Ixtapa

Reservations: ☎800-231-9860 (U.S.), ✉*www.nh-hotels.com*

A 260-room balconied wedge-shaped tower rises above a land-scaped garden, giving each room an ocean view. Guests enjoy a large beachside pool with waterfall, exercise gym, and tennis and racquetball courts, plus a fine poolside restaurant.

Melia Azul Ixtapa

Reservations: ☎800-336-3542 (U.S.), ✉*www.solmelia.com*

This 250-room modern high-rise offers balconies and great views, plus forty-seven junior suites and forty-eight two-bedroom suites, making it perfect for families. An all-inclusive resort, it offers several restaurants and activities for the whole family.

Qualton Club

Reservations: ☎755-552-0083, ✐*www.qualton.com*

Located ten minutes from the Zona Hotelera on Playa Linda, this all-inclusive, very family-oriented, low-rise resort spreads out over seven acres facing Isla de Ixtapa. It has two restaurants, four bars, two tennis courts, and a disco, plus two swimming pools. A complete activity program for adults and children keeps everyone busy and happy.

Villas/Rental Options

Luxurious villas and condominiums dot the hillsides rising above both the Bahía de Palmar and Bahía de Zihuatanejo. Two major condominium developments in Ixtapa are Punta Ixtapa (Ixtapa Point), designed by Mexican architect Diego Villaseñor, at the northern end of Bahía de Palmar, and Trapiche Ixtapa, designed by Mexican architect Julio Madrazo, at the southern end. For rental properties, go to ✐*www.paradise-properties.com.mx.*

Something for Everyone

Sports lovers and outdoor buffs can be active all day long in Ixtapa/ Zihuatanejo. Activities range from premier golfing, tennis, scuba diving and the full scope of water sports, horseback riding, fishing, and even bird watching. For those who just want to relax, there are sixteen beaches to lie on and let the world go by.

Things to Do

One of Ixtapa's attractions is its offshore islands. For example, Isla Grande, more commonly known as Isla de Ixtapa, is a Robinson Crusoe's paradise, uninhabited except for exotic birds and a few sun worshippers. You can get to the island by shuttle boat from the pier at Playa Linda. Boats depart from 8 A.M. to 5 P.M. for a round-trip fare of $3. In addition to its beautiful beaches, there are also many other natural attractions, such as the rugged rock formations found all along the coast.

 **TRAVEL TIP**

If you plan to take a tour, don't go with someone on the beach or the street. Check with your hotel tour desk for tours.

For the Kids

Though Ixtapa is a resort more for adults, there are some activities for children. Magic World, a new water park, offers a wave pool, toboggans, and a pirate ship for kids to climb on. Kids can even swim with dolphins at Delfiniti. Those who can't swim can also have an encounter with the dolphins through a special program for three- to seven-year-olds called Delfiniti Kids.

Happy Planet in downtown Zihuatanejo offers interactive games for small children.

Since Ixtapa/Zihuatanejo is one of the best places for sea turtles to come ashore to lay their eggs, it's a great place for kids to learn about turtle conservation. There are quite a few active groups in the area, such as the Asociación de Ecologistas de Zihuatanejo (Zihuat Ecology Association), members of which help collect eggs and build temporary pens on the beaches to protect the eggs until they hatch, after which they release the baby turtles into the ocean.

Fun in the Sun

More than any other beach resort in Mexico, Ixtapa/Zihuatanejo is the place to have fun in the sun. You can swim in the ocean or in luxurious hotel pools, jog along the beach, or play beach volleyball. In fact, there isn't much to do indoors except maybe take a nap while waiting out a tropical afternoon rain shower.

Beach It

An assortment of beaches await you in Ixtapa/Zihuatanejo, beginning with three-mile-long Playa El Palmar (Palm Tree Beach) in Ixtapa. Even though this broad beach faces the open ocean, the surf is gentle enough for children. Six miles beyond the Zona Hotelera, you'll find Playas Quieta, Don Juan, Don Rodrigo, Las Cuatas, and Linda. The waters off Playa Quieta (Calm Beach) especially are clear and perfect for scuba diving. Though it's a public beach (like all beaches in Mexico), you can only gain access through the Club Med gate, which is locked at night. The strong waves at Playa Linda are good for surfing.

 RAINY DAY FUN

On a rainy day, you can go see a movie at the Cinema Flamingos on the Boulevard in Ixtapa (Plaza Flamingos, ☎755-553-2490) or visit El Museo Arqueológico de la Costa Grande, located at the end of Playa Principal in Zihuat, where you can learn about local pre-Columbian history for $1 admission. (Open Tuesday to Sunday from 9:30 A.M. to 7 P.M.)

Four beaches line the Bahía de Zihuatanejo—Playa Principal, Playa La Ropa, Playa La Madera, and Playa Las Gatas. Adjoining the small Plaza de Armas in Zihuat (as Zihuatenejo is locally known) is the usually crowded, half-mile-long Playa Principal (Main Beach), along which you'll find most of the beachside restaurants. East of town lies small Playa La Madera (Wood Beach), a favorite of campers, although officially camping is only allowed at Playa Linda (Beautiful Beach), north of Ixtapa, and Playa Larga (Long Beach), south of Zihuat. Following the curve of Bahía de Zihuatanejo, five minutes from town, is Playa La Ropa (Clothes Beach), more than a mile of pure paradise framed by a backdrop of hotels and banana and coconut plantations and dotted with quaint seaside restaurants.

One of the calmest and most beautiful of local beaches, thatched *palapas* and feathery palms line its yellow-sand, half moon stretch. Parachutes for parasailing ($15 for ten minutes) lie waiting for customers as others zip over the waves on Hobie Cats and Jet Skis.

South of Zihuat, you'll find Playas Manzanillo, El Riscalillo, Larga (Long Beach), and Blanca (White Beach), each with its own special charm. Playas Manzanillo and El Riscalillo are somewhat secluded. Playa Larga, the longest beach in the area, is especially good for long beach walks or jogging and has many seafood restaurants where you can have lunch after your walk. Playa Blanca, another long beach, also has many seaside restaurants that are great for letting you just sit back with a cold beer and enjoy the day.

Just beyond is Playa Las Gatas (Cats Beach), lying further south and the most Polynesian-like of Zihuat's beaches. Once the private bathing area of Tarascan princesses, it now offers great swimming, snorkeling, and scuba diving in its calm waters and on its offshore reef. Afterward, you can enjoy grilled shrimp at one of a dozen seaside restaurants. To reach it, you need to take a ten-minute ferry ride for $4 across Bahía de Zihuatanejo from the municipal pier in Zihuatanejo.

Boat It

No visit is complete without a trip to Isla Grande, also known as Isla de Ixtapa, a scenic island and wildlife preserve a mile off Playa Quieta. This exotic hideaway comes complete with a crescent beach and open-air restaurant. If you would rather see Zihuatanejo from the water, you can hop aboard the Tri Star catamaran at 10 A.M. for a cruise of the bay with lunch and open bar for $50 per person. The Tri Star also offers sunset party cruises with snacks and bar only, departing at 5 P.M. from the main pier in Zihuat, for $40 per person (✆755-554-2694).

≡FAST FACT

Playa La Ropa, one of the finest beaches on the west coast of Mexico, is uncrowded, wide, and clean. Literally translated as "clothes beach," it takes its name from an incident in the eighteenth century, when a Spanish galleon loaded with silks from China foundered offshore and the cloth washed up on the beach.

Snorkel, Scuba, Fish

Water sports of all types from jet-skiing to banana boat riding to windsurfing are popular in Ixtapa/Zihuatanejo. Rentals, available at Playas El Palmar, Linda, and Quieta in Ixtapa and Playas La Ropa and Gatas in Zihuat, run from $10 dollars an hour and up. Windsurfing is best at Playa Linda and Las Escolleras.

With water temperatures of 79°F, you'll find the best snorkeling in the shallow waters off Playas Las Gatas and Manzanillo and off the shores of Isla de Ixtapa. You can rent equipment for the day on Playa Las Gatas and on Isla de Ixtapa.

TRAVEL TIP

Avoid solid foods for at least twelve hours before you dive. Also, don't dive if you have an ear or respiratory infection. Lastly, don't fly for at least twenty hours after your last dive.

Scuba diving is surprisingly good here, with opportunities for divers of all levels at over thirty dive sites. Whether you dive to the wreck of the *Fandango* in the Bahía de Zihuatanejo or the shallow reefs off the coast at Playas Las Gatas or Manzanillo, you'll find a site of interest. Dives begin at $50, including equipment, one tank, and a guide. NAUI and PADI certification courses are available at the Zihuatanejo

Scuba Center. Equipment rentals and instruction are also available from the following dive shops:

- **Carlo Scuba:** Playa Las Gatas, Zihuatanejo, ☎755-554-6003
- **Catcha L'ola:** Plaza Kiosko, L12, Ixtapa, ☎755-553-1384
- **Centro De Buceo Oliverio:** Playa Cuachalalate, Isla de Ixtapa, ☎755-554-3992
- **Ixtapa Aqua Paradise:** Plaza Los Patios, L137, Ixtapa, ☎755-553-1510
- **Nautilus Divers:** Juan N. Alvarez #33, Zihuatanejo, ☎755-554-9191

Ixtapa/Zihuatanejo ranks among the top three places in the world for deep-sea fishing. Anglers hook sailfish most of the year, but black and blue marlin, dorado, and yellow-knife tuna are also plentiful.

⚊FAST FACT

Writers Ernest Hemingway and Zane Grey both came to Zihuatanejo to catch sailfish long before there was even a road to the village.

You'll pay as much as $600, including fishing license, bait, and drinks, for seven hours on a charter boat, depending on the size and number in your party. Grouper, roosterfish, wahoo, mackerel, barracuda, and bonito swim the waters closer to shore. You won't need a license to fish close to shore, but you should bring your own equipment.

Golf

If you like to play golf, you'll find two challenging resort courses in Ixtapa:

- **Club de Golf Palma Real Ixtapa:** This eighteen-hole traditional course designed by Robert Trent Jones Jr. is also a wildlife reserve where alligators live in the water hazard lakes (✆755-553-1163).

- **Club de Golf La Marina Ixtapa:** Canals crisscross this challenging eighteen-hole, links-style course designed by Robert Von Hagge (✆755-553-1410).

If you wish to rent clubs, the fee is $30 at both courses.

Tennis

Ixtapa offers limited tennis facilities. The Barceló, NH Krystal, and Dorado Pacifico Hotels along Bulevar Ixtapa have guest-only courts as well as some public courts, many lit for night play. Court rental fees are $4 to $7.50 per hour, with reservations mandatory, especially during high season.

Ecotourism

With its emphasis on outdoor activities, Ixtapa/Zihuatanejo offers a perfect setting for ecotourism activities like horseback riding, mountain biking, cave exploration, and rappeling. You can rent horses for $15 an hour from Rancho Playa Linda to the north of Ixtapa, from which you can ride with a guide along the Rio Pantla. You can also go horseback riding along Playa Larga near Zihuatanejo.

At Parque Aventura in Ixtapa, you can walk through the treetops via a hanging bridge or fly through them on a zip line thirteen to thirty feet above the forest floor.

For a really unique thrill, you can go tandem skydiving over Playa El Palmar. You'll fall at approximately 120 miles per hour while attached to a licensed skydiver, then land on the soft sand of Playa El Palmar (✆755-553-0257, ✐*www.skydive-ixtapa.com*).

Shopping

There are now seven shopping centers between Ixtapa and Zihuatanejo, with over a thousand shops selling everything from hardware to local handicrafts to fine Gucci leathers. At the handicraft markets in Zihuat (Av. Cinco de Mayo) and in Ixtapa (along Bulevar Ixtapa), you can see Mexican families hard at work making pottery and other crafts for sale. The former has over 200 vendors and the latter over eighty.

 TRAVEL TIP

When shopping in either Ixtapa or Zihuatanejo, watch out for special sales and promotions. Signs will read either *"oferta"* (on sale), *"rebaja"* (reduced price), or *"liquidación"* (close-out). Remember, you can bargain for items at handicraft markets but not in regular shops.

When you want to shift gears, take the fifteen-minute ride by minibus or taxi into Zihuatanejo. Here, you'll find enough boutiques lining the cobblestone streets to fill an entire day of browsing. Sparkling silver jewelry, luxurious blankets, and unique wood carvings are available at the FONART Shop (government handicrafts shop). You can also try the small street market near the *zócalo* behind the *malecón*, Paseo del Pescador, the main beach promenade running along Playa La Madera and Playa Principal. Prices here tend to be lower than in Ixtapa. As a break from shopping, be sure to stop at a waterfront café for a leisurely lunch of red snapper and beer while listening to a band of strolling musicians.

Calles Alvarez and Pedro Ascensio, two streets in Zihuatanejo filled with great handicraft shops, are a favorite of visitors. Here, you'll find colorful ceramic wall plates, ironwood fish and bird sculptures, clay or wooden ceremonial masks, bark paintings, beautifully decorated boxes, and hand-tied hammocks in various sizes. And there's nothing like a pair of handmade *huaraches* (leather sandals) to keep your feet cool. Be careful when purchasing silver jewelry, however. While all of it looks shiny and beautiful, some is just plated, or *plata*, and other pieces are *alpaca*, or nickel silver. Be sure to look for the number .925 stamped on the piece, indicating sterling silver, and buy in a shop rather than from a handicraft vendor. Generally, shops remain open from 9 A.M. to 2 P.M. and 4 to 8 P.M. Mondays through Saturdays.

Time to Eat

In Ixtapa/Zihuatanejo, you can choose from over 150 restaurants. Since the waters off Ixtapa are renowned for superb fishing, it's only natural that the restaurants throughout the resort offer superb seafood. Menus often include ocean-fresh lobster, clams, oysters and other excellent fish dishes, such as red snapper and rooster-fish. Restaurants also serve Italian, French, and Mexican dishes. In Ixtapa, you'll find a good selection in the shopping centers and hotels along Bulevar Ixtapa.

 JUST FOR PARENTS

For a getaway from the kids, spend an evening dining and relaxing at Villa del Sol, a sprawling cottage-like hotel fronting Playa La Ropa in Zihuatanejo. Fine food and wines in an atmosphere of Old Mexico makes for a romantic evening (☎755-555-5500).

You have a wide choice of restaurants to choose from in Zihuatanejo. Locals gather at the shaded and inexpensive *enramada* (arbored restaurants) known as *los arbolitos* (the little trees) that face the municipal beach in the center of town. Which one to go to is left to the most enticing aroma. Strolling musicians entertain on Friday afternoons.

Local Dining Suggestions

- **Bogart's:** This chic restaurant in the Krystal Hotel has a romantic, *Casablanca*-like ambience. Specialties include

Persian crepes, duck Shanghai, and Caribbean lobster (Blvd. Ixtapa, ☎755-553-0333).

- **Coconuts:** This perennial in-spot features a dine-in-garden courtyard with palm trees. A favorite of the local café society and set on an elegant terrace with palm trees and hand-painted parasol lampshades, it serves excellent red snapper, seafood pate, black bean soup, and salads (Agustin Ramirez s/n, Ixtapa, ☎755-554-2518).

- **El Faro:** This replica of a nineteenth-century lighthouse features an international menu, including prime U.S. beef, seafood casseroles, and pasta (Marina Ixtapa, ☎755-553-1027).

- **La Perla:** This palapa-roofed beachside restaurant on La Ropa Beach is known for the freshest and tastiest seafood and best sunset views in town (Playa La Ropa, ☎755-554-2700).

- **Teosintle:** Authentic dishes are served here from the state of Guerrero (Carreterra Zihuat-Acapulco, ☎755-554-3712).

- **Pizzas Ragazzi:** This full-service pizzeria serves the best pizza in Ixtapa (Los Arcos Ixtapa Shopping Center).

- **Villa de la Selva:** This elegant hillside restaurant is set in a charming home that once belonged to Mexico's former president Luis Echeverria. Known for its sauce-smothered seafood and flaming café royal (Paseo de la Roca, Ixtapa, ☎755-553-1190).

Dining Precautions

Since Ixtapa/Zihuatanejo caters to Americans and Canadians, the restaurants practice good hygiene. All the major hotels have water purification facilities, and bottled water is available everywhere.

Where to Go After Dark

Ixtapa's nightlife is sophisticated, sweet, and simple. While the resort frequently imports big-name entertainers, most visitors go dancing in one of several discos along the boulevard. Euphoria is a chic disco overlooking the ocean by the Marina Lighthouse that's popular with locals and visitors alike. But the most spectacular one is still Christine Club Ixtapa (✆755-553-0333), where many dance to the wee hours. Since this is the best disco in the resort, be prepared wait in line during high season.

During high season (November to April), you can take in a fun-filled Fiesta Méxicana in Ixtapa at either the Barceló (✆775-555-0000), Dorado Pacifico (✆755-553-2025), or Presidente Intercontinental (✆775-553-0018) starting around 7 P.M. and featuring an elaborate buffet dinner with open bar, live mariachi music, and folkloric dance performances, as well as handicraft bazaars for shopping. They start at $40 per person, with children under twelve at half price. Be sure to make reservations.

 TRAVEL TIP

If you want to hire a trio to play music for your family in a restaurant or on the beach, be sure to agree on a price before you request any songs.

If you would rather just drink and dance to a live band, Ixtapa's hotels all have lounges with a laid-back atmosphere. And there's always Señor Frogs and Carlos 'n' Charlies (✆755-553-0692 for both), both located near Ixtapa's hotels.

For nighttime fun in Zihuatanejo, head to either Sacbe or Black Bull, the first with international music and the second with Mexican ranchero music. Cover charges at clubs usually range from as low as $5 per person to upward of $25.

CHAPTER 16

Acapulco

ACAPULCO, THE OLDEST OF Mexico's beach resorts, has always been synonymous with extravagance. It's beautiful—a broad blue bay is surrounded by sleek high-rise hotels against the backdrop of emerald hills. It's glamorous—high fashion goes hand-in-hand with worldly sophistication. It's upbeat—dozens of discos pound their beat until dawn. It's loud—horns honk in traffic day and night. After fifty years of development, Acapulco isn't exactly a Robinson Crusoe hideaway or a place for "getting away from it all." Over 4.5 million people visit the resort yearly.

About Acapulco

The resort of Acapulco hugs its half-moon bay following a seven-mile beachfront boulevard, the Costera Miguel Alemán (known locally as the Costera), lined with high-rise hotels and condominiums. Beyond the park, the boulevard meanders along palm-studded beaches to the cruise dock and on to the *zócalo*, or main square, which faces Caleta Beach.

The resort has grown into three distinct areas: Acapulco Tradicionale (Old Acapulco) in the old part of town; Acapulco de Oro (Golden Acapulco) along the Costera; and Acapulco Diamante (Diamond Acapulco) along the road to the airport.

═FAST FACT

Acapulco Tradicionale, known simply as Old Acapulco, is where Johnny Weismuller, the famed Olympian who brought Tarzan to the silver screen, entertained his friends from Hollywood on Playas Caleta and Caletilla.

The area known by many tourists as The Strip, the bay front between Parque Papagayo (Papagayo Park) and the naval base, is known as Golden Acapulco. Bounded on one end by the Radisson Paraisso Hotel and on the other by the Hyatt Regency, Golden Acapulco offers high-rise hotels intermingled with trendy boutiques, beachside restaurants, and some of the best discos in the world.

Acapulco Diamante, the newest area, extends from the airport along a wide stretch of beaches and up into the hills overlooking the sheltered Puerto Marquez Bay.

Best Time to Go

Warm balmy breezes blow the air that ranges from 79 to 85°F most of the year. From mid-December to Easter, the high season, count on blue skies and plenty of sun. Even in the so-called rainy season, from June to September, the showers are short and mostly in the afternoon. But it can be uncomfortably hot and humid in midsummer.

Cuisine

You'll find all sorts of cuisine available at Acapulco's eateries, from American to Italian and French to Thai and Chinese. Fresh seafood, prepared in a variety of ways, is the order of the day, washed down with cold Mexican beer or *refrescos* (cold tropical fruit drinks). And, like all international resorts, Acapulco has its fill of American fast-food eateries.

If you're in Acapulco on a Thursday, be sure to try *pozole*, a savory soup made with hominy, one of Guerrero's most famous and traditional dishes, served for lunch at many local restaurants.

Cautions and Safety Concerns

Generally, Acapulco is quite safe. The streets are well lit and police-men are visible all along the Costera in the tourist zone. In recent years, the city has cracked down on prostitutes and beggars along the Costera, making it safer to walk any time of day. Use common sense, keep your valuables concealed, and only take as much money with you as you think you'll need.

As at other Pacific resorts, tides at Acapulco can be dangerous, with a strong undertow. The city uses a flag system to warn bath-ers—a black or red flag indicates danger, a yellow flag means cau-tion, and green or white flags mean it's safe to swim.

Getting Around Acapulco

Upon arrival, you'll take an airport van for the twenty to thirty-minute ride to your hotel. Though the trip into town costs only $7.50, the return by private, reservations-only airport taxi from Transportes Aeropuerto (☎744-462-1095) costs $15. A shuttle is also available for $10 round-trip. You'll find taxis everywhere, but they don't have meters, so make sure you establish the rate before getting in. Hotels have authorized taxi rates posted in their lob-bies. Hotel taxis are more expensive than if you hail one on the street, and they have set rates. Public buses ride up and down the Costera between the main square in town and the naval base. Hop on one that says "Zocalo" or "Centro" to go into town or one that says "Base" to go in the other direction. The fare is only three pesos (thirty cents) per person.

Family-Oriented Hotels

You'll find hotels catering to families in the center of Golden Acapulco, stretching from the Qualton Club all-inclusive near Papagayo Park to the Hyatt Regency by the naval base.

Costa Club Beach Resort

Reservations: ☎744-485-9050

This 506-room self-contained, all-inclusive resort on the beach in Golden Acapulco features a twenty-eight-story tower, two-story shopping mall, four pools, health club with sauna and jacuzzi, three tennis courts, four restaurants, three bars, all water sports, and a special program for kids. It's loud and noisy, with live music into the wee hours in the lobby bar.

Radisson Acapulco

Reservations: ☎800-333-3333 (U.S.), *www.radisson.com*

This 212-room hotel, consisting of a main building, thirteen cliff-side villas, plus an oceanfront *palapa* restaurant and nearby pools, clings to a steep cliff above Puerto Marques Bay. Each building has a flower's name. A tramway connects its upper and lower levels, making ascending and descending the rocky hillside a breeze. The hotel has two restaurants and three bars, two pools with swim-up bars, and a health club.

Fiesta Americana Condesa Acapulco

Reservations: ☎800-343-7821 (U.S.), *www.fiestamericana.com*

Located in the middle of Golden Acapulco along the Costera, this 487-room, eighteen-story oceanfront hotel offers spectacular views of Acapulco Bay from many rooms. Popular with families, it features oceanfront and children's pools, water sports, three restaurants, and three cocktail lounges. Activities for children center upon the pool area.

Fiesta Inn Acapulco

Reservations: ☎800-343-7821 (U.S.), *www.fiestainn.com*

This modern 220-room hotel is on the beach, next to the Fiesta Americana Condesa Hotel. It's a good family hotel with a large beachside pool with snack bar, plus an additional restaurant and kids' program.

Vidafel Mayan Palace

Reservations: ☎800-292-9446 (U.S.), *www.mayanresorts.com.mx*

Built in the Mayan style with lavish pools and luxurious junior suites with jacuzzi tubs, the Vidafel is a fantasyland for the whole family. The hotel stands at the other end of Revolcadero Beach from the Fairmont Acapulco Princess toward the airport. Enormous mirror-like pools and waterfalls are connected by Venice-like canals, with flower-laden boats to float you around the entire area surrounding the 380 rooms. Across the road from the resort, and connected to it by an elevated monorail, is an eighteen-hole golf course and twelve tennis courts.

Hotel Fairmont Acapulco Princess

Reservations: ☎800-866-5577 (U.S.), ✉*www.fairmont.com*

Ranked as one of the world's best resort hotels, this 1,017-room property sits on 480 acres near the airport. A magnificent sixteen-story pyramid-like building plus two ten-story towers rise above two large free-form pools with waterfalls. The resort also features a variety of restaurants and bars, plus two eighteen-hole golf courses, eleven tennis courts, a luxurious spa, and three additional pools, one fresh and two salt water. The beach is good for horseback riding but not swimming. The hotel is isolated and an expensive taxi ride to town.

Villas/Rental Options

Villas for rent cover the hills above Acapulco Bay in gated estates such as Tres Vidas en la Playa, Las Brisas, and Brisas Marques. Most come with a maid and gardener, a pool, and a great view of the bay. To find listings for villas, houses, and apartment rentals, go to ✉*www .casayvillas.com.mx.*

Something for Everyone

Visitors to Acapulco come more to relax and lie in the sun than to sightsee or participate in activities. Because so many Mexican families come here from Mexico City, there are now more activities for the whole family.

Things to Do

Acapulco offers families plenty to do. After a morning on the beach, you may want to stroll the Costera, which has special sidewalks that absorb the heat and make barefoot walking bearable. Or perhaps you'd rather dangle from a brilliantly striped parachute and parasail over the harbor.

RAINY DAY FUN

During a summer rain shower, you can pay $10 to watch the Basque game of jai-alai at Fiesta Alegre, an indoor stadium called a *frontón* on the Costera across from the Hyatt Regency Hotel.

You should also explore 400-year-old Fuerte de San Diego (Fort San Diego), which protected Acapulco from pirate attacks during the seventeenth century. You can see a sound and light show outside the fort at 7 P.M. Thursday through Saturday in winter and on Saturdays only during the summer. Admission is $3 per person, with Sundays free. (Open Tuesday through Sunday 9:30 A.M. to 6:30 P.M., ☎744-482-3828.)

To absorb some of the local flavor, spend some time savoring a tropical juice drink or coffee while watching the crowd from a café on the *zócalo* after visiting Acapulco's art deco–style cathedral dedicated to Our Lady of Solitude. Built in the 1930s, it has a mosque-like dome and Byzantine towers.

Your entire family will enjoy the Casa de la Máscara (House of Masks), a seven-room museum showcasing masks used in festivals and celebrations throughout the state of Guerrero, located one block from the entrance to Fort San Diego.

If you like the art of Diego Rivera, you'll find a mural he created called *Exekatikalli*, depicting the Aztec gods Quetzalcóatl and Tlaloc, on the wall outside the home of the late Dolores Olmedo, a long-time friend of the artist, at Inalambrica Number Six on the Cerro de la Pinzona.

■ TRAVEL TIP

Explore the greener side of Acapulco, especially if you're a bird watcher, by taking a two-and-a-half-hour "Jungle Tour" by boat of Laguna Coyuca (☎744-481-2103, ✎www.jungletour.com.mx). Transportation, lunch, and drinks are included.

From the coves of peaceful Caleta Beach, you can board a glass-bottomed boat to uninhabited Roqueta Island for about $3, where you can feast on Mexican delicacies, snorkel, and bathe in the warm waters of the Pacific.

For the Kids

There are three facilities for children in Acapulco: Parque Papagayo, Parque CICI Marino, and Mágico Mundo Marino. Papagayo Park is a large natural park about halfway between the naval base and the *zócalo* with fifty-five acres of rides, carnival amusements, a soccer field, basketball and volleyball courts, an auditorium, library, restaurants, swimming pools, three lakes for boating, a skating and cycling rink, a skyway, an aviary, and a small zoo. Admission is free.

≡FAST FACT

On late summer and early fall nights, sea turtles crawl onto Playa Larga (Long Beach), the eastern part of the longer Playa Revolcadero out beyond the Vidafel Mayan Palace Hotel, to lay their eggs.

CICI Marine Park (short for Centro Internacional de Convivencia Infantil) features whale, seal and dolphin shows (12:30, 3:30, and 5:30 P.M.), water slides, an aquarium, and a wave pool. Admission is $6 per person (open 10 A.M. to 6 P.M., ☎744-484-8210). Magic Marine World is an aquarium, with a seal show, water slides, and toboggan ride, built on a small island between Caleta and Caletilla beaches in Old Acapulco (open daily 9 A.M. to 6 P.M., ☎744-483-1215).

Cliff Divers

Not to be missed are the cliff divers of La Quebrada. Holding flaming torches, the *clavadistas* plunge 130 feet off the La Quebrada cliffs into the whirling waters of a shallow inlet bordered by jagged rocks below. You can see them at 1:00 P.M. and hourly from 7:30 to 10:30 P.M. for about $2 from the parking lot at La Quebrada or $5 from the terrace of the Plaza Las Glorias El Mirador Hotel. The late-night torch dives are the most dramatic.

Bungee Jumping

Dare to experience a once-in-a-lifetime moment and bungee jump from the fifty-meter tower of Hackett Paradise Bungee on Condesa Beach. Before you jump, enjoy the incredible view of all of Acapulco from the platform. (Open 12 P.M. to 12 A.M. weekdays, 12 P.M. to 2 A.M. weekends, ☎744-484-7529.)

Visit Taxco

From Acapulco, you can take a day trip to the colonial silver town of Taxco. Today, silver shops outnumber grocery stores or drugstores. There are said to be more than 100 in Taxco, along with stores selling imaginative work in tin and brass. Yet it's the town's colonial charm that will enthrall you. So magical is its spell that Taxco has been declared a national monument—not a cobble may be upturned without bureaucratic permission.

≡FAST FACT

A story is told of how a wandering Frenchman, who later changed his name to José de la Borda, slipped from his saddle while riding near Taxco and fell into one of the world's richest silver veins. His discovery made tiny Taxco rich.

You can see the main sights in town—the Museo Platería, Museo Guillermo Spratling, and the Casa Humbolt—as well as browse some of the many silver workshops, within several hours. To learn about the history of the Taxco silver industry, visit the small Museo Plateria (Silver Museum) before you browse the studios (open daily 10 A.M. to 6 P.M.). During the 1920s, William Spratling helped Taxco revive its ancient silvermaking craft. He collected examples of area archaeological pieces that are now displayed in his former home (open Tuesday to Saturday, 9 A.M. to 6 P.M. and to 5 P.M. on Sunday, ☎762-622-1660). At the Casa Humbolt, you'll see exhibits of art from the colonial era (open Tuesday to Saturday 10 A.M. to 3:30 P.M. and to 3 P.M. Sunday, ☎762-622-5501).

Festivals and Special Events

To experience authentic Mexican music and folk dancing, reserve an evening at the Gran Noche Mexica, held from two to four days a week depending on the season at the Acapulco Centro Convention Center at the east end of the Costera. Tickets for this excellent show go for $25 per person for the show with open bar, or $42 per person for open bar and buffet dinner. Kids pay half price. The performance begins at 8:15 P.M., with dinner served at 7:00 P.M. You can buy tickets through the Acapulco Tourism Office at ☎744-484-4416.

Fun in the Sun

Acapulco is *the* place people go to have fun in the sun. Its golden sand beaches are great for sunning and water sports.

Beach It

In Acapulco's younger days, the action centered on Playas Caleta and Caletilla, both downtown in Old Acapulco, and naturally protected Roqueta Island. Here, the gentle waves and soft sand are ideal for little children. Playa Los Tamarindos, lined with coconut palms, and Playa Los Hornos and Playa Hornitos (also called Playa Papagayo), lined with alfresco beachside restaurants, follow the northwestern shore of the bay.

Today, the emphasis has shifted to Playa La Condesa and Playa Paraiso, both punctuated by high-rise hotels, where tropical rhythms begin pulsing at noon. Playa Condesa offers powdery sand and *palapa*-topped seaside restaurants, where you can peel shrimp and sip fruit-garnished potions from coconut shells or drink salty margaritas or cold beer, all while listening to live music. At the east end of the bay lies Playa Icacos, a wider stretch of sand that runs past the naval base.

 JUST FOR PARENTS

Head out to Pié de la Cuesta, eight miles west of town, to take in *hora de la puesta del sol* (sunset hour). Northwest of the city proper, this romantic hideaway is the best place to watch the sunset while cuddled up in a hammock sipping a *coco loco*, a drink made with tequila and coconut milk served in a coconut shell.

You may want to rent a Jeep or grab a taxi and head south along the Carretera Escenica, the scenic highway to Playa Revolcadero, where the white surf of the open ocean pounds sugary sands. Once remote and apart from the action of Acapulco proper, it now features resorts of its own, like the palatial Vidafel Mayan Palace and the pyramid-shaped Fairmont Acapulco Princess. Horseback riding along this beach early in the morning is a favorite activity. With its strong currents and surf, swimming can be dangerous here.

Boat It

Motorboats pulling parasailers zip back and forth across Acapulco Bay, making sailing dangerous. If you want to sail or sailboard, go to Laguna de Coyuca or to Puerto Marqués, where the waters are calmer. For a more leisurely boat ride, try a three-hour narrated cruise on the Bonanza along the coast of Old Acapulco from Puerto Marqués on the east to the cliffs of La Quebrada on the west. For the price of $17 per person (kids under five feet tall are free), you get the tour, drinks, dancing, and a swim. Or take the Shotover Jet tour of Laguna Puerto Marques (☎744-484-1154, ✐*www*.*shotoverjet-acapulco.com*) on the way to the airport.

Snorkel, Scuba, Fish

Acapulco isn't the greatest place to go diving or snorkeling. The waters of the bay are often murky, especially during summer months.

If you'd like to fish, deep-sea charter boats leave from the docks along the *malecón* (waterfront) across from the *zócalo* about 8 A.M. and return about 2 P.M. You can fish for bonitos, pompano, yellowtail, barracuda, red snapper, and shark out in the Pacific. Larger 40-foot boats for a half-dozen fishermen rent for $250 and up per day, while smaller boats for three or four fishermen rent for about $200 per day. If you wish to reserve a boat ahead of time, contact Fish-R-Us at (☎877-347-4787 (U.S.), ✐*www.fish-r-us.com*). If you prefer freshwater fishing, go to Laguna de Coyuca (Coyuca Lagoon), a natural sanctuary surrounded by coconut groves, about twenty minutes west of town near Pié de la Cuesta beach, where you can hire a *panga* with an awning for about $20 and fish for catfish.

Parasailing and Personal Watercraft

For $20, you can sail high above Acapulco Bay for ten minutes dangling from a parachute, or for $50 dollars per hour you can skim the surface of the water on skis. At major beachside hotels, you'll find all sorts of personal watercraft to rent for $60 an hour.

Tennis

If you like to play tennis, Acapulco has five tennis clubs with a total of forty-four courts, ranging from regular courts to those lighted for night play to indoor, clay, and covered courts. Fees range from $5 to $20 per hour, and most hotels will allow you to play even if you aren't a guest.

Golf

Though Acapulco has only five golf courses, three of them are among the best in Mexico:

- **Fairmont Acapulco Princess Golf Club:** A fine eighteen-hole course, featuring water hazards on twelve holes (☎744-469-1000)
- **Fairmont Pierre Marques Golf Club:** Another excellent eighteen-hole course adjacent to the previous one, with water on thirteen holes and extremely well bunkered (☎744-469-1000)
- **Vidafel Mayan Palace Golf Club:** A lush rolling course by a lagoon near the airport (☎744-469-6000)
- **Tres Vidas Country Club:** The newest eighteen-hole course, with nine water hazards and scenic oceanside holes (☎744-444-5135)
- **Club de Golf Acapulco:** A well-maintained nine-hole course which is lighted for night play (☎744-484-0782)

Time to Relax

Acapulco has its share of luxurious spas. Two of the most luxurious, as well as the most expensive, are the Willowstream Spa at the Fairmont Acapulco Princess Hotel and the spa at the Hotel Villa Vera, in the hills above Golden Acapulco.

Shopping

One of the most popular activities in Acapulco is shopping. Try shopping at the Mercado Parazal (open from 9 A.M. to 8 P.M.) on Calle Velásquez de Léon near the *zócalo*. It's noisy, it's crowded, and it's fun. Sort through stacks of leather sandals, sticky-sweet candy in rainbow colors, handmade silver jewelry, and piles of bright handpainted pottery. If you'd rather shop closer to your hotel, browse the stalls of the La Diana Flea Market further up the Costera at the Glorieta Diana. Air-conditioned shopping centers like La Gran Plaza and Plaza Bahía, art galleries, and boutiques line the Costera. Acapulco is known for its resort wear. Name a sophisticated brand—Givenchy, Cartier, Calvin

Klein, or Gucci—and you'll find it in Acapulco. Most shops and boutiques open at 10 A.M. and stay open into the evening.

Time to Eat

Acapulco has more than 160 restaurants, serving everything from traditional Mexican food to Chinese, Japanese, Thai, Italian, French, and Lebanese cuisine. Many of the most popular eateries front the beach along the Costera. They're al fresco, casual, and lively, especially along Playa Condesa, but if you prefer a quieter place, there are enchanting restaurants off the main drag. Or you may prefer the elegance of dining al fresco at the magnificent El Campanario high above the bay. You can eat seafood in abundance here. In fact, preparing seafood *a la talla* (grilled) began in Acapulco. To enjoy it at its best, head to Barra Vieja, out beyond the Vidafel Mayan Palace Hotel, where restaurant owners grill fish on the beach.

Prices in the more sophisticated restaurants tend to be high, with dinner for two costing $75 or more. But there are plenty of relatively good inexpensive restaurants serving local food all along the Costera.

Local Dining Suggestions

- **Beto's:** Popular seafood lunch place by the beach along the Costera (Costera Miguel Alemán 99, Playa Condesa, ☎744-484-0473)
- **El Amigo Miguel:** A favorite local hangout downtown, serving the best seafood in town washed down with cold Mexican beer (corner of Juárez and Azueta, ☎744-483-6981)
- **El Campanario:** Dine al fresco in this Italianate mansion with a breathtaking view of the bay (Avenida Paraiso s/n Fraccionamiento Condesa, ☎744-484-8830).
- **Restaurante La Cabaña:** Excellent seafood and famous Acapulco ceviche served in a simple bistro on Caleta Beach in Old Acapulco, bedecked with photos of Johnny

Weismuller and other movie stars (Playa Caleta s/n Lado Oriente, Fraccionamiento Las Playas, ✆744-482-5007)

- **Ristorante CasaNova:** Set high above the bay on the road to the airport, serving Northern Italian cuisine with spectacular views (Carretera Escénica, Fraccionamiento Las Brisas, ✆744-446-6237)
- **Sanborn's:** An American-style family restaurant with good food, service, and prices (four locations along the Costera, ✆744-485-5360)
- **Tony Roma's:** International steak house, serving the best ribs in town (Costera Miguel Alemán in the Hotel Continental Plaza, ✆744-484-3348)

Dining Precautions

Most restaurants in the resort area of the city along the Costera are clean. Bottled water is available everywhere. Be cautious of buffets served outdoors in the heat of summer.

Where to Go After Dark

At night, the sounds of tropical, guitar, and rock music drift through the air, mingling with the sounds of the ocean and the traffic along the Costera. This is the best time to take a ride in a balloon-festooned *calendria* or horse and carriage.

Acapulco-after-dark doesn't heat up until after midnight. Whirl away into the wee hours on the floors of some of the world's hottest discos. Zucca, Palladium, Baby'O, and others are frenzied and fun. Most open at 10 P.M. and don't close until dawn. Some charge a small cover with drinks extra and others an all-you-can-drink cover. And don't forget to have your hotel concierge make reservations, or you may not get in.

For family fun, especially if you have teens along, go to either Señor Frogs (✆744-446-5734), with a bullring decor, or Carlos 'n' Charlies's (✆744-484-1285), a favorite party hangout since 1970. The latter offers all-you-can-eat tacos, tequila, and beer every Wednesday and Sunday from 2 to 6 P.M.

CHAPTER 17

Mexico City

MEXICO CITY— usually referred to as La Cuidad or simply Mexico or D.F. (short for Distrito Federal)—is the political, cultural, economic heart of Mexico—the very center of Mexican life. Over the last 700 years, it has evolved into one of the world's great cities. One in five Mexicans lives within its sprawling confines. Its international ambiance results from a blend of European and ancient cultures dating back 3,000 years. It's this mélange of cultures that sets it apart from other capitals of the world. Some claim that if you haven't seen Mexico City, you haven't seen Mexico, yet so few of the millions of Mexico's annual visitors have.

About Mexico City

Mexico City offers three distinct cultures—Aztec, Spanish, and Mexican. This magnificent city of wide, shady boulevards lined with modern glass and steel buildings spiced with touches of the past is also the oldest and highest capital in North America, as well as one of the world's most populous cities, with over 26 million people.

World War II brought a surge in industrialization and by 1968, Mexico City had made itself ready to host the Summer Olympics, which spawned some of its ultramodern architecture.

But since that time, the city's population has exploded, doubling in the last twenty-five years. Poorer Mexicans have come to the city seeking work, settling in *barrios* on its fringes. The city spread out, and what used to be suburbs have now been swallowed up by urban sprawl. Streets are rarely empty. All the traffic has produced one of the worst air pollution problems on Earth. And though it slows down just after midnight, by five, the buses and cars return to the streets, and the daily tempo of life begins all over again.

Best Time to Go

Although it almost never snows and daytime temperatures can reach 70°F, they can drop to the mid-40s at night. The weather is warmest from March to June, when it can reach 80°F during the day. During the rainy season from June to September, torrential downpours can last an hour or a day.

Cuisine

With such an influx of people from all different parts of Mexico, it's no wonder that the cuisine of the capital literally represents the country. However, some dishes have become specialities, like *caldo tlalpeno* (stewed chicken in broth flavored with *chipotles,* or smoked *jalapeños*), *budin Azteca* (chicken, tortillas, cheese, *tomatillos*, roasted chiles, and herbs baked in a *cazuela*), and *sopa de Azteca* (tortillas, chicken, avocado, and cheese).

Cautions and Safety Concerns

Mexico City has had a rash of muggings and kidnappings in recent years, many involving taxis. Do not walk on dark streets at night. Even in well-lighted places, walk with someone. Leave your jewelry at home and only carry enough cash to pay for what you need. Also, don't hail taxis at night. Instead, ask the restaurant or club to call one for you and write down the number of the taxi they're sending and wait for that particular one. In case you're the victim of a crime in Mexico City, you can call the bilingual operator of the Procudaduría del Turista (✆55-5625-8153).

 TRAVEL TIP

Use ATMs in daylight and preferably only those in well-lit and well-trafficked shopping centers.

And remember, the thinner air at the city's 7,346-foot altitude will cause you to tire easily and have mild headaches. For the first couple of days, avoid alcohol, drink plenty of water, eat lightly, and rest often.

Getting Around Mexico City

Considering its size, it's not surprising that you can easily get lost in Mexico City. And with traffic congestion and the constant street name changes, driving is impossible. Luckily, there are thousands of safe taxis to get you to the major sites.

Airport, hotel, and radio taxis have set rates. Although these may be somewhat higher than rates of street taxis, they're safer and more efficient. After claiming your bags at the airport, look for a large "Taxi" sign, where you can purchase your fare into town for about $10. When you get in a taxi, make sure the driver's identification and photograph are visible and legible, and if it has a meter, that it's working. Metered street taxis, usually painted green and white, charge in pesos according to the distance. Rates may be higher on Sundays and evenings after 10 P.M. Drivers don't expect tips.

Street names change as they cross the city's 240 designated *colonias* (neighborhoods), located in sixteen *delegaciones* (districts). Downtown is a veritable United Nations, with streets named after European cities, and rivers or countries in Latin America. Only Avenida Insurgentes retains its name as it runs north to south through the city. There are also many diagonal and curving streets running around many small squares, parks, and *glorietas* (traffic circles), creating odd-shaped blocks that often make it impossible to find street addresses.

🧳 TRAVEL TIP

You'll find that streets and numbers aren't always properly marked, so you should ask for a known landmark or cross street to make it easier to find your destination, whether walking or in a taxi.

Inexpensive buses and *colectivos* run throughout the city. These can be confusing even though they show their fixed routes on their windshields. And while the subway or *metro* offers another option for getting around, it has had a high crime rate in the past. Generally, avoid traveling during rush hours from 8 to 10 A.M. and 6 to 8 P.M. A good alternative is the trolley buses, operating from 6:30 A.M. until midnight on nineteen routes throughout downtown.

Family-Oriented Hotels

Mexico City offers every kind of accommodation you can imagine. For your family, however, you'll probably be more comfortable in one of the city's larger hotels, located in four major areas—the Centro Histórico, the Zona Rosa, the area along the Paseo de Reforma, and the area bordering Bosque de Chapultepec.

Fiesta Americana Reforma

Reservations: ☎800-343-7821 (U.S.), ✍*www.fiestamexico.com*
This twenty-five-story, 587-room hotel will put you high above the Paseo de Reforma. Facilities include three restaurants, a nightclub, a rooftop supper club, lounges, and a health club.

Krystal Zona Rosa

Reservations: ☎800-231-9860 (U.S.), ✍*www.wotw.com/krystal*
This comfortable 302-room high-rise in the heart of the Zona Rosa has two restaurants, a rooftop pool, and a nightclub.

Majestic (Best Western)

Reservations: ☏800-528-1234 (U.S.), ✍*www.majestic.com.mx*

This beautiful and cozy seven-story eighty-five-room hotel in a converted colonial building, with a rooftop restaurant overlooking the Zócalo.

Presidente InterContinental

Reservations:☏800-327-0200 (U.S.), ✍*www.interconti.com*

This thirty-two-story tower with 659 rooms overlooks the Bosque de Chapultepec; it has seven restaurants, a rooftop pool, a lobby bar with music, and a shopping arcade.

Sheraton Centro Histórico

Reservations: ☏800-325-3535 (U.S.), ✍*www.sheraton.com*

One of the city's newest, this twenty-story high-rise overlooks Alameda Central, with several restaurants and a fitness center.

Something for Everyone

If you wanted to take advantage of everything there is to do in Mexico City, you'd need to stay a month. But you'll find plenty of activities for your whole family to enjoy during a few days to a week. While the capital's appeal is timeless, its sheer size makes it somewhat intimidating. Mexico City is not easily conquered. It's so big that it can take weeks to explore it in its entirety. To get a sense of the city, the best option is to tackle the areas containing the biggest concentration of attractions. You'll find most grouped into three major areas—Centro Histórico, Bosque de Chapultepec, and the Zona Rosa.

💼 TRAVEL TIP

For about $10, take the open-air, double-decker Turibus tour of Mexico City. The whole tour, with English narration by earphones, lasts one hour, but you can get off and on at designated stops along the way from the Zócalo to Bosque de Chapultepec from 8:30 A.M. to 10:00 P.M.

Things to Do

Mexico City is a place to be savored, a cornucopia for the senses. But you may feel overwhelmed by it all. If possible, devote a day to each major area of the city—taking an overall tour first may be the best way to orient yourself to the sights.

The Plaza de la Constitución (Constitution Square) or Zócalo (written with a capital "Z" to distinguish it as the original) is not only the heart of the city but of the country. The largest square in the Americas and the city's meeting place, it was, before the arrival of the Spaniards, the site of the Halls of Moctezuma, the core of the Aztec world. Surrounded by two city halls, the Palacio Nacional, and the Catédral Metropolitana with its Sagrario, it has witnessed Mexico's history through the fight for independence to the Revolution. It was even the site of the first bullfight in Mexico.

💼 TRAVEL TIP

Join the free two-hour walking tour of the Centro Histórico on Sundays at 10 A.M. (📞55-5510-2541). Or board a trolley tour, departing daily (except Mondays) every thirty minutes from 10 A.M. to 4 P.M. across from the Museo de la Ciudad.

The thirteen-acre Zócalo is also the epicenter of the Centro Histórico, a 600-square-block area of 1,500 designated historic buildings, many restored to their former glory. The *cátedral*, an encyclopedia of artistic styles begun in 1573 that took over three centuries to construct, dominates the square. Combining Spanish Renaissance and early nineteenth-century French Neoclassical styles, it features the Altar de los Reyes (Altar of the Kings), considered to be one of the best examples of Mexican colonial art and the Altar del Perdon (Altar of Pardon), both built and carved by Jeronimo de Balbas in 1737. Paintings surrounded by golden columns, sculptures, moldings, angels, and other baroque ornamentation decorate the interior. The eighteenth-century El Sagrario is the cathedral's church.

On the east end of the Zócalo, the Palacio Nacional, one of the first buildings built by Cortés (in 1693), houses offices of the president and the finance ministry. Diego Rivera vividly portrayed his vision of daily life in pre-Columbian Tenochtitlán in his mural *El Gran Tenochtitlán*, which you see on the second floor (✆55-5542-6466). Across from the palace stands the Nacional Monte de Piedad (The National Pawn Shop), built more than two centuries ago.

Located just off the Zócalo, the most impressive testimony of the Aztec period are the ruins of the Templo Mayor de Tenochtitlán (Great Temple of the Aztecs), destroyed by the conquistadores and now part of an extensive museum. In 1978, a power company crew burying a cable came upon a huge altar stone buried where the temple had stood. A massive archaeological dig revealed thousands of artifacts, including life-size figures of eagle warriors along with the skulls of their sacrificial victims. You can see them in the museum behind the site. One of the most intriguing finds is an eight-ton stone disc representing Coyolxauhqui, Goddess of the Moon. (Open daily 9 A.M. to 5 P.M., closed Mondays, ✆55-5542-4787.)

Avenida Francisco Madero, the main street of the Centro Histórico, was once known as the Calle de los Plateros (Street of the Silversmiths) and has, since colonial times, been a shopping street. At its west end, the ornate Casa de los Azulejos (House of Tiles), formerly a viceregal palace, now contains several restaurants and shops. Just west of the Casa de los Azulejos stands the magnificent Palacio de Bellas Artes (Palace of Fine Arts). A monument to the art deco style, it's both an opera house and art gallery showing paintings by Diego Rivera, José Climente Orozco, and David Alfaro Siqueiros. This impressive marble palace is home to the world-famous Ballet Folklórico de Amalia Hernández and the Mexican symphony and opera. The theater's stunning twenty-two-ton beaded stained glass curtain, designed by Tiffany, shows the volcanoes surrounding Mexico City (✆55-5512-2593).

TRAVEL TIP

To get a feel for the Belle Epoque in Mexico, step into La Opera, a bar on Cinco de Mayo that dates back to the days of the Mexican Revolution. You can still see bullet holes in the ceiling made by Pancho Villa when he stormed in on his horse (✆55-5512-8959).

Alameda Central, laid out in 1541 over the remains of an Aztec marketplace, extends beyond the Belles Artes. During colonial times, members of the Spanish Inquisition burned heretics at the stake in the Plaza del Quemadero (Bonfire Plaza), off to one side. If you're strolling through the Centro Histórico, you'll find this shady oasis to be a pleasant place to rest. A few blocks west of the Alameda stands the enormous Monumento de la Revolución (Monument to the Revolution), with a museum in its base.

Originally designed to connect Maxmilian's residence with the Zócalo, the tree-lined Paseo de la Reforma, lined with modern office buildings and hotels, runs through downtown from west to northeast. Bronze monuments to Columbus, Cuauhtémoc, the last of the Aztec emperors, and others grace its *glorietas*. The most impressive is the Monumento de la Independencía (Independence Monument) at the entrance to the Zona Rosa, known as El Angelito (The Little Angel), a slender column topped by an eight-ton golden statue of the Goddess of Liberty.

The Zona Rosa (Pink Zone), a twenty-one-block neighborhood of chic boutiques, hotels, and restaurants catering to tourists, lies halfway between the Zócalo and Bosque de Chapultepec. Unfortunately, this is also the area where you're most likely to be robbed, for thieves prey on the high concentration of unsuspecting tourists lured into a false sense of security by the area's designation.

Further beyond the Zona Rosa lies the expansive 2,100-acre Bosque de Chapultepec, which means "hill of the grasshoppers" in Nahuatl—the world's largest urban park. You can see remnants of the city's turbulent past—occupation by England, Spain, France, a revolution, and a civil war—at Castillo de Chapultepec, Maxmilian's residence on Cerro de Chapulín (Grasshopper Hill). The boy figures of the *Monumento de los Niños Heroes* (Monument to the Heroic Children) guard its terrace, from which you can get a sweeping view of the city. This enormous park, filled with gardens, lawns, and woods, was once Maxmilian's hunting grounds and is now home to a zoo, botanical garden, and amusement park. You'll find Sundays especially lively, when families gather for picnics, boating on the lake, and to watch street performers. The park also contains the largest concentration of museums in the city as well as Los Pinos (The Pines), the official home of the president of Mexico.

≡FAST FACT

The Basilica of Our Lady of Guadalupe is the second-most visited religious site after the Vatican.

Another must-see is the Santuario de Nuestra Virgen de Guadalupe (Basilica of Our Lady of Guadalupe), considered by Latin American Catholics to be the holiest site in the Western Hemisphere. It was here in 1531 that Juan Diego received a cloak from the Virgin with her image on it. Wander into the ultramodern church, then visit the museum with its hundreds of antique *retablos* in the original basilica next-door (℡55-5577-6022).

Museums

Mexico City has over 130 museums, where you can find exhibits of art and history that show off its larger-than-life past. Most are closed on Mondays but are open from 10 A.M. to 6 P.M. other days. The following are just a sampling.

Museums in the Centro Histórico include these:

- **Museo Templo Mayor:** A modern museum with exhibits of 7,000 artifacts found in the ruins of the Templo Mayor out front, including the Coyolxauhqui, the Aztec Goddess of the Moon, stone disk (☎55-5542-4784)
- **Museo de la Ciudad de Mexico (Mexico City Museum):** Formerly the eighteenth-century Palacio de la Santiago de Calimaya, contains works by Impressionist painter Joaquin Clausell (☎55-5512-0671)
- **MUNAL (The National Museum of Art):** Housed in the former Palacio de Communicaciónes y Trabajos Públicos (Office of Communications and Public Works), displays more than 700 works dating from the fifteenth to the twentieth century (☎55-5521-7320)
- **Museo Diego Rivera:** Located at the Jardín de Solidaridad, on the site of the Hotel Regis which was destroyed in the 1985 earthquake, contains the fabulous Diego Rivera mural *Dream of a Sunday Afternoon in Alameda Park*, originally from the Hotel Del Prado, also destroyed in the quake (☎55-5510-2329)

Museums in Bosque de Chapultepec include these:

- **Museo Nacional de Antropológia (National Museum of Anthropology):** Mexico's most famous museum, with exhibits of artifacts representing thirty centuries of Mexican human evolution to help you understand the colorful and heroic past of pre-Columbian Mexico (☎55-5553-1902)

- **Museo de Artes Moderno (Modern Art Museum):** Works created by some of the most outstanding Mexican painters, such as Orozco, Rivera, Toledo, and Siqueiros (☎55-5553-6233)
- **Museo Nacional de la História (National History Museum):** Located in Castillo de Chapultepec, shows the panorama of Mexican history, from the Conquest to the Revolution, through paintings, uniforms, sculptures, old coins, musical instruments, antique carriages, flags, and historical documents (☎55-5553-6224)
- **Museo Rufino Tamayo:** Works by the world-renowned Mexican painter as well as those of over 160 other contemporary artists (☎55-5286-6519)

For the Kids

When you visit Mexico City, join your children in discovering all that the city has to offer. Bosque de Chapultepec offers the largest concentration of kids' activities. Row across the lake, with swans and geese gliding alongside your boat. Afterward, visit Parque Zoológico de Chapultepec (Chapultepec Zoo), the best in Latin America. Here, you'll see over 1,300 species of animals—including panda bears and a rare black rhinoceros—over 200 of which roam in natural habitats. Admission is free (closed on Mondays, ☎55-5553-6229).

☂ RAINY DAY FUN

Mexico City has special movie houses and theaters for children, with an ongoing variety of family movies and shows to capture their attention.

Nearby is La Feria de Chapultepec, an amusement park where you can ride the world's largest wooden rollercoaster, Montaña Rusa, an impressive ferris wheel, and a minitrain for a $15 all-day pass. (Open Tuesdays to Fridays 11 A.M. to 7 P.M., weekends 10 A.M. to 9 P.M., ☎55-5230-2121.) Close by, you'll find the interactive El Papalote Museo del Niño (Butterfly Children's Museum), where your children can travel through fantasy and technology through over 380 exhibits in the arts, science, and technology, walk through a five-story maze, and view films about Mexico culture on an IMAX screen (☎55-5237-1781). The Centro de Convivencia Infantil is a kids' playground, complete with its own small zoo, where your little ones can get their faces painted. A waterpark, Divertido, has a wave pool, giant slide, and a log ride, guaranteed to give you a good splash.

On Sundays, kids can laugh at puppet shows and eat cotton candy in Alameda Central. And at Six Flags Amusement Park, Reino Aventura, six international-themed villages, plus forty-five rides, a water show, and the thrilling El Escorpión (The Scorpion) will keep them entertained for hours. (Open daily 10 A.M. to 7 P.M., ☎55-5728-7292.)

Visit Xochimilco

La Cosa que Flota Jardínes de Xochimilco (The Floating Gardens of Xochimilco), a few miles east of Avenida Insurgentes, are a reminder of Mexico City the way it was in Aztec times. Actually, the gardens don't float, but they once did. The Aztecs, needing more farmland, placed earth-covered rafts in the swampy waters and planted vegetables in the soil, creating *chinampas*. Eventually, the roots extended to the lake bottom through the shallow waters. Today, you can ride through the canals on colorful but touristy flower-bedecked barges called *trajineras* for $10 per hour, or you can take a guided tour in a traditional *panga*. The 412-acre Parque Ecologico de Xochimilco (Ecological Park of Xochimilco), features a fine museum and a look at the restoration of planting areas using age-old techniques.

Be sure not to miss the incredible collection of Diego Rivera's work at the Museo Dolores Olmedo Patiño, set in a sixteenth-century hacienda with extensive gardens (☎55-5555-0891).

Other Parts of the City

Avenida Insurgentes leads to some of Mexico City's more attractive suburbs. San Ángel, a village of narrow winding cobblestone streets, walled mansions, and beautiful gardens, has retained the gracious ambiance of its colonial past. Today, it attracts artists, writers, and intellectuals but is best known for its Bazar del Sábado (Saturday market), where artisans sell a wide variety of fine arts and crafts. You should also visit Museo-Estudio Diego Rivera, the muralist's former home where he and ex-wife Frida Kahlo lived separately after their divorce (☏55-5548-3032).

 **TRAVEL TIP**

You can take a free guided walking tour of San Ángel on Saturdays at noon, 2 P.M., and 4 P.M. (☏55-5277-6955)

Museo Frida Kahlo, also known as Casa Azul (Blue House), the home of controversial painter Frida Kahlo, the wife of artist Diego Rivera, stands on a quiet street corner in Bohemian Coyoacán. Now a museum, it shows a part of her life through her paintings, diary, and home decor (☏55-5554-5999). The Museo Leon Trotsky, the refugee home of the Communist leader while in Mexico and where he was later assassinated, stands behind fortified walls around the block. The Museo Nacional de las Intervenciónes (The Interventions Museum), housed in a former monastery, displays a history of Mexico through the country's various foreign invasions, through arms, flags, paintings, lithographs, maps, and historic documents (☏55-5604-0699).

Reminiscent of Paris's Latin Quarter, Coyoacán is home to many students of UNAM (Mexico's National University). Bookstores and cafés serving espresso line its twin shady plazas, Plaza Hidalgo and Jardín Centenario. You'll also see outdoor displays of paintings, handcrafted silver, and leather by local artists.

Bullfights and Horse Races

On Sundays from November to March you can enjoy a bullfight at the world's largest bullring, Plaza Mexico You can also attend a *charreada* at noon on Sundays at Rancho del Charro in Bosque de Chapultepec. You can purchase tickets for either event from your hotel's travel desk for $10 in the *sol* (sun) or $20 in the *sombra* (shade).

Visit the Past

Avenida Insurgentes leads to Teotihuacán, "Place Where the Gods Are Born." This ceremonial center was once one of the most important cities on the continent and thrived from about the sixth to the seventh century. Although much is unknown, there are signs that its people came from the east approximately 2,000 years ago and worshiped the rain god. When the Aztecs discovered the city, it was already long abandoned.

The Museo de Teotihuacán showcases artifacts discovered at the site. Exhibits include a reproduction of a burial site, sculptures of animals thought sacred to the Aztecs (such as jaguars, eagles, serpents and frogs), richly ornamented ceramics, and well-preserved fragments of murals showing mythological figures.

The two most impressive structures at Teotihuacán are the Pirámide del Sol (Pyramid of the Sun), standing 205 feet high, with 365 steps leading to a temple and astronomical observatory on top, and the Pirámide de la Luna (Pyramid of the Moon), 140 feet high with 112 steps. The Avenida de la Muerte (Avenue of the Dead), containing twenty-three temples, connects to the pyramids. Sculptural decoration based on the theme of the serpent in motion and masks of Quetzalcoátl and the god Tlaloc fill the Templo de Quetzalcoátl.

Time to Relax

The following luxury hotels have full-service spas:

- **Fiesta Americana Grand Chapultepec:** ✆800-343-7821 (U.S.), *✍www.fiestamexico.com*

- **Habita:** &800-525-4800 (U.S.), *⊘www.slh.com/habita*
- **Hotel Residencia Polanco:** &55-203-9144, *⊘www.mexico boutiquehotels.com*
- **Meliá Mexico Reforma Hotel:** &800-336-3542 (U.S.), *⊘www. solmelia.com*

Shopping

Mexico City has excellent options for shopping. You'll find some of the largest, most modern shopping malls in Latin America—Perisur, Galerias Insurgentes, and Plaza Loreto—along Avenida Insurgentes, once the main Aztec thoroughfare into the city.

≡FAST FACT

The largest of the city markets is La Merced, covering several blocks in the eastern part of town.

In the Centro Histórico, shops displaying jewelry, leather goods, perfumes, and gourmet candy line Calles Cinco de Mayo, Madero, and Correo Mayor. And even if they're beyond your budget, you'll enjoy window shopping along Calles Florencia, Hamburgo, and Londres in the Zona Rosa.

If your taste leans toward the upscale, then head for Colonia Polanco, with its thirty blocks of deluxe boutiques along Avenida Presidente Mazaryk. Collections by world-famous designers, dress-makers, and jewelers will dazzle you. Colonia Polanco also sports some fabulous shopping malls—Pabellon Polanco, Plaza Polanco, and Plaza Mazaryk.

If you're searching for typical Mexican handicrafts, try the Mercado Ciudadela Artesaniás, outside the Balderas subway station downtown, or the equally good Artesaniás Buenavista, next to the railroad station. You'll also find a good FONART shop across from Alameda Central.

Time to Eat

Most of Mexico City's over 2,000 restaurants serve *desayuno* (break-fast) from 7 A.M. to noon, *almuerzo* (lunch), considered the main meal, from 2 to 4 P.M., and *la cena* (dinner) after 7 P.M. Some restaurants require more dressy attire, so come prepared if you want to eat at fancier places. In general, Capitalinos (as residents of the city are called) are more conservative.

═FAST FACT

Chinese coffee shops, called *café chinos*, serve the best hot choco-late in three ways—*Mexicano* (with water), *Frances* (with milk), and *Español* (spiced with milk).

You'll find branches of some of the world's most famous restau-rants concentrated in the Zona Rosa, while trendy bistros call Colonia Polanco home. If you're looking for a more bohemian atmosphere, check out the restaurants in Colonias Roma and Condesa.

Local Dining Suggestions

- **Hacienda de los Morales:** Elegant dining on fine Mexican cuisine in a restored hacienda in Mexico City's poshest neigh-borhood (Polanco, Vazque de Mella 525, ☏55-5096-4554)
- **La Fonda del Refugio:** Fantastic traditional Mexican dishes served in a cozy Mexican-art-filled environment (Zona Rosa, Liverpool 166, ☏55-5525-8128)
- **El Danubio:** The best grilled seafood and *comida corrida* served in a nostalgic setting, with autographed walls (Colonia Roma, República de Uruguay, ☏55-5521-0912)
- **Sanborn's:** Excellent family restaurant in the historic Casa de Azulejos, as well as other locations (Centro Histórico, Madero 4, ☏55-5512-2300)

- **Café de Tacuba:** One of the Centro Histórico's most picturesque eateries, serving traditional Mexican food to the accompaniment of *mariachis* and *estudiantinas* evenings (Centro Histórico, Tacuba 28, ☎55-5518-4950)

Dining Precautions

With so many restaurants, it's hard for the Mexican government to police them all. Use common sense when choosing one, and don't drink the water unless you're sure it's purified. Major hotels and restaurants all have water purification systems. You'll find bottled water sold everywhere.

Where to Go After Dark

When evening falls, Mexico City offers you a variety of choices for entertainment. You can enjoy typical folk songs in a peaceful plaza, or modern music at a crowded disco. For an unforgettable experience, visit Plaza de Santa Cecilia, better known as Plaza Garibaldi, where *mariachis* gather to tout their music for potential patrons. *Mariachis* often stroll into cafés lining streets (like Calle Tacuba) just off the square.

 **TRAVEL TIP**

Check the lists for the latest events in weekly publications such as *Tiempo Libre* and *Dónde* or in the Friday and Saturday editions of *The News,* the city's English-language newspaper.

Paseo de Reforma, as well as Avenidas Chapultepec, Florencia, and especially Insurgentes offer endless nighttime entertainment.

You'll find clubs playing hard rock and reggae, as well as sexy salsa and merengue.

And of course there are the not-to-be-missed performances of the world-famous Ballet Folklórico, held Sunday at 9:30 A.M. and 8:30 P.M. and Wednesdays at 8:30 P.M. in the Palacio de Belles Artes. Tickets cost $10 to $20 per person (☏55-5512-2593).

CHAPTER 18

Guadalajara

AS MEXICO'S SECOND-LARGEST CITY and the capital of the state of Jalisco, Guadalajara is also one its most progressive, a center of business and industry. *Tapatíos*, as the people of Guadalajara call themselves, proudly refer to it as Mexico's biggest small town. Because of a long period of isolation from Mexico City, the city has been able to preserve a characteristic independence, self-reliance, and European atmosphere. Besides creating the popular folk dance Jarabe Tapatío (Mexican hat dance) and the tradition of *charreada* (Mexican rodeo), it's the home of the *mariachi*. Benefitting from the best of Mexican culture, it's a city of beautiful parks, broad avenues, and light-colored buildings. Even the urban renewal of recent years has done little to spoil its friendly and genteel atmosphere.

About Guadalajara

Spread over a low hill in the mile-high fertile valley of Atemajac, Guadalajara is known as the *ciudad de las rosas* (city of roses). Its plazas, parks with fountains, and tree-lined boulevards make it a green city.

Despite its astounding growth, Guadalajara has managed to retain much of the gracious atmosphere of its colonial past. The traditional heart of the city, the Metropolitan Zone, containing many 400-year-old buildings, has been completely renewed. Though skyscrapers rise above the city's colonial skyline, Guadalajara has managed to modernize without endangering its quality of life or altering the centuries-old city plan.

For many, Guadalajara represents the soul of Mexico, for it's home to three things that most people think of when they think of Mexico—*mariachis*, tequila, and, of course, the *charro*, the Mexican cowboy dressed in a silver-studded outfit topped by a wide sombrero. But it's also a city of learning. With three universities and many other schools, it's a major center for education and the arts.

Best Time to Go
Guadalajara has a marvelous spring-like climate with daytime temperatures ranging from the 80s in June to the 70s in December. Nights can be chilly, from the mid-40s in January to the low 60s in July. From June to September, afternoon rains are common.

Cuisine
You'll find the regional cuisine of Jalisco much like that of other cities in the central plateau. But you should try some of the local specialities, like *birria* (goat or lamb wrapped in *nopales,* or cactus leaves, then cooked slowly in a sauce of chiles, cumin, and tomatoes), *pollo pipián* (chicken with pumpkin and sesame seeds), or *torta ahogada* (shredded meats in a salty baguette covered in tomato sauce and onions, served hot in a shallow bowl and drenched in fresh cream). Tamales are also a local favorite.

Cautions and Safety Concerns
Generally, Guadalajara is a safe city if you stay in the main downtown area. Protect your valuables since pickpockets can be present anyplace there are crowds, especially at Plaza de los Mariachis. There, you may get so engrossed in the music that you don't realize your wallet is being stolen. Bilingual tourist police patrol Guadalajara's Centro Histórico and will assist you with directions or answer questions.

Getting Around Guadalajara

Taxis with set, published rates are plentiful, although some still have meters. A typical fare around town is about $5 to $7, depending on the distance. Be sure to settle on the fare before you get in. While Guadalajara has many buses, three types will get you to tourist sites. The first is the Linea Turquesa (Turquoise Line); these buses have the letters "TUR" painted on their pale turquoise bodies. Costing $1, they're air-conditioned and have padded seats. They run frequently between the Centro Histórico, Tlaquepaque, and Tonalá. A second set of buses, the Par Vial (electric buses) run along a rectangular route downtown, hitting all the major sites.

 TRAVEL TIP

If you feel like seeing Guadalajara at a slower pace, hire a *calandría* for $15 an hour to take you on a leisurely horse-drawn ride around downtown. They depart from in front of the Museo Regional de Guadalajara, the Mercado Libertad, and the Jardín San Francisco.

The third, the Linea Dorada (Golden Line), depart from the Plaza Tapatía every fifteen minutes and can take you to all the major sites for about fifty cents. And finally, you can hop aboard the Tranvía, an old-time trolley on wheels, at the Plaza Guadalajara for an hour-long narrated journey through the Centro Histórico, departing at 11 A.M. and 1, 4, 6, and 7:30 P.M.

Family-Oriented Hotels

Because Guadalajara is a business center, its hotels cater more to businesspeople, so they're quite luxurious and have all the amenities you'd expect of big-city hotels.

Hotel Fiesta Americana

Reservations: ☎800-343-7821 (U.S.), ✍*www.fiestamexico.com*

This very Mexican 391-room hotel boasts a glass interior elevator with great views, a pool, gardens, and two restaurants and bars.

Hotel Camino Real

Reservations: ☎800-722-6466 (U.S.), ✍*www.caminoreal.com*

This older hotel features 224 spacious rooms in a low-rise garden setting, with pool, indoor and outdoor dining, and antique-filled lounge.

Hotel Quinta Real

Reservations: ☎800-457-4000 (U.S.), ✍*www.quintareal.com*

This colonial-style hotel has seventy-eight plush suites, some with fireplaces and sunken jacuzzis, as well as a great restaurant and beautiful gardens.

Hotel Vista Plaza del Sol

Reservations: ☎888-300-6394, ✍*www.vistahotel.com*

This family-oriented hotel has 371 rooms, a disco, and a cafeteria serving breakfast and buffet lunch.

Something for Everyone

Guadalajara is a vibrant city with lots for families to do. If you like history, you'll find plenty of fine museums balanced with great activities for kids.

Things to Do

Begin your exploration of Guadalajara in the Centro Histórico, a thirty-block area of restored buildings downtown. Dominating this area is the Catedral Metropolitana, with its Sagrario, begun in 1558 and finished in 1616. It shows a remarkable mingling of different styles, including Gothic, Tuscan, Moorish, and Corinthian. When an earthquake toppled the twin towers early in the twentieth century, Manuel Gómez Ibarra rebuilt them as Byzantine, yet another style. The cathedral houses many art treasures donated by King Fernando VII of Spain in appreciation of the financial support the city gave Spain during the Napoleonic Wars. Paintings attributed to Cristóbal de Villalpando, Miguel Cabrera, and Bartolomé Murillo hang in its eleven different chapels. Though all are ornate, the Capilla Nuestra Señora de las Rosas (Chapel of Our Lady of the Roses), housing the statue of the same name given by King Carlos V, is magnificent. You can get a superb view of the city by climbing to the top of the one of the bell towers.

TRAVEL TIP

Take the free two-hour guided tour of the Centro Histórico on Saturdays at 10:15 A.M. to get a quick orientation to the downtown sights.

The central feature of Guadalajara is a magnificent group of four squares—Plaza de Armas, Plaza Guadalajara, Plaza Liberación, and the Rotunda de los Jaliscienses Illustres—arranged in the shape of a cross, with the city's colonial public buildings set around them. The Palacio del Gobierno looks out on the Plaza de Armas, the finest of the four, with its wrought-iron bandstand, a gift from the French Government in 1910. Step into its patio on a weekday to see the magnificent mural of Father Hidalgo proclaiming the abolition of slavery painted by José Clemente Orozco, a native of the state of Jalisco, from 1936 to 1939. He completed another mural of the heroes of the three great Mexican wars ten years later.

Behind the cathedral stretches the Palacio de Justica (Jalisco Supreme Court) and Palacio Legislativo (Legislative Hall), both overlooking the Plaza Liberación. Next to them stands the city's first cathedral, Iglesia de Santa María de Gracia.

Beautiful old Indian laurel trees fill the Plaza Guadalajara in front of the cathedral. And to one side stands the Rotunda de los Jaliscienses Illustres, a circular monument of seventeen columns containing the remains of celebrated Jaliscans. Three blocks over stands the Templo de Santa Mónica, with its baroque façade, twisted Salamonic columns, and its rich and intricately carved ornamentation of corn cobs, grapes, angels, double eagles—all symbols of religious orders. On the way, visit Casa Museo Lopez Portillo, the nineteenth-century home of a wealthy *Tapatío* family, showing what life was like back then. (Open Tuesday through Sunday, 10 A.M. to 7 P.M., ✆33-3613-2411.)

TRAVEL TIP

Listen to the city band for an hour on Tuesday and the state band on Thursday and Sunday evenings at 6:30 P.M. in the Plaza de Armas. Go early to get a seat.

Behind the Teatro Degollado (Degollado Theater) stretches the 650-foot Plaza Tapatía, a five-block pedestrian mall filled with shops, cafés, department stores, and museums, highlighted with contemporary outdoor sculptures. Here you'll discover the pulse of contemporary Guadalajara. At the plaza's far end stands the Intituto Cultural Cabañas, which has 1,244 rooms and two chapels.

One of Guadalajara's best-loved landmarks, the old Cabañas Orphanage, a Neoclassical building built by Manuel Tolsá in 1803, has no fewer than twenty-three flower-filled patios connected by tiled corridors covering six acres. It served as an orphanage until the 1970s, then became the Intituto Cultural Cabañas, a cultural institute with galleries, a fine arts school, performing arts center, and a museum. Inside its vaulted hall you'll see yet another mural by Orozco, called *Man of Fire. Tapatíos* maintain that the fresco is one of the most dramatic works of art in the Western Hemisphere. Another of his murals, *The Four Horsemen of the Apocalypse,* is equally impressive. Be sure to also visit the museum. Admission is $2. (Open Tuesdays through Saturdays, 10 A.M. to 6 P.M., Sundays until 3 P.M., ✆33-3617-4322.)

Museums

Because of its many educational and arts institutions, Guadalajara has many fine museums. The following are the principal ones:

- **Casa José Clemente Orozco (Museum Workshop of José Clemente Orozco):** Orozco is Guadalajara's most renowned artist. Almost 100 of his paintings are on display here in the workshop where many of them were painted. (Open Tuesdays through Sundays, 10 A.M. to 7 P.M.)
- **Museo de Arqueológia del Occidente de Mexico (Archaeological Museum of Western Mexico):** Located in front of Parque Agua Azul, it displays ancient artifacts from the states of Colima, Jalisco, and Nayarit. (Open daily, 10 A.M. to 6:30 P.M.)
- **Museo de Artes Populares (Jalisco Museum of Popular Art):** Display of contemporary handicrafts and good exhibition of paintings on the second floor. All articles are for sale. (Open Tuesdays through Saturdays 10 A.M. to 6 P.M., Sundays, 10 A.M. to 3 P.M.; ☏33-3614-3897.)
- **Museo de la Ciudad (City Museum):** Housed in a former seventeenth-century Capuchin convent, this museum tells the history of the city from the sixteenth to the twentieth centuries. (Open Tuesdays to Saturdays, 10:00 A.M. to 5:30 P.M., Sundays, 10:00 A.M. to 2:30 P.M.; ☏33-3658-2531.)
- **Museo Regional de Guadalajara (Guadalajara Regional Museum):** This lovely museum is housed in the former seminary of San José, dating from 1700. Fourteen galleries around the colonial patio display archaeological and paleontological artifacts. (Open Tuesdays through Saturdays, 9:00 A.M. to 5:45 P.M.)

For the Kids

Take the kids to Guadalajara's beautiful Parque Agua Azul, with its acres of trees and grass, flower gardens, carnival rides, and swimming pool—all within the city limits. There's even a butterfly house where your children can experience the beauty of these creatures up close. Afterward, attend a musical or dance performance in the park's amphitheater. Museo Infantil (Children's Museum), also known as the Museo Globo del Niño (Sphere of the Child Museum) features interactive exhibits on prehistoric animals, geography, and space, plus all kinds of toys (open daily 10 A.M. to 6 P.M., ✆33-3669-1381). Or take your kids on a ride around the grounds on the rubber-tired mini-train. The park is open daily from 7 A.M. to 6 P.M.; admission is $1 for adults, half price for kids.

JUST FOR PARENTS

If you love orchids, you must visit the orchid house in Parque Agua Azul.

Parque Natural Huentitán lies just seven miles northeast of the city. This huge park includes the Zoológico Guadalajara. With more than 1,500 animals and over 230 species, this zoo will delight your little ones. They can even feed and pet animals in the Zoológico del Niños (Children's Zoo). Admission is $4 for adults, $2.50 for kids. (Open Wednesdays through Sundays, 10 A.M. to 6 P.M.; ✆33-3674-1827.)

The park also has the Planetario Guadalajara (Guadalajara Planetarium) with hourly shows from 10:30 A.M. (3✆33-674-4106) and the Centro de Ciencia y Tecnología (Science and Technology Center), plus Selva Mágica (Magic Jungle), an amusement park with seal, dolphin, and bird shows at 2, 4, and 6 P.M. (✆33-3674-0318). Take along your swimsuits and a picnic lunch, or buy some goodies at the park, and go to nearby Barranca de Huentitan, which is connected to Barranca de Oblatos, an enormous 2,000-foot-deep gorge filled with lush tropical vegetation and hot springs. Admission is $3 for adults, $2 for children. (Open Tuesdays through Sundays, 10 A.M. to 6 P.M., ✆33-3674-4488).

You'll find an American-style water park, Tobolandia, on the out-skirts of the village of Ajijic on Lake Chapala. The usual water slides and rides will keep your kids happy while you enjoy the fresh air. Admission is $5 for adults, half price for kids (☎33-3766-2120).

RAINY DAY FUN

Duck in out of the rain for an hour or so of ice skating at Iceland Pista de Hielo. Lessons are available, skates included. If you don't want to skate, have a *helado* in the ice cream parlor.

Visit Tequila and Lake Chapala

Endless fields of blue agave lead the way to the town of Tequila, thirty-five miles from Guadalajara. The picturesque town shares its name with the drink that's yet another Guadalajara innovation. Several distilleries—among them Cuervo, Herradura, and Orendain—produce over 20 million gallons of tequila per year and offer tours and tastings.

JUST FOR PARENTS

Tequila is the national drink of Mexico. Discovered more than 200 years ago, it's distilled from the *piñas*, or core, of the agave plant and comes in four types, ranging in age from three to five years, costing a few dollars to over $100 a bottle. One plant produces five bottles.

A great way to get to Tequila is by train. The Tequila Express makes a two-hour trip to Tequila on weekends at 10:30 A.M. from the Estación de Ferrocarriles de Guadalajara (Guadalajara train station). The nine-hour tour includes a stop at the seventeenth-century Hacienda San José Refugio, home of Tequila Herradura (✎*www .casaherradura.com.mx*), and unlimited margaritas, beer, sodas, and snacks, and, of course, plenty of tequila. The ride costs $55 per adult and $30 per child (☎33-3880-9010, ✎*www.tequilaexpress.com.mx*).

Another worthwhile side trip from Guadalajara is to Laguna de Chapala (Lake Chapala), thirty miles from Guadalajara. Chapala, which in Nahuatl means "splashing waves," mostly lies in the state of Jalisco, although a portion of it lies in the state of Michoacán. Today, the northwest shore hosts the largest colony of resident *norteamericanos* outside the United States and Canada, especially at the little fishing village of Ajijic.

TRAVEL TIP

If you don't have time to go to Tequila, you can take a tour of the Sauza bottling plant in Guadalajara at 10 A.M. on weekdays (☎33-3615-6990).

Ajijic, the lake's most picturesque village, has a small artists' colony and thermal hot springs. While wandering its narrow streets, you can peek into weaving workshops where townspeople produce handwoven fabrics and embroidery. Life moves slowly here, so slow down and enjoy it.

Bullfights and *Charreadas*

Charros compete in ten events every Sunday at noon at Aceves Galindo Lienzo, Guadalajara's *charreada* stadium. Go see riding and rope twirling from some of Mexico's best (☎33-3637-0563). You can see a bullfight on most Sundays from October to March at 4:30 P.M. at the Plaza de Toros el Nuevo Progreso. Ticket prices range from about $5 on the sunny side to $80 on the shady side. You can buy them at the Hotel Francés on Thursdays from 10 A.M. to 7 P.M. or at the bullring (☎33-3637-9982).

Golf

Many consider Guadalajara to be the inland golf capital of Mexico. The consistently fine weather allows play most of the year.

Its five public courses are seldom crowded on weekdays. To play at a private club, you'll need to show your U.S. club membership card. Here are a few of your options:

- **Guadalajara Country Club:** Though private, this, the oldest course, allows limited public use and is a favorite of beginners and advanced players (☎33-3817-2858).
- **Club de Golf Altas:** The tree-lined fairways of this Joe Finger eighteen-hole course offer respite from the sun (☎33-3689-2620).
- **Las Cañadas:** This twenty-seven-hole beauty nine miles north of the city spreads out in a valley surrounded by mountains (☎33-3685-0285).
- **Club de Golf Santa Anita:** This eighteen-hole course surrounded by luxury homes is four miles south of the city (☎33-3686-4123).
- **Club de Golf El Palomar:** This fine eighteen-hole course is located in the hills overlooking Guadalajara (☎33-3684-4434).

Tennis

If you want to get in a game or two of tennis, you'll find excellent facilities in and around Guadalajara. Most of the major hotels have courts, and there's the Club Deportivo de Guadalajara (☎33-3625-8881) and Club de Tenis Royal (☎33-3647-5348), but you'll find the best facilities at the El Tapatío Hotel & Resort in Tlaquepaque, which offers ten lighted clay courts (☎33-3837-2929, ✎*www.hotel-tapatio.com*).

Time to Relax

The Rancho Rio Caliente Spa, located seventeen miles from Guadalajara, offers all the usual spa treatments in a natural environment of thermal springs and pine forests. Whether you decide to stay in one of its fifty garden rooms, floating in the pool or relaxing in one of four hot springs, or just spend a day at the spa, you'll come away relaxed and energized (☎800-200-2927 [U.S.]).

Shopping

Guadalajara's Mercado Libertad (Liberty Market), also known as the Mercado San Juan de Diós, is one of the largest public markets in the world. Covering four square blocks, it offers just about everything from clothing to food to arts and crafts—even medicinal herbs. Housed in a huge modern building with over 1,000 stalls on three levels, each of them privately owned, it offers you good prices if you're willing to bargain and is open daily. The Casa de las Artesanías, within Parque Agua Azul, shows the vast range of Jalisco handicrafts, which are also for sale. (Open weekdays from 10 A.M. to 6 P.M.; weekends from 10 A.M. to 5 P.M.)

 TRAVEL TIP

For a real Mexican treat, go upstairs in the Mercado de la Libertad and make the rounds of the *fondas* (food stalls), the Mexican version of a food court.

If you like glass, head for the Fabrica Cristal (Glass Factory), where you can watch handmade glass being blown, and then purchase it as cheaply as anywhere else. If you're going to be in Guadalajara long enough, you can have the artisans custom-make glassware for you in whatever color and design you want. They'll even ship it for you.

American-style malls have come to Guadalajara—the Plazas Patria, Mexico, Universidad, Bonita, and the sleek La Gran Plaza. Be on the lookout for children's clothing stores filled with embroidered clothing and handknit sweaters.

And for a flea-market experience of a lifetime, head to El Baratillo, the world's largest flea market. Here, on Sundays from 6 A.M. to 2 P.M., you'll find thirty blocks of everything and anything, especially antiques.

Tlaquepaque

San Pedro Tlaquepaque lies five miles east of Guadalajara. Once a separate town, it is now part of the city. Tlaquepaque is famous for its hand-blown glass and painted ceramics, but the main reason you'll want to come here is to shop. Over 300 stores line the pedestrian-only Calle Independencía and other streets in the center of town, where you can find a wide variety of quality arts and crafts items including fine pottery, *huaraches*, blown glass, and *equipales* (barrel leather chairs). Shop owners will ship your purchases home if asked. Be sure to visit the small free Museo Regional de la Cerámica to see exhibits of traditional pottery from nearby Tonalá and other villages, to get an idea of what you can buy. (Open Mondays to Saturdays, 10 A.M. to 6 P.M., Sundays 10 A.M. to 3 P.M., ☎33-3335-5404.) After visiting the museum, head across the street to La Rosa Fábrica de Vidrio Soplado, a glass-blowing workshop where you can watch artisans making jars and bottles from 9:30 A.M. to 2:30 P.M. weekdays. And to learn about the history of Tlaquepaque, visit La Casa de la Cultura, in El Refugio (The Refuge) that used to be a women's insane asylum. (Open Mondays through Fridays, 9 A.M. to 8 P.M., Sundays, 9 A.M. to 3 P.M.; ☎33-3619-3611.)

 **TRAVEL TIP**

Take a break from shopping and have lunch under the circular roof of the nineteenth-century El Parián, a series of linked restaurants and bars. As you eat, listen to music being played in the bandstand in the Jardín Hidalgo, the town's main square, diagonally across the pedestrian thoroughfare.

Tonalá, one of the oldest pueblos in Mexico, lies seven miles beyond Tlaquepaque. Noted for its fine pottery, many of the artisans who sell their wares in Tlaquepaque have their studios there. Be sure to stop at the free Museo Naciónal de la Cerámica (National Ceramic Museum) and the Museo Regional de Tonalá. (Both are open weekdays, 9 A.M. to 3 P.M.) Tonalá holds a huge pottery market every Thursday and Sunday. Come ready to bargain.

Time to Eat

When you get hungry in Guadalajara, you won't have to go far to find delectable food. The city offers an incredible array of restaurants serving not only Jalisco cuisine but more exotic fare, too. Generally, you should plan to eat lunch between 3 and 4 P.M. and dinner after 9, the way the Tapatíos do.

Local Dining Suggestions

- **Guadalajara Grill:** A mixture of good Mexican and American food is served in a three-level dining room decorated with old photographs of Guadalajara (Avenida Lopez Mateos Sur 3771, ☎33-3631-5728).
- **La Destillería:** Regional food is served in a simulated tequila distillery (Avenida Mexico 2916, ☎33-3640-3110).
- **La Fonda de San Miguel:** Enjoy excellent regional Mexican dishes served in the courtyard of a restored eighteenth-century convent in an atmosphere of refined elegance (Donato Guerra 25, ☎33-3613-0809).
- **Maximino's:** The city's most elegant, this restaurant is set in a two-story mansion, with individual dining rooms decorated with crystal chandeliers and antiques. Serves international and French cuisine (Lerdo de Tejada 2043, ☎33-3615-3435).
- **Parilla Argentina:** This, one of the best of Guadalajara's steak houses, serves a mixed *parrillada* (grilled meats) or tender steaks (Fernando Celada 176, ☎33-3615-7361).

Dining Precautions

Dine where the locals eat. Restaurants packed with locals are a sure bet. To be on the safe side, avoid food from street vendors. The major hotels have water purification systems, but drink bottled water everywhere else.

Where to Go After Dark

While Guadalajara has all the clubs and discos other cities have, it has one place that's special—the Plaza de las Mariachis (Plaza of the Mariachis). Here, you can sit at a sidewalk café and listen to the strolling mariachis play music that was born here or, better yet, hire them to serenade you.

≡FAST FACT

To find out what's happening in the city, check the English-language *Guadalajara Weekly* or *Guadalajara Colony Reporter*.

Or perhaps you'll choose to attend a performance at the Teatro Degollado (Degollado Theater), Guadalajara's major cultural center and home of the Filarmónica de Jalisco (Jalisco Philharmonic Orchestra) (☎33-3658-3812), as well as the city operatic and theatrical groups. You'll find performances scheduled almost every night, with tickets starting at about $1. For a real treat, plan to attend a performance of the Ballet Folklórico de la Universidad de Guadalajara on Sunday at 10:00 A.M. or 6:30 P.M. Ticket prices range from $5 to $20 (☎33-3616-4991, ✑*www.ballet.udg.mx*). Or see the Ballet Folklórico Nacional del Instituto Cultural Cabañas on Wednesday at 8:30 P.M. at the Instituto Cultural Cabañas for $6 to $8 (☎33-3626-9280).

A city this size has plenty of clubs and discos. If you prefer to dance to live music, try Maxim's Disco or the Café Tecuba or the salsa rhythms at Copacabana. To see a Mexican show, complete with mariachi and ranchero music and *charro* demonstrations, go to Mariachi Mexicanísimo. The Ex-Convento del Carmen, near the Centro Histórico, offers cultural events almost every night (✆33-3614-7184).

CHAPTER 19

Monterrey

SOME SAY THE STREETS of Monterrey are paved with gold, but more likely, they're paved with pesos, for Monterrey is Mexico's wealthiest city. Often referred to as the "Sultan of the North," Monterrey is a progressive city—the most Americanized one in Mexico. Here, you won't find the laid-back lifestyle of the rest of Mexico. Though Monterrey isn't a beautiful or a charming city, it's a sophisticated one, a businessman's town. *Regiomontaños,* as the residents of Monterrey are called, say the nearest town, Saltillo, is "one hour and three centuries away."

About Monterrey

A modern vibrant city with streets full of traffic, Monterrey has excellent hotels, huge stores, and fine museums. The locals point out that Monterrey, at least in atmosphere, more closely resembles San Antonio, Texas, than other cities in Mexico. In fact, there are more Texas newspapers on sale in Monterrey than there are papers in Spanish.

In spite of its location in the desert, the city has become the great industrial center of northern Mexico, the gateway to the south and the most dynamic urban center in the country. With a population of nearly 4 million, it's Mexico's third-largest city.

Situated in the Santa Catarina Valley in the Sierra Madre Oriental mountain range, Monterrey is flanked by the hulking 7,800-foot Cerro de la Mitra (Mitre Peak) to the west and the distinctive

5,700-foot Cerro de la Silla (Saddle Peak)—the city's emblem—to the east. Legend says a local citizen lost a peso on the topmost ridge of Cerro de la Silla and kept digging frantically until he discovered it, thus forming its saddle-shaped crest.

As northern Mexico's powerhouse, Monterrey is a bustling, hard-driving, hard-working, wealthy city, which boasts an opera season longer than in any center twice its size in the United States, as well as one of the highest literacy rates in Mexico. The city has nine newspapers, seven television channels, and over twenty radio stations, making its citizens some of the best informed in Mexico. It's also frequently chosen as sites for Lions Club, Rotary, and Kiwanis Club conventions and regional meetings.

Best Time to Go

An average day in Monterrey is in the low 90s. Though the air is hot by any measure, it's also dry and not oppressive. Temperatures range from highs of 68°F in January to 100°F in August. It can dip below freezing on winter nights. The best months to visit are March, April, and October. May and September are the rainiest months.

Cuisine

Northern Mexico is considered cattle country, and you'll discover beef's influence in its unique cuisine. Fajitas and *cabrito,* or baby goat, are favorites. *Norteño*-style cooking means charcoal-broiled steaks and thin tortillas made of wheat flour rather than cornmeal. Another favorite is *cortadillo norteño,* cuts of beef stewed in tomato sauce.

Another delicious dish, *machacado con huevo,* scrambled eggs mixed with dried beef and salsa and tortillas, will get your day off to a nutritious start. And be sure to order one of the local beers—Bohemia, Tecate, Carta Blanca, and others. Finally, don't forget to satisfy your sweet tooth with *glorias, marquetas, natillas, turcos,* pumpkin in *tacha,* and *camote* (sweet potato) *en piloncillo* and *semitas,* as well as luscious pecan turnovers.

☰ FAST FACT

Cooking *al pastor* means to roast meat vertically on a spit then serve it thinly sliced.

Cautions and Safety Concerns

Though walking around Monterrey's lighted streets is safe, it's best to take precautions and not to walk alone on darker streets. And while you can certainly hail a taxi during the day, avoid doing so at night. Ask the restaurant to call one for you.

Getting Around Monterrey

Monterrey is the best connected city in northern Mexico. A modern network of roads and highways connects it not only to the rest of Mexico but also to the Texas border, only 120 miles away. You'll find that renting a car is the best way to get around. The city has not only good signage but also a sophisticated electronic traffic monitoring system. Transportation from the airport in Monterrey is regulated. The only other way for you to traverse the forty-five-minute drive into town, other than by rental car, is by airport taxi. Prices for the twelve-mile one-way trip are fixed at about $6. For pick-up service *to* the airport, call Transportes Mont Trans (📞81-8345-7398) or Autotransportes Aeropuerto (📞81-8340-3840).

💼 TRAVEL TIP

Take an old-time trolley tour of the Zona Rosa from in front of the Howard Johnson Hotel, downtown.

In addition, the city offers excellent taxi and bus services. Most taxis have meters, but ask the driver for the fare before you get in.

Seventeen bus lines ferry passengers between Monterrey and sur-rounding towns. The Ruta 1 (Route 1) city buses will get you to most attractions. Be sure to ask before getting on.

Family-Oriented Hotels

Because Monterrey is such an international business center, hotels are modern, state-of-the art facilities able to cater to both business travelers and families. You'll find top hotels clustered together down-town near Avenida Morelos, the main street, now a pedestrian mall.

Sheraton Ambassador Hotel and Towers

Reservations: ✆800-325-3535 (U.S.), ✍*www.sheraton.com*

This colonial-style, 229-room hotel, located downtown, features a gym with running track, pool, spa, and indoor tennis court, as well as a restaurant, a coffee shop, and a bar.

Intercontinental Presidente Monterrey

Reservations: ✆800-980-6429 (U.S.), ✍*www.intercontinental.com*

This 362-room contemporary hotel, located in a residential neighbor-hood, features a heated indoor pool, outdoor tennis court, health club with gym and sauna, coffee shop, gourmet international restaurant, and a lobby bar complete with a waterfall. Baby-sitting service is available.

Crowne Plaza

Reservations: ✆800-227-6963 (U.S.), ✍*www.crowneplaza.com*

Located on a main highway not far from downtown, the Crowne Plaza offers 393 rooms on seventeen floors, plus an indoor pool, gym with sauna and whirlpool, tennis court, coffee shop, steak house, a lobby bar with live music, and a nightclub. Baby-sitting and high-speed Internet service are available.

Hampton Inn Monterrey Norte

Reservations: ✆1-800-426-7866 (U.S.), ✍*www.hampton-inn.com*

Located in the northern industrial area of the city, this 235-room hotel offers free continental breakfast, phone with voice mail, a pool, and a gym. Plus, children under eighteen stay free with an adult.

Holiday Inn Norte

Reservations: ✆877-270-6405 (U.S.), ✑*www.holidayinn.com*

This 195-room suburban hotel, with a free shuttle to downtown, kids eating free, baby-sitting services, and an outdoor pool, is great for families.

Fiesta Americana Centro Monterrey

Reservations: ✆800-343-7821 (U.S.), ✑*www.fiestaamericana.com*

This 307-room twelve-story hotel, located on a quiet square one block from the Gran Plaza, features a twenty-four-hour coffee shop, gourmet restaurant, lobby bar, indoor pool, and gym. Baby-sitting service, kids program, and cribs are also available.

Something for Everyone

Monterrey offers a lot for families. Besides numerous and varied museums, there are also several outstanding theaters and venues for the performing arts, as well as special places to take your kids. And because it's home to several institutions of higher learning, including the Monterrey Institute of Technology, you'll find the modern parts of the city unlike any other place in Mexico. Futuristic architecture and imaginative museums along with a good infrastructure make Monterrey a great family destination.

Things to Do

Though the oldest part of the city began along the Rio de Santa Catarina, today Monterrey's heart is the 100-acre, six-block-long Gran Plaza. Also known as the Macro Plaza, this ambitious multilevel urban renewal complex of many monuments and fountains mixes colonial with ultramodern. On its north end stands the Palacio de Gobierno

(Government Palace), a turn-of-the-twentieth-century building with fresco-lined patios.

At its south end stands the baroque Catedral de Monterrey on Plaza Zaragoza. Here, you'll also find the historic state capitol, the tiny Dulces Nombres (Sweet Names) Chapel, and the Casino Monterrey. In stark contrast are the ultramodern Teatro de la Ciudad (City Theater), the Centro Biblioteca (Central Library), and the Palacio Municipal (City Hall), with its impressive sculpture, *Homage to the Sun,* by Ruffino Tamayo. The Faro de Comercio (Lighthouse of Commerce), a 228-foot-tall orange stucco obelisk designed by Mexican architects Raúl Ferrera and Luis Barragán, from which a green laser beam shines forth each evening, stands across from the cathedral. The plaza beneath it is the site of frequent concerts. You can sit next to the fountains, attend a show at the theater, or shop in the mall underground.

Streets west of the plaza comprise the Zona Rosa, the downtown shopping area with many pedestrian walkways, restaurants, and hotels. Pancho Villa once rode his horse into the elegant lobby of the Radisson Gran Hotel Ancira.

TRAVEL TIP

Taking a horse-drawn carriage ride is a leisurely way of seeing the sights around the Gran Plaza and Barrio Antiguo.

Monterrey's contemporary architecture is a symbol of its success. One of the most notable examples is the concrete Basilica de la Purísima, located at Calle Serafín Peña and Avenida Hidalgo Poniente. Designed by Mexican architect Enrique de la Mora, its steel and glass were all made in the city.

The El Obispado (Bishops' Palace), built in 1789, is the only landmark completed during colonial times. Today, it houses the Museo Regional de Nuevo León, the state's regional museum, containing exhibits on Mexican haciendas and the Revolution. Admission is about $3 but free on Sundays. (Open Tuesday through Saturday 10 A.M. to 1 P.M. and 3 to 6 P.M., Sunday 10 A.M. to 1 P.M. ✆81-8333-9588.)

 TRAVEL TIP

You can also take a guided tour of the Cervecería Cuauhtémoc Moctezuma (Cuauhtemoc Brewery), at Avenida Alfonso Reyes 220 Norte, Tuesday through Saturday at 11 A.M. and 3 P.M. (✆81-8328-5355). After touring the plant, you get to taste the freshly brewed beers under the shade of century-old trees in the company's beer garden.

The Cuauhtemoc brewery spawned a glass factory for bottles, a steel mill for caps, a carton factory, and eventually several industrial conglomerates, including Alfa, which gave the city the Centro Cultural Alfa (Alfa Cultural Center), the best museum of science and technology in the country.

Monterrey is also a big college town with seven universities, including the Instituto Tecnológico de Monterrey. Patterned after MIT, it's one of the largest and best colleges of technology in Latin America. There's also the Universidad de Nuevo León and the private Universidad de Monterrey, with its fine medical school.

≡FAST FACT

For general information about McCarran International Airport, call ✆702-261-5211. For parking information, call ✆702-261-5121. For flight information (all airlines), call ✆702-261-INFO.

Be sure to see some of Monterrey's large collection of modern sculpture, much of it on the Gran Plaza. Did you know Monterrey has a lead crystal factory? The main producer, Kristaluxus (✆81-8351-6396) offers factory tours at 10:30 A.M., Monday through Saturday. Afterwards, you can buy their wares at discounted prices.

For the Kids

For a business city, Monterrey has a surprising number of activities for kids. At Plaza Sésamo (Sesame Place) (✆81-8333-3700), an amusement and water park, you can take your little ones on a variety of rides and to meet *Sesame Street* characters. There's also Parque La Pastora (✆81-8337-4340), with its zoo, and Bosque Mágico (The Magic Forest; ✆81-8367-4622), with over thirty-five rides and special shows. Your kids will love visiting the Puppet House Museum in the Barrio Antiguo (✆81-8343-0604).

Museums

Museo de Arte Contemporáneo de Monterrey (MARCO), the Museum of Contemporary Art, stands on the Gran Plaza next to the cathedral. Once inside, you'll be surprised by its dramatic architectural features, as well as its fine collection of paintings and sculptures by renowned international artists. You can also attend performances here. Admission is about $3.50. (Open 11 A.M. to 7 P.M., Tuesday through Sunday, and to 9 P.M. Wednesday and Sunday, ✆81-8342-4820.)

Learn about the region's history in the Museo del Obispado (Bishop's Palace Museum). This jewel of colonial architecture, built more than 200 years ago, stands on a peak overlooking the city. And be sure not to miss the Museo de Histórica de Mexico (Mexican History Museum), the best of its kind in Mexico and situated in an ultramodern building on the site of the city's origin.

TRAVEL TIP

To find out about current museum exhibits and other happenings around town, pick up a copy of *What's on Monterrey,* available in hotels and restaurants.

The Museo de Monterrey (Monterrey Museum), within the confines of the original Cuauhtémoc Brewery, showcases over 1,000 works by local and national artists. And right next door is the famous El Salón de Fama del Beisbol (Mexican Baseball Hall of Fame), filled with memorabilia of the sport's legends.

To get to the Centro Cultural Alfa at Avenida Roberto Garza Sada 1000, you'll have to travel to the Monterrey suburb of San Pedro Garza Garcia, Monterrey's wealthiest neighborhood. This excellent museum houses historical, scientific, and technological exhibits. Admission is $4. (Open 3 to 9 P.M. Tuesday through Friday, 2 to 9 P.M. Saturdays, and 12 to 9:30 P.M. Sundays; ✆81-8303-0002.)

One of Monterrey's most famous industries is glass. The Glass Museum presents fascinating exhibits on the history of glass, its manufacture, and the current products available (✆81-8329-1000).

Another cultural highlight is the Pinacotheca Nuevo León (State Art Museum), with its collection of original paintings by artists from the state of Nuevo León. It's located in the Parque Niños Héroes (Child Heroes Park), along with the automobile and wildlife museums (✆81-8331-3890). The latter has a collection of 100 species in their natural habitat. Admission is about $8 for adults and free for children under twelve. (Open Monday through Sunday 9 A.M. to 7 P.M., Av. Alfonso Reyes 1000, Norte Colonia Regina, ✆81-8351-2817.)

Ecotourism

The wide range of natural attractions in and around Monterrey will amaze you. Although the city isn't primarily known as a tourist destination, visiting the unique caverns, hot springs, waterfalls, and nearby mountains will provide memorable experiences for your family.

You can't help seeing the summits of the Sierra Madre Oriental mountains anywhere you look in Monterrey. To really appreciate them, you need to take an excursion to Chipinque Ecological Park, part of the National Summits Park of Monterrey, twenty minutes from the city. Here, you can walk, jog, mountain bike, climb, and camp. If you're a bird watcher, there are 120 different local and migrating species. And if you're into photography, you'll discover amazing vistas in all directions. Admission is about $3 (✆81-8335-6979).

☰FAST FACT

Some of the best hiking, climbing, biking, and spelunking in Mexico exists within reach of Monterrey.

Also close to the city is Potrero Redondo, where you can walk along forest paths, swim at any of several turquoise-colored wells, and enjoy rappelling off the cliffs. You can also hike through the canyon.

If you enjoy exploring underground, then you shouldn't miss the Grutas De Garcia (Garcia Caves), a magnificent series of underground caverns formed over 60 million years ago. To reach it, you must ascend 2,275 feet by cable car, followed by a 1.3-mile journey into the Earth. Once inside, you'll marvel at the whimsical stalactites and stalagmites on your ninety-minute tour (in Spanish only). Admission, including cable car ride and tour, is about $4 for adults and less for children. Other area caves include Gruta de la Terrosa, Gruta de Tabasco, and Gruta de la Cebolla.

For the best rock climbing, head to Cañon Potrero Chico (Potrero Chico Canyon), about twenty-five miles from Monterrey, with enormous cliffs nearly 2,937 feet high. These are considered to be Mexico's highest and attract climbers from around the world. Cañon de Huasteca (Huesteca Canyon), with its impressive 1,000-foot rock walls, is nearby.

If you like to hike, you'll find a trail leading to Cascada Cola De Caballo (Horsetail Falls), a spectacular eighty-two-foot-high waterfall surrounded by picnic areas and panoramic views. If you'd rather take the easier way up, you can hire a horse or horse-pulled cart to reach the waterfall. Admission is about $3.50. (Open daily 9 A.M. to 5:30 P.M., ✆81-8347-1599.)

Golf

The *regiomontaños* are as enthusiastic about golf as Americans. Monterrey's two best courses are private. In order to play at them, you must obtain an invitation from a member. However, the nine-hole course at Hacienda El Mirador is open to the public. Though there are no carts available, there are caddies, and you can rent clubs (☎81-8349-9467).

Bullfights

Bullfights are held intermittently in Monterrey at the Plaza de Toros Monumental (☎81-8374-0450), which has a retractable roof so that events can take place in all kinds of weather. Normally, bullfighting season runs from May to December. You can purchase tickets for $15 to $30 for the Sunday afternoon *corrida* at the tourist office adjacent to the Gran Plaza. Ask at your hotel if there will be a bullfight during your stay.

TRAVEL TIP

If you're into soccer, be sure to see an exciting professional match at one of Monterrey's stadiums.

Every Sunday morning, you can see *charros* (cowboys) compete in regional competitions at Rancho Siete Leguas and Rancho El Realito in the suburb of Villa de Guadalupe. Ask at your hotel for schedules and locations.

Time to Relax

Since Monterrey is a business town, its hotels have health clubs with exercise rooms, saunas, and whirlpools, catering more to men than women. The Fiesta Americana Centro Hotel offers massage services as well.

Shopping

Regiomontaños love to shop. High-quality Mexican and international goods fill the city's modern malls and shopping centers. You'll find boutiques in a five-block area downtown known as Plaza Morelos. Here, trendy boutiques line up beside coffeehouses, clothing and jewelry stores, bookshops, and boot shops. The Galerias Monterrey stands out as the most popular mall, followed by Pabellon Tec and Plazas San Pedro, La Silla, and Fiesta San Agustin. Each has several large anchor stores, plus dozens of shops and restaurants, cafés, and snack bars.

The Mercado Colón (Columbus Market), a traditional Mexican market between Avenida Juárez and Cuauhtémoc, has rows of vendors selling everything from fruits and vegetables to kitchen utensils, herbs, and even religious objects. For regional handicrafts, such as copper, glass, pottery, and leather items, the Casa de las Artesanias de Nuevo León at Avenida Allende and Dr. Coss has more than you could ever want.

Time to Eat

Monterrey's location amid near prime cattle ranches gives restaurants a special flavor all their own. Expect to pay $55 to $75 for a full dinner for two at top places, $45 at moderate ones, and $40 or less at inexpensive restaurants.

Local Dining Suggestions

- **El Tío:** Moderately priced regional specialties are served in a garden patio setting (Av. Hidalgo and Mexico, Colonia Obispado, ☎81-8346-0291).
- **La Fe Palenque:** This restaurant has the wild folk atmosphere of a Mexican *ranchero*, where traditional Mexican food, accompanied by Mexican music, entertainment, and cockfights, is served in an amphitheater-like room (Av. Morones Prieto Pte 2525, ☎81-8345-1347).

- **Luisiana:** This is the most elegant restaurant downtown, with soft piano music and a taste of New Orleans. Though no Cajun dishes are served, you'll find steak, seafood, and occasionally rattlesnake on the menu (Av. Hidalgo Oriente 530, ☎81-8343-1561).
- **El Rey de Cabrito:** This inexpensive restaurant serves the best *cabrito* in town (Constitución Oriente 317, ☎81-8345-3232).
- **Sanborn's:** This reliable chain family restaurant has good food and local specialties (Escobedo 920, ☎81-8343-1834).

Dining Precautions

In a modern city such as Monterrey, there's little danger of problems with food or water. All hotels and most restaurants have purified water.

Where to Go After Dark

On Saturday nights, locals head for small clubs and cafés in the Barrio Antiguo, such as La Fonda de San Miguel on Avenida Morelos (☎81-8342-6659), where they listen to live jazz and folk music. Most of the major hotels also have nightclubs or piano bars.

 JUST FOR PARENTS

For a special Saturday night out, go to see Flamenco dancers and guitarists at El Mesón del Olivo while dining on suckling pig and paella (Juan I. Ramon Oriente and Dr. Coss 805, ☎81-8343-7474).

For a taste of the wild west, try the Norteño Rodeo Disco (☎81-8351-8080), one of Monterrey's rodeo-style clubs. For a fun time, take the family to either Señor Frog's on Plaza Fiesta San Agustín or Carlos 'n' Charlies on Avenida San Jeronimo 1106 (☎81-8347-9205).

Puebla

LOCATED EIGHTY-FIVE MILES FROM Mexico City, Puebla (capital of the state of the same name) remains Mexico's most Spanish city—a city of churches surrounded by volcanoes. Though a sprawling city of nearly 3 million, its elaborate and abundant colonial architecture, including no fewer than 100 churches, former monasteries and convents, and its blending of pre-Columbian and Spanish cultures, gives it a unique and distinctive personality. Besides being Mexico's most beautiful colonial city, it's also one of its most historic.

About Puebla

Known by many names throughout its history—La Ciudad de Angeles (City of Angels), La Ciudad de Azulejos (City of Tiles), La Heroico Ciudad de Zaragoza (Heroic City of Zaragoza)—today, the city is simply known as Puebla. An old city with a long history, it remains the ecclesiastical center of Mexico. Phenomenal growth in recent years has made Puebla Mexico's fourth-largest city, but it's still one of its most beautiful.

Best Time to Go

Puebla enjoys sunny days with temperatures in the 70s and 80s and nights in the 40s and 50s throughout the year. From November to March, there's almost no rain. But from April through October, it rains most afternoons.

Cuisine

The cuisine of Puebla mixes flavors, smells, textures, and colors into a mélange of good eating. While you'll find dishes direct from Spain, alongside them will be dishes spiced with curry from India, cumin from Arab countries, or even those with rich sauces from France.

But Puebla is best known for its *mole poblano* (a rich sauce made from an imaginative mix of red chiles, peanuts, almonds, cinnamon, tomato, onion, garlic, *ajonjoli,* or sesame seeds, chocolate, and many other herbs and spices) that's poured over boiled chicken or turkey and served on holidays.

You'll also find an infinite variety of soups prepared with string beans, pumpkin, pork loin, brains, almonds, mushrooms, and peas.

And last but not least, Puebla is famous for its traditional *dulces* (sweets). Beginning in the eighteenth century, nuns at the Convento de Santa Clara made delicious sweets. Today, you'll find shops selling these goodies along Calle Santa Clara, near the former convent.

Cautions and Safety Concerns

Puebla's water system isn't as pure as some other Mexican cities that see a lot of American tourists. But you can buy bottled water everywhere, and the major hotels all have their own water purification systems. When eating out, ask for *agua mineral* or bottled water and no ice. Also avoid the tempting sno-cones, popsicles, and ice cream sold by street vendors, unless they're pre-packaged. Finally, carry some antibacterial towelettes with you to wash your hands before eating.

Getting Around Puebla

Streets running from east to west are called *avenidas*, and those running north to south are called *calles*. The Avenida de la Reforma and Avenida Avila Camacho divide the town into northern and southern halves.

📼 TRAVEL TIP

From the Mexico City airport, you can take a deluxe air-conditioned Estrella Roja (Red Star) bus to Puebla every half hour for $15 one-way. A stewardess serves snacks and refrescos while you watch a movie on the way.

Puebla has a unique taxi system. Instead of making a deal with the driver for the price of a ride, you buy a ticket from kiosks selling government-authorized rides to specific destinations for a flat fee. You'll find a map at the kiosk that tells you the fare zone for your destination. You can hail a taxi on the street, but make sure it's a marked one. Or you can take the bus for just forty cents—exact change only.

Family-Oriented Hotels

Puebla has some excellent hotels. Though they may not have special programs for kids like those in the resort areas, they get lots of Mexican families as guests, so they welcome children.

Camino Real Puebla

Reservations: ✆800-722-6466 (U.S.), ✐*www.caminoreal.com*

Occupying a restored sixteenth-century convent in the Centro Histórico, this magnificent eighty-four-room hotel has the modern comforts blended with the romance of historic Puebla. Just two blocks from the *zócalo*, its facilities include three restaurants, health club, and lounge with live music.

Crowne Plaza Puebla

Reservations: ✆800-465-4329 (U.S.)

Located three miles northwest of downtown, this 216-room, five-story hotel has a large free-form pool set in a lush garden that occupies its central courtyard, a children's playground, one tennis court, two restaurants, and a popular pub with live jazz.

Holiday Inn Centro Histórico

Reservations: &800-465-4329 (U.S.), *www.holidayinnpuebla .com.mx*

This fully restored turn-of-the-century French-style, seventy-one-room, seven-story hotel just two blocks from the Cathedral offers a lobby courtyard with filigreed decoration, a stained glass skylight, and chandeliers. There's a small pool on a fourth-floor terrace, as well as a gourmet restaurant and an English-style pub.

Real de Puebla Best Western

Reservations: &800-528-1234 (U.S.)

This modern five-story, 183-room hotel located thirteen blocks from the *zócalo* has a pool, gym with sauna and tanning salon, two restaurants, and two bars.

Something for Everyone

The key to activities in Puebla is history. Your family will learn more about Mexican history here than just about anywhere else.

Things to Do

City life centers on the magnificent Plaza de la Constitución, Puebla's *zócalo,* with well-tended gardens, tall shade trees, and a seventeenth-century fountain. With arched colonnades on three sides, it's the heart of a 100-block Centro Histórico (Historic District). But you'll find the majority of historic sites within a four-block radius of the plaza. Before its remodeling in 1854, it was the site of a huge *tianguis* (Nahuatl for "marketplace"), where bullfights and hangings also took place.

On the plaza's south side stands the enormous Catedral de la Concepción Inmaculada (Immaculate Conception Cathedral), the second largest in Mexico. The cathedral has Mexico's tallest bell tower, rising 228 feet, and is famous for its rich gilded interior with fourteen chapels, marble floors, and carved choir stalls. The spectacular Neoclassical main altar, designed by Manuel Tolsá and José Manzo, depicts the kings and queens of seventeenth-century Europe. Its huge dome, faced with Talavera tiles, gleams in the sun.

Also on the southern side of the square is the Palacio del Obispo (Archbishop's Palace), the seventeenth-century residence of Bishop Juan de Palafox y Mendoza. Now a cultural center, it contains the Biblioteca Palafoxiana (Palafox Library), created in 1646 by the bishop and once the finest collection of manuscripts in the New World. Today, you'll see over 43,000 books in Spanish, French, English, and Creole, including rare fifteenth-century works. Admission is $2.

Two blocks east of the *zócalo* rises the Jesuit Iglesia de la Compañía, dating from 1767, with a churrigueresque façade and a blue-and-white tiled dome. In the sacristy, you'll see the tomb of La China Poblana, a young woman who made a costume of a white frilled and embroidered blouse, sequined red and green skirt, a *rebozo* (shawl), red hair bow, and silver and gold jewelry that has since become the national female folk costume of Mexico.

Two blocks north of the *zócalo* stands the Iglesia de Santo Domingo de Guzmán (Church of Santo Domingo), dating from 1534 and originally part of a Dominican monastery. Don't miss its Capilla del Rosario (Chapel of the Rosary) from 1690, a dazzling mix of painted tiles, gilded plaster, polychromed statues, onyx stonework, and carved woodwork, considered to be one the most splendid examples of the churrigueresque style in Mexico. A particularly notable feature is an orchestra of cherubs from the center of which emerges the figure of God the Father. On the church's main altar rests a richly attired figure of the Virgen del Rosario (Virgin of the Rosary) surrounded by saints and apostles.

You'll come upon the Exconvento de Santa Mónica (Convent of Saint Monica), founded in 1609 and redone in 1680, a few blocks further. Although the Reform Laws of 1857 abolished monasteries and dissolved the convent, the nuns continued to run it in secret for eighty years, until they were discovered. It now contains the Museo de Arte Religiosa (Museum of Religious Art). Don't miss the exquisite tiled courtyard and numerous cells, tunnels, and hidden passages where the nuns lived in secret. Admission is $5 (☎222-246-2044).

≡ FAST FACT

Churrigueresque is a style of baroque architecture—named after Spanish architect José Benito Churriguera—brought from Spain by the conquistadors. Building designers covered facades with garlands, shells, and balustrades. Indian workers added their own interpretation to produce a style now known as Mexican baroque.

The largest convent in Puebla, the Ex-convento de Santa Rosa (Convent of Saint Rose), two blocks away, now houses the Museo de Arte Popular (Museum of Folk Art), featuring a fine collection of folk art and regional costumes from throughout the state. Admission is $2. (Open daily, except Monday, 10 A.M. to 4:30 P.M.; ☎222-246-4526.)

Museums

Puebla features a myriad of museums with exhibits about its history and culture. You'll discover the largest grouping at the Centro Cívico 5 de Mayo, Puebla's Civic Center, located in an extensive park on the Cerro de Guadalupe (Hill of Guadalupe) fifteen blocks northeast of the *zócalo*. The complex consists of eight facilities, four of which are museums. Besides the Museo de Antropología (Anthropology Museum) and the Museo de Historia Natural (Natural History Museum), the complex contains Fuerte Loreto, with the Museo de la Intervención (Museum of the Intervention), featuring exhibits of documents and uniforms relating to France's occupation of Mexico, and Fuerte Guadalupe. If you listen closely, you just might hear the sounds of fighting from the Battle of Puebla. On May 5, 1862, Mexican forces fought off the French, a victory that Puebla today celebrates as Cinco de Mayo.

≡FAST FACT

A common misconception is that Cinco de Mayo is a Mexican national holiday. In fact, it's a regional one, celebrated mostly in the state of Puebla and several other places in Mexico.

The Museo Regional de la Revolución (Regional Museum of the Revolution), housed in the eighteenth-century Casa de los Hermanos Serdán, three blocks from the *zócalo* on the way to the Civic Center, is the birthplace of the Mexican Revolution. It depicts the life of Aquiles Serdán and his family, who died on November 18, 1910, following a fourteen-hour gun battle with 500 police and federal troops. Notice the bullet holes on the front of the house.

The Casa del Alfeñique (Almond-Cake House), a late-eighteenth-century structure designed by Antonio de Santa María Incháurregui, houses the Museo Regional (Regional Museum). The building's colored tiles, red brick, and white stucco decoration are an excellent example of the *Poblano* style of Mexican baroque. Today, you can browse through displays of pottery, furniture, arms and armor, and *china poblana* costumes—including the original—on the first two floors. Admission is $2 for adults, half price for kids (✆222-241-4296).

📰 TRAVEL TIP

Most of Puebla's museums open daily, except Monday, from 10 A.M. to 4:30 P.M. Most have free admission on Sundays.

Puebla also offers museums that mix technology with art, such as the Museo Amparo (Amparo Museum), housed in an elegant colonial mansion, with its interactive, state-of-the-art multimedia exhibits of pre-Columbian and colonial art in four languages. Originally it served as a hospital, then a college for women, and finally as the

Colegio Ezparza before being converted into one of the best archaeo-logical museums in the country. Admission is $5 for adults, half price for kids. (Open daily 10 A.M. to 5:30 P.M., except Tuesday, ✆222-246-4210.) Other technologically advanced museums include the Museo Arte de San Pedro (San Pedro Museum of Art), showing one of the best painting and sculpture collections in Latin America. The Museo Poblano De Arte Virreinal (Museum of Poblano Art), housed in a seventeenth-century hospital, displays colonial art.

For the Kids

Your kids will love going to Africam, a wild animal safari park on the outskirts of the city. As the most important zoo in Latin America, it showcases over 2,000 wild animals from 250 different species, many of which are native to Mexico and on the endangered list. Here, they roam freely as if it was their natural habitat, divided by regions into Asia, Africa, and North America. Take the safari bus ride with a guided tour to learn all about them. The park also has a special area where you can see endangered species, as well as a discovery area featuring interactive displays and games enabling your children to learn more about them. Younger kids especially like the Butterfly Pavilion and Bat Cave, while adults enjoy the extensive botanical gar-den featuring many plants from the state of Puebla.

RAINY DAY FUN

When it rains on summer afternoons, take your kids to El Planetario (The Planetarium) in the Civic Center complex.

In addition to the animals, your kids can ride a pony or a llama, take a boat ride, watch animal shows, and go on a photo safari. Spend the day and bring a picnic lunch or eat in the restaurant. Africam provides transportation from Puebla, just fifteen minutes away. Admission is $7.50 for adults, $7 for children (open daily, ☎222-235-8713).

Antiquing

There are few places in Mexico to go antiquing. Puebla is an exception. Shops specializing in *antigüedades* (antiques and collectibles) surround Plazuela de Los Sapos (Little Plaza of the Toads) and continue up Callejon de Los Sapos (Alley of the Toads).

TRAVEL TIP

While browsing Callejon de Los Sapos, be sure to stop into Meson de Sacristia de la Compañia, a combination bed-and-breakfast and antique shop, where all the items in the rooms are for sale. Ask for a tour, as each room displays a different decor (☎222-242-3554).

A flea market fills the plaza and surrounding streets on weekends. Allow a couple of hours to browse the shops and the market, then stop at the cantina on the corner to taste its famous raisin liqueur.

Visit the Past

Not far from Puebla, you'll find two major archaeological sites, both worth seeing. The first is Cholula, an ancient holy city dating from as early as 400 B.C. The great city of Cholula once stood at the foot of what appears to be an earthen hill five miles west of Puebla. In fact, under this "hill" stands the largest pyramid ever built, covering over forty-six acres. Archaeologists believe that people of Toltec ancestry constructed what's now called the Gran Pirámide de Tepanampa (Great Pyramid of Tepanampa), also known as Pirámide de Tlatchihualteptl, in successive stages from A.D. 1 to 800. You can explore it either through a labyrinth of interior tunnels or above-ground by walking through excavations at the pyramid's base. High atop the hill rises the blue-and-white Nuestra Señora de Los

Remedios (Our Lady of the Remedies), a church built in 1666 and a classic symbol of the Spanish conquest. Climb to the top for an awesome view of the town with its many church steeples. Hire a guide for about $8 and take a tour inside the pyramid. Admission is $5 and free on Sundays (open daily 10 A.M. to 5 P.M.).

An hour east of Puebla lies what archaeologists believe is the largest ancient urban center yet discovered in Mesoamerica, dating from A.D. 600 to 950. An Olmec–Xicalanca city, Cantona covers about ten square miles divided into three urban units. The ruins display a sophisticated urban design that includes an extensive roadway network, over 3,000 individual patios, or residences, twenty-four ball courts, and an elaborate acropolis with ceremonial buildings and temples. Much of the site resembles a fortress, complete with a moat and several guard stations, since the city developed during a period of great social upheaval following the fall of Teotihuacán in the eighth century.

Bullfights and *Charreadas*

To see a bullfight, go to Plaza de Toros El Relicario (Relicario Bullring) on Sunday afternoons (✆222-236-8818). For *charreadas*, join several thousand people on most weekends at the stadium Lienzo Charro (✆222-235-2288).

Shopping

Most smaller shops close during the traditional lunch hour from 2 to 4 P.M., but they open at 10 A.M. and stay open in the evenings until 8 P.M. A pedestrian shopping street runs for several blocks downtown, and there are three malls—Plazas Loreto and Dorado, and the Zona Esmerelda—with shops, restaurants, and movie theaters. The Mercado de Artesanías "El Parián" ("El Parián" Handicrafts Market), remains the longest established market, founded in 1796. Its brick-and-stone stalls are your one-stop shopping destination for *poblano* crafts, including embroidered clothing and textiles, Talavera ceramics, onyx items, and traditional candies. You're expected to bargain here, so allow plenty of time to browse the stalls (open daily 10 A.M. to 7:30 P.M.).

To get a glimpse of art being done by *Poblano* artists today, visit the Barrio del Artista (The Artist's Neighborhood), fifty studios where artists produce, display, and sell their work, located behind the Teatro Principal, dating from 1759, and near El Parián (open 10 A.M. to 4:30 P.M.).

Talavera Pottery

Talavera pottery has been produced in Puebla ever since the seventeenth century, when Franciscan friars taught the local Indians the special techniques they brought with them from Spain. Vases, cups, plates, serving bowls, and tiles are just some of the myriad of items being made. Artisans must handpaint the pottery's intricate designs using natural dyes derived from minerals. It can take several days to produce one piece. Dozens of workshops and studios scattered throughout the city produce vividly colored tiles and dishware in the Talavera style. To learn more about how it's made, visit La Escuela de la Talavera Poblana (Puebla Talavera Craft School) at the Patio de los Azulejos one block west of the *zócalo*. And to view the best exhibit of Talavera in Puebla, visit the Talavera Room of the Museo Bello y González (Bello and González Museum). Admission, including a guided tour, is $2. (Open Tuesday through Sunday, 10 A.M. to 4:30 P.M., ✆222-241-9475.)

Time to Eat

Good restaurants abound in this City of Tiles. With such a rich cuisine featuring so many dishes, you'll want to sample them all.

Local Dining Suggestions

- **El Mesón de la Sacristía:** Delicious *poblano* food is served either inside the restored colonial mansion or outdoors on the patio (Callejon de los Sapos, ✆222-242-3554).

- **Fonda de Santa Clara:** One of Puebla's most popular eateries, specializing in regional cuisine, this is the best place to taste *poblano* food (Avenida 3 Poinente No. 307, ☎222-242-2659).
- **Macs:** Locals pack this place at lunch for its filling $5 daily *poblano comida corrida*, but they also serve a larger weekend spread for $10 (Camacho and Portal Morelos, ☎222-246-0211).
- **Sanborns:** This spacious family restaurant belongs to the Anderson chain and is set in a colonial courtyard, serving a wide variety of foods, from *poblano* specialties to the best burgers in town (Avenida 2 Oriente No. 6, ☎222-242-9436).

Dining Precautions

Poblano restaurant owners take pride in their food and most serve it in clean surroundings. Be adventuresome and try some of the local delicacies.

Where to Go After Dark

If you like *mariachi* music, Puebla has several squares where roving troubadours play for you beginning around 6 P.M. La Plazuela de los Sapos is the closest to the *zócalo*—just two blocks. Sit at a table at one of the small cafés and enjoy. Or walk to Plaza de Santa Inés, near the La Escuela de la Talavera Poblana and four blocks from the *zócalo*, or take a taxi to Plaza del Alto, a dozen blocks from it. If your taste is more to rock or blues, then head to Corcores or Café La Obra.

CHAPTER 21

Guanajuato

GUANAJUATO IS A FEAST for the senses, a living museum of a colonial gem 6,700 feet up in the mountains six hours northwest of Mexico City. Brimming over with romantic ambiance, Guanajuato, capital of the state of Guanajuato, is one of Mexico's truly beautiful cities. The charm of secluded courtyards, white walls accented by wrought-iron balconies, red tile roofs gleaming in the sun, and recessed windows guarded by ornate metal filigree will take you back to the days of the conquistadors. During the peak of its silver mining industry, Guanajuato ranked as one of the wealthiest cities in the world. Today, the city's architecture shows evidence of that wealth.

About Guanajuato

Built in a gorge during the Viceregal period, Guanajuato has a special topgraphy that has forced its residents to build their city over and under the terrain. Unlike other Mexican cities, Guanajuato feels like a bit of Old Spain in Mexico.

Today, Guanajuato oozes culture from its markets to its churches to its museums.

Best Time to Go

You can visit the Guanajuato area just about any time of the year although occasional hailstorms occur in November, December, January, and February. Though winter days can be mild, nights can get chilly with frost.

Cuisine

You'll find the cuisine in Guanajuato very Mexican. Enchiladas, lentils done in a variety of ways, tamales, and tacos are all favorites. A popular snack, *vasitas de elote* (supper in a cup), consists of cooked kernels of corn scraped from the cob then sprinkled with chili powder.

Cautions and Safety Concerns

Because of Guanajuato's hilly, cobblestoned streets, it's wise to wear rubber-soled walking shoes. And unless you visit during the Cervantino Festival, when crowds pack the streets for sixteen days each October, you'll find the city quite safe and well lit.

Getting Around Guanajuato

Guanajuato is the only city in Mexico with underground streets and a system of tunnels. These roadways—one going in and one going out following the original course of the Río Guanajuato for nearly two miles—whisk you to various parts of the city, keeping its romantic, narrow streets relatively clear of traffic.

Taxis are less expensive in colonial cities like Guanajuato. You'll be able to get anywhere in town for $2 to $3. And while the city is ideal for walking, you may get tired going up and down the hilly streets.

 **TRAVEL TIP**

You'll find Guanajuato more pedestrian-friendly on weekends, when the city blocks traffic from the streets around the Jardín de la Unión.

Family-Oriented Hotels

While Guanajuato doesn't have hotels specifically designed for families, you'll find accommodations not only comfortable but also luxurious, for reasonable rates.

Gran Plaza Guanajuato

Reservations: ✆473-733-1990, ✍*www.hotelgranplaza.com*

This attractive and modern colonial-style two-story hotel has ninety-five rooms, plus a courtyard with a pool and slide set in a garden, a restaurant serving gourmet Mexican cuisine, and complimentary shuttle service to downtown.

Hotel Castillo de Santa Cecelia

Reservations: ✆473-732-0485

This eighty-eight-room hotel, perched on a hillside with lovely views of the city, resembles a medieval castle and occupies the site of a former hacienda. Larger rooms have vaulted ceilings, canopied beds, and great city views. It also includes a restaurant, nightclub, heated swimming pool, and a shuttle to downtown.

Hotel Misión de Guanajuato

Reservations: ✆473-732-3980, ✍*www.misiongto.com*

This low-rise colonial-style 138-room hotel combines Mexican colonial and modern decor, with a restaurant and bar, pool, and tennis court.

Hotel Posada Santa Fe

Reservations: ☎473-732-0084, ✑*www.posadasantafe.com*

Located off the Jardín la Unión, this colonial-era, fifty-room hotel, furnished with antiques, once housed the Prussian Consulate. Facilities include two restaurants, including one with outdoor tables and fine regional food, and a rooftop terrace with jacuzzi.

Something for Everyone

Guanajuato offers lots of atmosphere. It's great for strolling and wandering, a marvelous place to contemplate Mexico as it once was and, in many ways, still is.

Things to Do

The best way to explore this small, provincial city is literally to lose yourself in it. Around every corner is a new surprise. Reminiscent of Segovia, Guanajuato's maze of corkscrew lanes, winding around hillsides, blossom into picturesque little plazas bedecked with mustard yellow, tan, or pink houses or fade into alleys or staircases. Guanajuato is made for walking. Each tiny side street seems to lead to pocket gardens, quaint houses, and monuments. You'll find a church on just about every plaza. Mine owners, seeking to outdo each other, built these temples to God as a way of seeking the esteem of their peers and the blessing of the Church. You'll find Guanajuato feels more like a medieval village than a colonial town.

Life here centers on the Jardín de la Unión (Union Garden), Guanajuato's *zócalo,* a small elegant triangular-shaped park ringed with cozy outdoor cafés, wrought-iron benches, and old Indian laurel trees. If you're there on a Tuesday or Thursday evening at 7 P.M., or on Sunday at noon, sit at one of the cafés and sip a cool drink while listening to the band playing in the Victorian gazebo.

On one side stands the Teatro Juárez, an opera house in Neoclassical style begun in 1873 and inaugurated in 1903, during the opulent era of the Porfiriato, with a performance of Giuseppe Verdi's *Aïda*. Moorish decoration surrounds you as you enter the red, blue, and gold Belle Epoque interior, complete with a Parisian crystal chandelier. Admission is $2. (Open Tuesdays to Sundays, 9 A.M. to 1:45 P.M. and 5:00 to 7:45 P.M.; ℡473-732-0183.)

 ## JUST FOR PARENTS

Dress up and attend a symphony concert, ballet, or opera at the Teatro Juárez. Check with the tourism office for performance dates and times.

Next door rises the elegant Franciscan Iglesia de la San Diego, built in 1633. A flood almost destroyed it and, in the rebuilding during the eighteenth century, workers added a churrigueresque façade. And if you look up, you'll see the imposing thirty-three-foot El Monumento del Pípila, a rose-stone sculpture of the city's hero holding a torch. Go behind the theater and take the funicular up to the monument for a panoramic view of the city. (Tuesdays to Saturdays, 9 A.M. to 10 P.M., Sundays, 10 A.M. to 9 P.M.)

From here the Avenida Benito Juárez will lead you to the Plaza de la Paz (Peace Square). The Basilica de Nuestra Señora de Guanajuato, a beautiful seventeenth-century baroque church painted a striking yellow, contains the oldest piece of Christian art in Mexico—a jewel-studded wooden statue of the Virgen de la Guanajuato, dating from the eighteenth century. Admission is $2 (open 10 A.M. to 6 P.M.). The imposing white stone stairway leading to the main building of the Universario de Guanajuato, constructed in 1732 by the Jesuits, begins behind the plaza.

Also along the Plaza de la Paz is the Mansión del Conde de Rul y Valenciana, the Neoclassical mansion of the La Valencia Mine owner, the Conde de Rul y Valenciana (Count of Rul and Valencia). Built by Francisco Eduardo Tresguerras at the end of the eighteenth century, the former mansion is now home to the Corte Suprema de la Justicia (High Court of Justice). On either side of the Avenida Juárez are a number of picturesque plazuelas. Off the Plazuela de los Angeles opens the Callejón del Beso (Kissing Lane), so called because its narrowness—only two feet wide—allowed a couple to kiss from windows on each side.

Museums

The city has many fine museums. Most are open from 10 A.M. to 6:30 P.M. Tuesday through Saturday and 10 A.M. to 2:30 P.M. Sunday, with an admission of $2 to $3 per adult, half price for children. Try to see at least some of the following during your visit:

- **Museo Ex-hacienda San Gabriel de Barrera:** Once the home of the Conde de Valenciana (Count of Valencia), founder of the rich La Valenciana mine, it shows colonial-era artifacts inside while seventeen gardens in different styles, ranging from Italian to Arabian to Chinese with footpaths, statuary, and fountains, await you outside (℡473-732-0619).
- **Museo del Diego Rivera:** The birthplace of noted Mexican artist Diego Rivera now shows original nineteenth-century furniture on the first floor and 100 early paintings and mural sketches by Rivera on the second (℡473-732-1197).
- **Museo Inconográfico del Quijote:** Housed in a renovated colonial mansion close to the Jardín de la Union, this museum features over 600 works of art, including some by Salvador Dalí and Picasso, collected by Spaniard Eulalio Ferrer Rodriguez, that glorify the characters from the literary works of Miguel Cervantes. A bronze statue of Cervantes stands guard outside (℡473-732-6721).

- **Museo de las Momias (Mummy Museum):** In this, one of Mexico's most macabre museums, the dearly departed of Guanajuato remain on display for all to see. Glass cases contain nightmarish mummified bodies from the turn of the century with gruesome facial expressions. Admission is $5. (Open 9 A.M. to 6:00 P.M., ✆473-732-0639.)
- **Museo del Pueblo de Guanajuato (Municipal Museum):** The Casa de los Marqueses San Juan de Rayas, the former seventeenth-century home of the Marqués San Juan de Rayas, owner of the Raya silver mine, has a churrigueresque façade with murals by José Chávez Morado. It now contains Chávez's priceless collection of religious and civil art, illustrating the development of folk art in Guanajuato (✆473-732-2990).
- **Museo Regional la Alhóndiga de Granaditas:** The Alhóndiga de Granaditas, a plain building erected between 1798 and 1803 and originally used as a granary, then as a prison and then a fort, is famous for its role as the site of the first battle of the Mexican fight for independence. Admission is $3, with children under thirteen free (✆473-732-1112).

For the Kids

You can take a guided tour of the Observatorio de la Astronomia (Astronomical Observatory) operated by the Astronomy Department of the University of Guanajuato (✆473-732-9607).

Visit Dolores Hidalgo and San Miguel de Allende

Rent a car and drive down Mexico's La Ruta Independencia (Route of Independence) to the small town of Dolores Hidalgo, named for the freedom-fighting priest, Father Hidalgo, who began the fight for independence, and further on to San Miguel de Allende. You can make this a long day trip or an overnight, or book a guided tour at your hotel.

TRAVEL TIP

> Look for ads in the bilingual newspaper *Atención San Miguel,* where you'll find information regarding organized tours of the surrounding area.

Three miles from Guanajuato on the Dolores Hidalgo road is the Iglesia de San Ceytano (Church of La Valenciana), built in 1788 by the first Conde de Valenciana (Count of Valencia), Antonio Obregón y Alcocer, owner of the famous La Valenciana silver mine. As you enter the side doorway to the church from the garden, you'll see an elaborately shaped and decorated scallop-shell and a statue of San José. A highlight of the interior is the doorway to the sacristy, with its carved stone drapery above a Moorish arch, decorated with bands of elegant ornamentation in *tezontle* stone (open 9 A.M. to 6 P.M.).

You'll come to the Bocamina de Valenciana (Valencia Silver Mine) not far from the church. Discovered in 1766 by Antonio Obregón y Alcocer, a miner who became the first Conde de Valenciana, it became the most productive mine in the world, employing up to 3,300 miners in shafts penetrating 1,650 feet. Admission is $1. (Open Tuesdays through Sundays, 10 A.M. to 6 P.M., ✆473-232-0580.)

Dolores Hidalgo, known as the Cradle of National Independence, is the first stop on Mexico's Independence trail that traces the course of the revolution against Spain. It was from Dolores Hidalgo that the Grito de Dolores (shout for independence) echoed across the nation early on September 16, 1810—signaling the start of the Mexican Revolution.

Father Miguel Hidalgo y Castilla, the parochial priest who proclaimed the *grito,* summoned his parishoners earlier than usual, then gave the famous call to rebellion, initiating the uprising against the Spanish Crown. Today, Hidalgo is Mexico's most revered hero, and the town of Dolores Hidalgo, renamed in his honor in 1824, has almost become *the* place of pilgrimage for Mexicans. Visit the Casa

Hidalgo, the house where he lived from 1804 until 1810, which displays many of his personal effects, as well as documents from that era (☎418-182-0171).

Thirty miles beyond Dolores Hidalgo, you'll come to San Miguel de Allende. Its bright colors and languorous atmosphere make it the most typically "Mexican" of the colonial cities. Smaller than most, it's one of the few towns in Mexico to be designated as a national monument, enabling it to preserve its character as a colonial town almost intact.

The charm of the town, its mild year-round climate, and its superb, clear light, have attracted many artists and writers. Thus, it has become a center of intellectual and artistic life, with a number of schools teaching painting, sculpture, music, literature, and drama.

═FAST FACT

For a $10 donation, you can visit some of San Miguel's most interesting homes on a two-hour house and garden tour, sponsored by the Biblioteca Pública (Public Library) (☎415-152-0293).

If you look beyond the box-shaped pruned trees around the *zócalo*, you'll see the birthplace of Ignacio de Allende, with its *alfénique* decoration. Step inside to see the exhibits of the Museo de la Casa de Allende, featuring colonial-era furnishings and documents from the fight for independence (☎473-152-2499). A bit beyond stands the Convento de la Concepción (Convent of the Conception), the largest Mexican convent, begun in the middle of the eighteenth century but not completed until the end of the nineteenth. The magnificent dome of the church, also designed by Gutiérrez, was the final piece. Today the former convent houses an art school, Escuela de Bellas Artes (☎473-152-0289). Farther beyond the convent stands La Casa del Mayorazgo de la Canal, the former home of Don Manuel Tomás de la Canal. Built in 1735, today it houses the Instituto Allende, the second of San Miguel's important art schools (☎473-152-0190;

&*www.intituto-allende.edu.com.mx*). Notice its spacious patio and unique arches. Beyond lies the shaded green expanse of the Parque Benito Juárez, originally called the Paseo del Chorro (The Water Spring). Local Indian women wash clothes by hand in the spring-fed tubs of the public *lavandería* (laundry).

To see a superb example of Mexican churrigueresque architecture and decoration, visit the Santa Casa de Loreto, a copy of the original House of the Virgin in Loreto, Italy, built in 1736 by Manuel Tomás de la Canal, then the town's richest citizen. Be sure to step into the Camarín, an octagonal room containing six altars, one Neoclassical and five baroque, with exquisite *retablos* of carved and gilded ornamentation.

🧳 TRAVEL TIP

Take a unique walking tour or perhaps a tour to visit local working haciendas or artisans' workshops with the Instituto de Viajes de San Miguel. Tours, conducted in six-passenger vans, often include lunch (📞415-152-0078).

One of the most important sites along La Ruta Independencía is the nearby sixteenth-century baroque Oratorio de Atotonilco (Augustinian monastery church of Atotonilco), the first stopping place of the independence army after it left Dolores. Its six chapels contain statues, folk murals, and impressive seventeenth- and eighteenth-century paintings.

Time to Relax

The only European-style spa in Guanajuato is Spa Hotel Hacienda de Cobos, where you can get a massage or a facial and then relax in the circular skylit conservatory (📞473-732-6815). You'll also discover hot springs between Dolores Hidalgo and San Miguel de Allende. Called *balnearios,* some have waterslides, wave pools, and mineral pools. In Dolores Hidalgo, visit the Balneario El Oasis, and near San Miguel, go to Hacienda Taboada (☎473-152-0888), a spa built on mineral springs used by the Chichimec and Otomi Indians, where you can also stay overnight and partake of the usual spa treatments, or to Balneario La Gruta (☎473-152-2530), a natural hot spring—all on the highway from Dolores Hidalgo.

Shopping

If you love to shop, head first to the Mercado Hidalgo, one of Mexico's best markets. Built in 1910, this cast-iron art nouveau-style structure, with an interior balcony that encircles the entire building, overflows with stalls selling produce, crafts, and food. Don't miss the candy and leather vendors.

Guanajuato also has workshops that produce traditional majolica-style pottery, as well as shops selling silver jewelry, both in the city and at La Valenciana Mine. Especially look for the traditional *pajaritos* (small birds) jewelry and baroque silverwork.

Dolores Hidalgo is famous for its Talavera pottery, which is distinct from that made in Puebla, and a whole lot less expensive. You'll discover workshops as you walk the streets around the *zócalo.*

≡FAST FACT

To see craftspeople making and decorating Talavera ware, stop into Talavera Cortés at Distrito Federal 8 in Dolores. (Open weekdays 7 A.M. to 4:30 P.M., Saturdays 7 A.M. to 1 P.M.)

San Miguel has one of the biggest and best concentrations of craft shops in Mexico. Brass and tin, the town's specialty, shine brightly, but you'll also find locally handwoven fabrics and well-designed jewelry in the shops occupying colonial buildings surrounding its square. Go to the large outdoor Mercado de Artesanías, located outside the

Mercado El Nigromante, or visit some of the many townhouses that have been converted into handicraft shops and art galleries.

Time to Eat

You'll find most of Guanajuato's restaurants in hotels near the Jardín de la Unión and on the highway leading toward Dolores Hidalgo. If you'd like some free *botanas* (snacks) around lunch time, go to the Clave Azul at the Plaza San Fernando.

Local Dining Suggestions

- **Casa del Conde de la Valenciana:** Excellent regional cuisine is served in a Mexican atmosphere (Carretera a Dolores Hidalgo, Km. 5, ✆473-732-2550; *www.condevalenciana. com*).
- **El Gallo Pitagorico:** Fine Italian and international cuisine is served overlooking the *jardín*, with free *botanas* with drinks in the late afternoons and early evening (Jardín de la Unión, ✆473-732-9489).
- **El Truco:** Popular local hangout where you'll find good food, especially the *comida corrida*, and good coffee, served in three separate dining rooms of a restored colonial house. Live guitar music nightly (Calle Truco 7, ✆473-732-9374).

Dining Precautions

Guanajuato, Dolores Hidalgo, and San Miguel de Allende all get lots of tourists. The high number of expatriates living in these communities, especially San Miguel, assures that most restaurants are clean and safe. But you'll still need to drink bottled water in all three towns.

Where to Go After Dark

In this cultural mecca, you'll find not only folkloric dance but ballet, theater, opera, and philharmonic orchestras as popular as discos.

Mariachis often play until the wee hours of the morning at *plazuelas* throughout the town. The action begins late at romantic *salsa* clubs like El Bar or La Dama de las Camelias and continues at crowded discos like El Capitolio, Guanajuato Grill, or Galería on the weekends.

JUST FOR PARENTS

Spend a romantic evening dining on paella by candlelight in the Spanish baroque atmosphere of Tasca de Los Santos, one of Guanajuato's fancier restaurants (Plaza de la Paz 28, ☎473-152-2320).

Join students at Café Bosanova or Van Gogh at the Plaza San Fernando, or go to Café Dada or La Galería for a coffee or a cool drink. If you're in the mood to just listen to music, stop in at El Santurario or Ché Café.

For both an entertaining and educational evening, take part in a two-hour *callejonada* (alley stroll) led by *estudiantinas* (student musical groups) who stroll the *callejones* of Guanajuato on weekend nights in costume, strumming their guitars and serenading local residents. Groups leave the Jardín de la Unión at about 8 P.M. A wine-carrying donkey follows the group, and when the group stops at a *plazuela*, everyone gets a drink. You'll have to pay a small charge for the wine.

And every Sunday evening when the university is in session, go to Plazuela de San Roque to see students performing *entremeses* (interludes), short farces written in Spanish to be performed at intermissions during the Cervantino Festival. The performances, featuring seventeenth-century costumed actors and sound effects, last about ninety minutes and are free.

CHAPTER 22

Mérida

MÉRIDA HAS BEEN A gateway for immigrants into Mexico whose traditions have all influenced life here. And even though Mérida has rich colonial architecture, it's one of Mexico's most up-to-date cities. By combining the architecture of the old with the pragmatism of the new, Mérida shows a respect for tradition.

About Mérida

Spanish nobleman Francisco de Montejo, "El Mozo" ("The Younger"), founded Mérida on January 6, 1542 upon the remains of the Mayan city of Ichcaanziho or T'ho. He renamed it Mérida because its buildings resembled those in Mérida, Spain. Using the carved stones from the Mayan buildings, the conquistadors built their own churches, government buildings, and homes.

Today, Mérida is the capital of the state of Yucatán, a thriving port city, and gateway to the archaeological wonders of the Maya.

Best Time to Go

Because Mérida has a semitropical climate, afternoon rains occur from May to October. Hurricanes often blow in from the Gulf of Mexico in September and October. The best time to visit is from November through April, when high temperatures reach the low 80s and lows are in the mid-60s.

Cuisine

Food in Mérida is something else again. Any time, day or night, a Yucatecan dish can turn into an unforgettable culinary experience. The *auténtico sabor* (authentic flavor) of the typical Yucatecan dishes come from a mouthwatering blend of European and Mexican flavors. Though the culinary heritage of the Maya lives on, there's a significant influence from dishes brought to Mexico by Syrian and Lebanese immigrants, as well as dishes from New Orleans, France, and Cuba.

JUST FOR PARENTS

If you like Yucatecan cuisine, you can learn to cook it by attending cooking classes held in the colonial kitchen at Los Dos. A seven-hour class costs $75, an eleven-hour $125, with food, drinks, ingredients, and workbook included (☎999-928-1116; ✐*www.los-dos.com*).

One of the Yucatán's trademark dishes is *pollo pibil* or *cochinita pibil*—chicken or pork marinated in *achiote*, sour orange juice, peppercorns, garlic, cumin, and salt, then wrapped in banana leaves and baked. There's also the traditional *poc chuc*, tender slices of pork marinated in sour orange juice, then grilled and served with a tangy tomato sauce and pickled onions. Another popular dish is *huevos motuleños*, a tortilla covered with refried beans and a fried egg and then smothered with tomato sauce, peas, chopped ham, and shredded cheese. *Frijoles con puerco*—the Meridano's version of pork and beans—has chunks of pork cooked with black beans, served with rice and garnished with cilantro and onion.

With Mérida's high summer heat, cold drinks like *horchata* (ground rice, raw sugar, cinnamon, and water), a classic Mayan specialty, are popular, as are *licuados* (fresh fruit pureed with water).

Cautions and Safety Concerns

If you're traveling to Mérida during the summer, be sure to drink lots of water. The heat and humidity can take their toll quickly. Tour archaeological sites in the morning, if possible, to avoid the afternoon heat.

Getting Around Mérida

Taxis and vans will take you into town from the airport for $10 dollars per vehicle, or you can take the bus. For the most part, taxis in Mérida are expensive. While taxis in town used to have set, published rates, several new companies have begun to use meters. You can identify them by the *taximetro* sign on the roof of the car.

≡FAST FACT

All east-west streets are odd-numbered, while north-south streets are even-numbered.

Your hotel should have a list of prices. If you're not using a metered taxi, agree on the price before you get in the car. You can also hire taxis for $12 an hour.

Family-Oriented Hotels

Mérida has many attractive hotels, some with colonial gardens and flowering patios, along with new high-rise hotels that line Paseo de Montejo. These are more likely where you'll want to stay with your family.

Fiesta Americana Mérida

Reservations: ☎800-343-7821 (U.S.), ✐*www.fiestamexico.com*

Located on Paseo de Montejo, this five-story, 350-room hotel offers a spectacular glass atrium lobby, pool, health club, and tennis courts, restaurant, and coffee shop.

Hyatt Regency Mérida

Reservations: ✆800-223-1234 (U.S.), *✍www.hyatt.com*

This seventeen-story high-rise just off the Paseo de Montejo has 300 rooms, plus elegant public areas with marble floors, archways, and fountains. It features two restaurants, a bar with live entertainment, a health club, two tennis courts, and a large pool.

Casa del Balam

Reservations: ✆800-624-8451 (U.S.), *✍www.yucatanadventure* *.com.mx*

This seven-story, fifty-seven room high-rise offers a distinct colonial atmosphere with a tree-filled interior courtyard with a bubbling fountain. Facilities include a small L-shaped pool, a bar, a rooftop sun deck, and a restaurant specializing in Yucatecan cuisine.

Hotel Misión Mérida

Reservations: ✆800-448-8355 (U.S.), *✍www.hotelesmision.com* *.mx*

Just two blocks off the *zócalo*, this colonial-style hotel offers spacious rooms with red tile floors and wood wicker furnishings. An interior patio has a large pool and garden, good restaurant, bar, and shops. It's a good family hotel in the center of the action.

Something for Everyone

Mérida lies at the center of the Mayan world in the Yucatán. Surrounding it are archaeological sites dating back thousands of years. But its colonial history is just as interesting.

Things to Do

Start your tour of the city at the Plaza Mayor, or, as it was once called, the Plaza de la Independencia, Mérida's *zócalo*. The Catedral de San Idelfonso, built by Pedro de Aulestia and Miguel de Auguero between 1561 and 1598, making it the oldest cathedral in North

America, stands on the east side of the Plaza. Peek into the Capilla del Cristo de las Ampollas (Chapel of the Christ of the Blisters), to the left of the main altar to see the sixteenth-century Mayan wood-carving of Christ. According to legend, someone carved this from the wood of a tree in Ichmul that the Maya saw burning but undamaged.

 **TRAVEL TIP**

Take a free guided walking tour of Mérida's Centro Histórico (Historic District), Monday to Saturday at 9:30 A.M. (✆999-942-0000, ext. 133).

To one side of the cathedral stands the former archbishop's house, now the Museo de Arte Contemporáneo (Museum of Contemporary Art), also known as the Museo MACAY (MACAY Museum), which displays modern Yucatecan art. Admission is $3. (Open Tuesday to Sunday, 8 A.M. to 5 P.M., ✆999-928-3258.)

Opposite the cathedral on the plaza's north side stands the Palacio Municipal, Mérida's City Hall, built in 1735, with its clock tower and colonnades. Nearby is the Palacio de Gobierno (Government Palace), built in 1892, which displays twenty-seven abstract murals. Painted in 1978 by Fernando Castro Pacheco, the murals shows his interpretation of the Yucatán's bloody history. A block beyond stands the Convento de las Monjas, a former sixteenth-century convent.

On the south side is the Casa de Montejo, built in 1549, the former home of Francisco de Montejo, a Spanish Conquistador who founded Mérida in 1542, now a bank. You can stroll, shop, and people-watch while doing the Calle 60 Stroll—one of the "must-dos" while in Mérida. Beginning at the *zócalo*, stroll north Calle 60 to Parque Hidalgo. Stop for a *café*, a *cerveza*, or a *refresco*, and sample some *botanas* (snacks) while you people-watch.

🧳 TRAVEL TIP

> Take an hour ride from Parque Hidalgo through the historic district in a *calesa* (horse-drawn carriage) for $25.

Just beyond stands the beautiful Iglesia de Jesús, also known as Iglesia de Tercer Orden (Church of the Third Order), with its magnificent frescoed interior. Built in 1618, it's a good place to see a Yucatecan wedding. Parque de la Madre (Motherhood Park) offers some shade as you gaze over at the Teatro José Peón Contreras (José Peón Contreras Theater). The University of the Yucatán's main building, across the street, offers summer courses in archaeology and Spanish and a folkloric dance performance on Friday evenings.

Parque de Santa Lucia (Saint Lucy Park), up next, offers a free Yucatecan serenade every Thursday evening at 9 P.M. Across the street stands the Iglesia de Santa Lucia (Church of Saint Lucy), which the Spaniards originally built for the exclusive use of their African slaves.

Continue your stroll to Calle 47 to Parque Santa Ana surrounded by antique shops and art galleries. Purchase a snack and cold drink from the vendors in the park. Walk over one block to Paseo de Montejo, Mérida's main avenue, considered to be Mérida's tree-lined version of Paris's Champs-Elysées, flanked by French-style old chateaux and monuments that tell of the grandeur of the Yucatán's turn-of-the-century *henequén* (a hemp fiber used to make rope) boom. At the corner of Paseo de Montejo and Calle 43 stands the Palacio Cantón, built by General Francisco Cantón, a former governor of the Yucatán. Now it houses the Museo de Antropología e Historia, showing exhibits of Mayan history and anthropology housed in a restored mansion. Admission is $5. (Open Tuesday to Saturday, 8 A.M. to 8 P.M., Sundays 8 A.M. to 2 P.M.; ☎999-923-0557.) If you're tired, take a *calesa* back to your hotel or to La Ermita De Santa Isabel (Santa Isabel Chapel), south of the *zócalo*. Its gardens contain Mayan statues. Travelers to and from Campeche used to stop here to pray for a safe journey.

💼 TRAVEL TIP

For about $10, take the Turibus open-air double-decker bus tour of Mérida. The whole tour, with English narration by earphones, lasts one hour, but you can get off and on at six designated stops along the way from 8:30 A.M. to 10:00 P.M., beginning near the Hotel Fiesta Americana Mérida.

You'll find Mérida's downtown is closed to traffic on Sundays, allowing you to stroll its streets, browse its shops, and attend one of many folkloric shows held in its parks.

For the Kids

Parque Centenario is *the* place for kids in Mérida. Besides a great zoo (open 8 A.M. to 5 P.M.), it has all sorts of entertainment, including a festival for kids with clowns and magicians, puppets and players, plus organized games with prizes on Sundays at 11 A.M. Pinocchio's Movie House, across from the park, shows kids' movies on Sundays beginning at 8 A.M.

Ecotourism

If you're a bird lover, this part of the Yucatán is like Nirvana. Natural undeveloped beaches are full of seagulls in flight and pelicans fishing in the shallow waters. Of all the places you can visit, Río Lagartos, 165 miles from Mérida, offers the most amazing sight— thousands of bright pink flamingos gathering in the estuary and flying overhead. The Mexican government declared this site a National Wildlife Refuge in 1979. You may also see spider monkeys, whitetail deer, crocodiles, as well as nineteen of the twenty-seven types of birds found in the world in this 90,000-acre refuge. Although you can drive to Rio Lagartos, 165 miles east of Mérida, you'll enjoy taking an all-day tour with lunch with Ecoturismo Yucatán (☎999-920-2772, *ecoyuc.com.mx).*

Bullfights

You can see a bullfight at the Plaza de Toros in Mérida between November and April. Tickets, available at the arena, on the *zócalo*, and at convenience stores, cost 15 to to 50 dollars.

Visit Nearby Sites

In Mérida, history is all around you. To understand more about the Yucatán, you should take one or more short excursions into the countryside. You can either rent a car and drive yourself or take a tour with one of the following companies:

- **Amigo Yucatán:** ☎999-925-1785, ✉*www.amigo-travel.com*
- **Orbitur:** ☎999-920-3085, ✉*www.orbitur.com.mx*
- **Turitransmérida:** ☎999-924-1199, ✉*www.turitransmerida. com.mx*

Along the way, you'll see magnificent haciendas. With the passage of time, many began to deteriorate—their owners abandoning them to rot in the tropical heat. Today, many have been restored as luxury hotels and inns. Of 362 haciendas, seventy-one retain their original detail and have been preserved.

Izamal

Forty-four miles east of Mérida lies the picturesque town of Izamal, perhaps the oldest town in the Yucatán. According to Mayan legend, Itzámna, the god of creation, created it and Mayan pilgrims journeyed there for centuries before the Spaniards arrived. More recently, it's known as La Ciudad de las Cerros (City of the Hills) because of the many pre-Columbian mounds that surround it. Out of a dozen, only one pyramid has been restored: Kinich Kakmó, believed to be dedicated to Chaac, the rain god.

In preparation for Pope John Paul II's visit in 1992, workers painted many of the town's buildings an egg-yolk yellow. Take a *calesa* ride around town on its cobblestoned streets to absorb its colonial ambiance. Then visit the Museo de la Ciudad (Town Museum), located in the Parador Turistica (Visitors' Center).

La Ruta del Conventos (The Convent Route)

La Ruta del Conventos will take you into the heart of the Yucatán. Traveling through the countryside on the outskirts of Mérida, you'll visit Mayan villages, ruins, and colonial churches dating back centuries. While the best way to see this route is by renting a car and driving yourself, you can also go on guided tours from your hotel.

Visit the Past

Surrounding Mérida are vestiges of the Maya's great civilization. While you can visit a number of archaeological sites separately, following La Ruta Puuc (The Hilly Route) will help tie them together and make the splendor of the Maya easier to understand.

Uxmal and La Ruta Puuc

The ancient city of Uxmal, along with those of Labná, Kabah, Sayil, and Xlapac, combine to form La Ruta Puuc, an exploration of the splendor of the Maya, less than an hour south of Mérida.

Each of the sites has restored Mayan pyramids and others covered with brush, trees, and jungle, so you can see how archaeologists found them. Intricate geometrical designs of cut and carved limestone are the hallmark of the Puuc style.

Admission to each of the sites on La Ruta Puuc is about $3 per person, except Uxmal, which is about $8.

There are three ways you can make this trip: rent a car; book a tour for $43 with Mayaland Tours (☎800-235-4079 [U.S.]); or take an air-conditioned bus for $11 round-trip from the city bus terminal, departing daily at 8 A.M., with thirty-minute stopovers at Sayil, Labná, and Xlapac, and a one-and-a-half-hour stop at Uxmal, returning to Mérida at 4:30 P.M. While this bus tour may get you back for dinner, it doesn't give you much time to explore the sites.

🧳 TRAVEL TIP

When you visit the archaeological sites around Mérida, be sure to wear a hat and comfortable rubber-soled shoes, take along plenty of drinking water, and wear sunblock. If you begin to feel the effects of the heat, get into the shade immediately.

Dzibilchaltun

Dzibilchaltun, fourteen miles north of Mérida is one of the most ancient Mayan centers in the northern Yucatán. Its name means "place where there is writing on the stones." Although what you see today focuses on its ceremonial center, it originally covered seven square miles and was connected to other Mayan centers by *sacbes* (ceremonial causeways or white roads). The Templo de las Siete Muñecas (Temple of the Seven Dolls), named for the seven figurines found there, is outstanding. Archaeologists believe Mayan priests held ceremonies here to reinforce their status as intermediaries between the Sun god and the Maya. The Museo de Sitio displays an exhibit of traditional Mayan culture, including a typical Mayan house. Admission is $6. (Open Tuesdays to Sundays, 8 A.M. to 4 P.M., ☎999-924-0994.)

Time to Relax

Several old *henequén* haciendas have been restored outside of town. One of them, Hacienda Xcanatun, just five minutes from Mérida, has a spa where you can go to relax in the lap of luxury. Try some of their Mayan treatments and take yourself back in time (☎999-941-0273, ✉*www.xcanatun.com*).

Shopping

The Yucatán is famous for hammocks, Panama hats, *huipiles* or embroidered women's blouses, guayabera shirts, and a variety of items made from *henequén*. Mérida's main shopping districts lie east and south of the *zócalo*, on Calles 57 and 59 between Calles 54 and 64. Or you may prefer to explore the Mercado García Rejón, an enormous handicrafts market southeast of the *zócalo*, with stall after stall of Yucatecan crafts at good prices.

RAINY DAY FUN

Wait out an afternoon shower at the Casa de Artesanias, a restored monastery with a courtyard art gallery.

But for a true taste of the Yucatán, browse the Mercado Municipal, a maze-like conglomeration of stalls selling just about everything. Plus, each Sunday you'll find special markets to shop, including the Bazaar of Arts and Crafts at Parque Centenario and the Antique and Crafts Bazaar at Parque de Santa Lucia. Businesses in Mérida stay open through the day, but some do close for a siesta (midday break) during the hottest months of July and August.

Time to Eat

Mérida is a gourmet's delight. You'll find a mix of Mayan and Continental cuisine. But it also has cantinas—no, not the kind where Hollywood gunslingers hung out and only men were allowed, but places where families go for an inexpensive lunch. Most open from 1 P.M. to 6 or 7 P.M. When you order a beer, you're also served four dishes of *botanas* (snacks). They include everything from refried beans with tortilla chips, macaroni in a tomato sauce, and cucumbers in lemon, to beets with lemon and cilantro, pureed pumpkin seed, *empanadas*, and *ceviche*. Each cantina has its own specialties and most have live bands. Also, being so close to the sea, you'll find Mérida loaded with fine seafood restaurants serving lobster, shrimp, octopus, and conch. Seafood tacos are especially good.

💼 TRAVEL TIP

Mexican waiters don't automatically bring the bill to you. This would be considered rude and might look like they're trying to rush you. So, when you want your bill, say "*La cuenta, por favor*" (The bill, please).

Local Dining Suggestions

- **El Cangrejito:** This hole-in-the-wall restaurant serves the best seafood tacos in town (Calle 57 No. 523, El Centro, ☎999-928-2781).
- **La Prosperidad:** This popular local eatery serves a value-packed *typica comida corrida* (meal of the day) (Calle 56 No. 456, ☎999-928-5283).
- **Los Almendros:** This charming eatery serves a wide variety of authentic Yucatecan dishes. Watch them make tortillas (Parque Mejorada, El Centro, ☎999-928-5459).
- **Muelle 8:** Fine seafood at reasonable prices is served in a Mexican atmosphere (Calle 21 No. 142, El Centro, ☎999-928-2781).

Dining Precautions

Mérida's restaurants, like the city itself, are clean. Bottled water is available everywhere.

Where to Go After Dark

Cool evenings in Mérida offer many opportunities for people-watching. The Teatro José Peón Contreras and Teatro Daniel Ayala both have dance and theater performances. Every Wednesday at 9 P.M., the Folkloric Ballet of the University of Yucatán presents a lively program of music and dance called *Yucatán and Its Roots* in the Teatro José Peón Contreras. If you like to dance, join the fun at El Jabín, Antrox, and Tequila Rock Discos, or perhaps try something a little more daring, like Latin salsa at the Mambo Café.

CHAPTER 23

Veracruz

MEXICO'S HOT AND SULTRY principal port city of Veracruz is much like pre-Castro Havana. It's a lively and attractive town with a blend of colonial and modern architecture. Located on the Gulf of Mexico, it's a Caribbean-style place, as unspoiled as a freshly sliced pineapple—a city of tiled roofs, pink and salmon-colored walls, and old churches, and a *joie de vivre* unlike any other in Mexico. Although it's a popular destination for foreign tourists, you're more likely to meet Mexican vacationers who are attracted to its sandy beaches, heaps of fresh grilled shrimp, the moderately priced accommodations that welcome families with children, and the bustling life of the streets. Day and night, the musical rhythms of marimbas and guitar-strumming trios fill the streets of Veracruz, making it an ideal place to sample the "real" Mexico.

About Veracruz

Where the rough Sierra Madre range turns abruptly into lush coastal plains, and the waters of the Bahía de Campeche rush up to meet rocky beaches and sandy dunes, the Old World first met the New with the arrival of Hernán Cortés on Good Friday, April 21, 1519. There, some 250 miles east of what's now Mexico City, in a land rich with Mesoamerican Indian tribal culture, Cortés planted a cross and called it La Villa Rica de la Vera Cruz (The Rich Village of the True

Cross) and established the first settlement at La Antigua, sixteen miles north of the present city.

Today, over a million people call Ciudad de Veracruz (Veracruz City) home, Mexico's oldest city. Its maze of old colonial-style buildings with balconies and iron grills lining clean cobblestone-and-palm-lined streets harken back to the days of early Nueva España. Its distinctly Caribbean personality combines elegant Spanish heritage with Afro-Cuban rhythms and the spicy flair of Mexico. Veracruz has seen its share of Spanish invaders, pirates, slave traders, and armies from France and the United States, who all mixed with the Pre-Hispanic indigenous peoples resulting in a mélange that defies description. Its residents, commonly called *Jarochos* (The Rude Ones), are a fun-loving, lively people who love to have a good time.

Best Time to Go

It rains a lot here, and the humidity is overpowering any time of year. And while Veracruz's Carnaval is going on, usually in February, it's almost impossible to find a place to stay. May through July, even though the temperature can reach the low 80s, the humidity can make it seem even hotter. From September through November, hurricanes blow in from the Caribbean, and the winds change to a northerly direction during the winter, making November to March the best time to visit.

Cuisine

The gastronomic mosaic that's Veracruz cuisine—a combination of indigenous, Creole, mestiza, and mulato—combines fresh seafood with aromatic herbs and spices and tropical fruits to produce a synthesis of ingredients like no other in Mexico.

While *maize* (corn), beans, and squash have been staples of the Mexican diet since ancient times, *Jarochos* have added a variety of tropical fruits, tomatoes, chiles, and avocados to the ingredients of their ancestors to produce sauces *a la Veracruzana*. African slaves brought plantains, yucca, sweet potatoes, and peanuts, important elements of West African/Caribbean cooking, and added them to produce such dishes as *pollo encacahuatado* (chicken in peanut sauce). Also, you must sample the myriad of local seafood.

 **TRAVEL TIP**

For a light snack, go to the Pescado Mercado Municipal (Municipal Fish Market), where you can try slurping up oysters on the half-shell from *ostionerías* (oyster bars) accompanied by a bubbling *refresca* (fruit drink) or icy *cerveza*.

Or perhaps you'll prefer snacking on tasty *gordas* (thick corn cakes stuffed with beans) or *picaditas Veracruzanas* (ingredient-topped tortillas with salsa), and *empanadas* (meat pies) sold at street stands. In this hot climate, the locals love to drink *licuados* (fruit milk-shakes) and *helados* (traditional milkshakes). Try a *toro*, a milkshake made with rum—delicious.

If you have a sweet tooth, you'll enjoy *lechero con canillas* (milk and strong coffee with a special sweet bread). And since the coffee grown in the cool highlands of Veracruz is the best in Mexico, you'll be in heaven if you're a coffee lover.

Cautions and Safety Concerns

Veracruz is as safe a city as any in Mexico. However, watch out for pickpockets during Carnaval.

Getting Around Veracruz

After arriving at Veracruz's airport, you can catch a van into town for about $6 per person. You'll find taxis unmetered, inexpensive, and plentiful. Agree on the price before you get into the cab. Or you may want to hop on inexpensive, reproduction wooden trolley cars on rubber wheels, called Los Tranvías del Recuerdos (The Tramcars of Memories), that ply the streets as part of the city's public transit system.

Family-Oriented Hotels

You'll find Veracruz hotels in two zones: downtown, within walking distance of the Plaza de Armas, and south of town along the coastal road leading to Boca del Río.

Continental Plaza Veracruz

Reservations: ☏800-882-6684 (U.S.)

Only five minutes from the beach and located conveniently next to the Veracruz Convention Center, this 260-room, eleven-suite high-rise hotel offers a variety of modern amenities, including a health club, covered pool, two bars, a restaurant, and a coffee shop.

Fiesta Americana Veracruz

Reservations: ☏800-343-7821 (U.S.), ✉*www.fiestamexico.com*

This hotel's 233 super-deluxe rooms and twenty-three suites, decorated in shades of tan and green with original artwork, open onto the interior courtyard of a seven-story high-rise on the beach ten minutes from town. A great family hotel with a fine seafood restaurant, a cantina, two beachfront pools, three hot tubs, a health club, lighted tennis court, kids' club, and water sports rentals.

Hotel Emporio

Reservations: ☏800-666-1986, ✉*www.hotelesemporio.com.mx*

Located on the *malecón* facing the harbor, this 202-room hotel has fifty suites with Jacuzzis and harbor views, plus one indoor and one outdoor pool, another Olympic-size pool with high dive, two restaurants, two tennis courts, a health club, a piano bar, and a disco.

Torremar Resort

Reservations: ☏800-666-1986 (U.S.)

This 230-room, nine-story high-rise resort on the edge of Playa Mocambo in Boca del Río offers a pool, a restaurant and lounge with live music, plus a coffee shop, a health club, a kids' club, and a playground.

Mocambo Resort Hotel

Reservations: ☎229-922-0202

Built in 1932, this hotel was one of the first beach resorts in Mexico and is still famous for its sprawling grounds. Set on the side of a hill overlooking Playa Mocambo, it features a terrace facing the ocean, 113 spacious rooms, two restaurants, a piano bar, a tennis court, one outdoor and two indoor pools, a Jacuzzi, and a sauna.

Posada Coatepec

Reservations: ☎228-816-0544

Located in Coatepec, this renovated eighteenth-century colonial home offers twenty-three elegant suites, each decorated with a different theme. Facilities include a garden with pool and courtyard, plus an excellent restaurant.

Something for Everyone

Popular with Mexican vacationers, Veracruz offers a relaxed atmosphere with a few major sights. The center of action here is the sixteenth-century *zócalo,* the Plaza de Armas, a lively arcaded square planted with towering palms and tropical flowers.

Things to Do

The city has been the stage for many events in Mexican history, including the drafting of the Mexican constitution. It tells you of its compelling history through its historical monuments and attractions and museums.

Veracruz begs to be explored. Along the older streets of town, the faded clay-coated walls of ocher, gray, pink, blue, and green shield out the intense heat of the sun. Iron bars cover the windows, but great wooden doors swing wide open, revealing barbershops, print shops, doctor's offices, even banks, all open to the public view. You can either walk from the *zócalo* or take one of the *tranvías* to the shady Parque Gutierrez Zamora about seven blocks away.

The bell tower of the La Ermita del Santa Christo del Buen Viaje (The Hermitage of the Holy Christ of Good Journey), containing the chapel of the dark-skinned Christ and protector of travelers since 1598, said to be one of the oldest churches in the New World, rises to one side. Unlike other plazas in town, this square offers a green oasis of shade trees, a fountain, and an ice cream parlor. Stop and have your shoes shined at one of the numerous shoeshine stands. Over a block on Calle Zaragoza, the Museo de la Ciudad (Museum of the City of Veracruz), formerly the old Zamora Orphanage, offers a look into pre-Hispanic Veracruz's past through excellent collections of archaeological material and art from the Olmec, Totonac, and Huaxtec cultures, including Totonac *yugos,* large horseshoe-shaped stones used in ancient ball games, and objects from the Mexican Revolution (open Tuesday to Sunday).

Three blocks northeast, the tiny Baluarte de Santiago (Santiago's Bulwark), now a museum, is the only remaining bulwark out of nine built in 1526 to protect the city. Here, you can view an exhibit of pre-Columbian jewelry and weapons.

RAINY DAY FUN

Most museums in and around Veracruz have free admission. Ask at your hotel if you are wondering about the admission for a certain museum.

Heading back to the *zócalo,* you come upon Los Portales de Miranda, an arcade named after its original owner, Francisco Xavier Miranda, a grain merchant. During the nineteenth century, *evangelistas,* or typists, sat under its cool overhang and wrote letters and documents for people who didn't know how to read and write.

Across from the Portales de Miranda on the southeast side of the plaza stands the eighteenth-century Catedral de Nuestra Señora de la Asunción (Our Mother of the Ascension), known to *Jarochos* as La

Parroquia. On the northeast side, the Palacio Municipal, Veracruz's Moorish-style town hall, built in 1627 and seat of the first city council in North America, invites you into its beautiful patio. Take a break and sip a cool drink at a café under Los Portales overlooking the square, while you listen to the melodic strains of a marimba band. Around you, *Jarachos* play dominos, munch on tropical fruit, sip rich coffee, and watch the people.

Afterwards, stroll along Calle Miguel Lerdo toward the harbor. Follow the aroma of fresh tobacco just off the *zócalo* to the Factoría Cigarro La Prueba (La Prueba Cigar Factory) at Miguel Lerdo 500, where you can watch workers rolling cigars. (Open Monday to Friday 9 to 11 A.M., ☎229-932-2061). Then stop at the Plaza de la Republica, where people acquired merchandise arriving into the port. Across the street, the nineteenth-century Aduana Marítima (Customs House), built in 1903, contains part of the old city wall. The plaza's most striking building, the Registro Civil, was Mexico's first civil registry building. Continue on to the *malecón*.

Veracruz's *malecón* will remind you of what old Havana must have been like. And well it should. The English firm of Pearson & Co., which also built Havana's *malecón*, completed Veracruz's Correo y Telégrafo (Post and Telegraph Office), with its stately European façade and giant golden lions guarding its entrance, as well as the handsome nineteenth-century Estación de Ferrocarriles (Railroad Station) in 1902.

Along the *malécon*, the yellow-and-white–trimmed turn-of-the-century Museo Constituciónalista Venustiano Carranza houses a lighthouse and museum dedicated to former Mexican President Venustiano Carranza, whose hulking statue stands in the front yard. It was at his residence in Veracruz that he met with fellow statesmen to hammer out the post-revolutionary Mexican Constitution from 1914 to 1915.

Across the street, boats depart for harbor cruises, costing $5 per person, that include a running commentary on port sights sung out by the guide like a sailor's chant. Here, also, boats go to Castillo de San Juan de Ulua, a fort on an island east of the harbor. You may also want to take a boat to Isla de los Sacrificios (The Isle of Sacrifices), so called because the Spaniards witnessed a human sacrifice there. Today, it's known for its sandy beaches.

If you love the Agustín Lara song *Granada,* you'll want to visit his museum, Casa Museo Agustín Lara, located in Boca del Río. He began playing the piano in brothels and eventually took up bullfighting. Lara described himself as being born under "a silver, rumba-inspired, *Jarocho* moon, a real troubadour." Here, you'll see sheets of his music, notes, and photos, as well as a replica of the radio studio from which he hosted *La Hora Azul* (The Blue Hour).

For the Kids

Veracruz's ultramodern Acuario (Aquarium), north of Playa Villa del Mar, continually packs in the crowds. Designed by Hiroshi Kamio, it includes 100 tanks featuring salt and freshwater fish from Mexico and other Latin American countries, a touch-me table, tropical rain forest, and closed-circuit television showing algae and small life forms. The aquarium's gigantic circular main tank, holding 325,000 gallons of salt water with fifteen species of sharks, sting rays, and groupers, is the largest in Latin America (✆229-932-7984).

Beach It

Though Veracruz has a variety of beaches, only those farther south, away from the port, are good for swimming. Even though those closest to town—Playas Hornos and Villa del Mar—have hard-packed sand and murky waters, you can still watch fishermen repairing their boats and mending their nets. If you want to swim, you're better off doing so in your hotel's pool.

Five miles south of Playa Villa del Mar lies the fishing village of Boca del Río and Playa Mocambo, one of the best beaches, alive with concessions and watersports activities. Both it and Playas Costa de Oro and Los Arcos have finer sand and sometimes heavy swells, making all three perfect for WaveRunners, windsurfing, and surfing. Weekends, they overflow with Mexican families, as vendors, selling seafood and beer, and dancers move to continuous tropical rhythms.

Beyond Boca del Río, along the Río Jamapa, you'll come upon the village of Mandinga, which means Devil's Corner. Here, on Laguna Mandinga, a mangrove lagoon, you can munch on huge shrimp and soft-shelled crabs, washed down with an ice cold *cerveza*, at al fresco *marisquerías* (seafood restaurants) along its shore, where local children may entertain you with an impromptu *son jarocho* dance to the mellow tones of a harp.

Visit Nearby Sites

You'll find several interesting sites relatively close to Veracruz that you can see in a day or two. Why not take an excursion into the mountains to Coatepec and Jalapa, staying over at an inn to enjoy the cool mountain air?

La Antigua

In 1519, Hernán Cortés first landed in the New World at La Antigua, a fishing village twenty minutes north of Veracruz by the coast road. Supposedly the first European settlement in North America, the quiet village straddles the Río Antigua. You can visit the crumbling remains of the Cortés's former home, now encased in tree roots, and La Ermita (The Hermitage), the first church built on Mexican soil (in 1529), where Cortés attended mass and baptized the first Indian. You can also see the barracks that housed General Antonio López de Santa Ana's troops, which he formed in 1835 to fight at the Alamo in Texas.

Coatepec

Surrounded by citrus orchards, sugarcane fields, and coffee and banana plantations is the charming eighteenth-century colonial town of Coatepec. Winding inlaid stone streets with balconies overhanging the sidewalks have become the hallmark of this town of 45,000 people. Today, craftsmen produce fine furniture, saddles, and hand-tooled leather portraits, as well as *caféto* handicrafts such as knives, letter openers, figurines, and even elaborate clocks, all carved from the blond wood of coffee roots.

 **TRAVEL TIP**

> The air in Coatepec, best known for its rich coffee, smells of freshly roasted beans. Visit one of the small coffee-roasting factories and be sure to take back a pound or two for yourself.

As you stand in the Parque Hidalgo, the town's main square, you face La Parroquia de San Jerónimo, a fine parish church built in 1702. On another side stands the Palacio Municipal (City Hall). Wander inside to catch a glimpse of the beautiful murals covering the walls on the lower level. Down the street stands the orange and brown-trimmed La Iglesia de la Virgen de Guadalupe (The Church of the Virgin of Guadalupe). Step into its cool interior to marvel at its silver-ornamented walls. Afterward climb Cerro de las Culebras, a steep hill with an observation tower, for a spectacular view of the countryside.

Jalapa

Ten minutes north of Coatepec lies cool, clean Jalapa (or Xalapa), the capital of the state of Veracruz and home to one of Mexico's finest public universities. On a clear day, this hill town offers a dramatic view of Mexico's highest mountain, the snowcapped 18,551-foot Pico de Orizaba. Often called the "Flower Garden of Mexico" due to its profusion of flowers and fruits in its parks and gardens, Jalapa spreads over a number of hills in a garden-like region surrounded by high mountains; it receives abundant rainfall and is often clouded over. The locals call the rain *chipichipi*.

Once a former stronghold of the Spaniards and a stagecoach stop, Jalapa's old town is a maze of narrow streets and lanes lined with colorful houses and lush gardens left over from the Spanish colonial period. This is in striking contrast to the broad boulevards and modern buildings in the newer sections of town.

One notable building is the massive late-eighteenth-century restored cathedral. This stands near the attractive Parque Juárez, the main square, on the other side of which is the long light-stoned colonial-style Palacio de Gobierno (Government Palace), containing interesting frescoes and faced by ornate fountains. The adjacent Jardín de Morelos (Morelos Garden) offers a fine view of the city. Other attractive parks are the Parque Hidalgo and Parque de los Berros.

Just north of downtown, past sloping streets and hidden alleys, stands one of Mexico's most impressive museums. The Museo de Antropología (Museum of Anthropology), a feast for the eyes and part of the University of Veracruz, houses one of the most complete collections of the history of regional culture in Mexico. It displays an impressive 29,000-piece collection of Olmec heads, Aztec and Huaxtec stone sculptures, as well as a large selection of stelae and cult objects, pottery vessels, and figures and articles made from semiprecious stones, bringing together collections of artifacts formerly stored around the state. The museum's landscaped atriums show seven giant twenty-two-ton carved stone Olmec heads in natural settings, and an eighteen-level orientation hall explains exhibits and puts them all in context. The cultures shown in this museum influenced future cultures throughout Mesoamerica. It's worth making a trip to Jalapa just to see it.

And six miles south of town you'll find the Ex-Hacienda El Lencero, the grand home of General Santa Ana, where he entertained visiting nobility and artists during his several terms as president of Mexico. Elegant furnishings from around the world fill its rooms. After touring the house, have a snack and some coffee in the restaurant housed in the former servants' quarters (open Tuesday to Sunday, 9 A.M. to 5 P.M.).

Visit the Past

An hour from Veracruz along the coast road stands the significant archaeological site of Las Ruinas de Zempoala (The Ruins of Zempoala), the last capital of the Totonacs. Cortés and his men made their first contact with the natives here. Covering two square miles, Zempoala consists of ten groups of buildings, including the thirty-six-foot-high Templo Mayor or Temple of the Thirteen Steps, the Templo de la Chimineas (Temple of the Chimneys), a six-story structure with a broad staircase and the remains of six columns, the Templo de la Dios Viento (Temple of the Wind God), a circular pyramid with ramps in front, and the Gran Pirámide (Great Pyramid), a later structure of superimposed platforms. A three-story structure of cement and boulders, Templo de las Caritas (Temple of the Little Faces), has niches once filled with small carved faces. Don't miss the small museum at the entrance.

Shopping

It's best to visit the Mercado Hidalgo, a block from Parque Zamora, early in the morning. Here, your eyes will catch the unusual shapes and names of some familiar and unfamiliar fruits and vegetables— *camotes* (sweet potatoes), *tamarindos* (tamarind fruit), *mandarina* (tangerines)—and the fragrance of fresh vanilla beans from nearby Papantla permeates the air. Wander through the enchanting witch-craft stalls and the rhythmical meat market, where the butchers beat their knives on chopping blocks to Latin tunes.

Time to Eat

Whether you enjoy fresh seafood in a quiet bistro, steak in an elegant restaurant, or a Cuban sandwich in an open-air café, you'll find dining in Veracruz an adventure for your taste buds. Café life here is the best in Mexico, so stop often and enjoy it.

TRAVEL TIP

Order the best *café con leche,* locally known as *café lechero,* at La Gran Café del Portal, a Veracruz landmark since its opening in 1926. Breakfast of fresh juice, coffee, and *pan dulce* (pastries) is a must.

Local Dining Suggestions

- **La Estancia de Boca:** Regional specialties, including fish stews served in *mulcahetes* (volcanic rock bowls) are served in a colorful Veracruzana atmosphere (Boulevard Ruiz Cortinez 3500, Boca del Río, ☎229- 922-6789).
- **Mariscos Villa Rica Mocambo:** Fresh-seafood lovers come here to dine on grilled shrimp and fish in this al fresco restaurant by Playa Mocambo (Calzada Mocambo ☎527-229-922-2113).
- **Antojitos Lolita:** A great eatery, serving a variety of *antojitos* and local specialties *a la Veracruzana* (Avenida 16 de Septembre 837, El Centro, ☎229-932-0760).
- **La Paella:** If you love paella, then head to this busy place decorated with bullfight posters just off the *zócalo* (Zamora 138, El Centro, ☎229-932-0322).

JUST FOR PARENTS

For a romantic evening without the kids, make reservations at La Mansión, and relive the elegance of the 1930s and 1940s while listening to the melodies of Agustín Lara as you eat thick steaks washed down with fine Mexican wines (Boulevard Ruiz Cortines, ☎229-937-1338).

Dining Precautions

Restaurant owners pride themselves in the freshness of their seafood, so your chances of getting ill from it are slim. However, the city caters more to European and Caribbean tourists than American, so you'd be wise to drink bottled water, available everywhere, whenever possible.

Where to Go After Dark

Late at night, the Plaza de Armas teems with life. Bright white flourescent bulbs light up cafés under Los Portales as you sit listening to a cacophony of music—guitars, marimbas, trumpets, mariachi bands. Hawkers sell strawberries and peanuts, while café patrons spin their fans in time to the music that begins at 8 P.M. and runs as late as 3 A.M. on weekends. On Tuesday, Thursday, and Saturday nights, people of all ages come to execute the elegant steps of the *danzón,* an Andalusian dance brought to Veracruz in the 1870s by refugees fleeing war-torn Cuba, to the accompaniment of the Manzanita Orchestra.

≡FAST FACT

The spirited song *La Bamba,* which rock star Ritchie Valens made a worldwide hit in the 1950s, originated in Veracruz.

To hear the lively rhythms of Cuban music, venture into the side streets off the *zócalo* to one of the Mexican/Cuban dance clubs, such as El Rincón de la Trova (The Inside Corner of the Troubador) and La Tasca. Or if your taste leans more to rock, head to the ZOO, Freeworld, and Ocean discos.

CHAPTER 24

Copper Canyon

THE COPPER CANYON, MEXICO'S most spectacular natural wonder, is even more accessible today than it was just twenty years ago. It offers you an outdoor experience so shockingly pure and majestic that you'll feel like an explorer entering an undiscovered civilization.

About Copper Canyon

Although the locals refer to this area in northwestern Mexico collectively as Las Barrancas del Cobre, or the Copper Canyon, it is, in fact, a 10,000-mile maze of more than twenty smaller gorges that combine to form a series of five interconnecting canyons, or *barrancas*. Situated in the state of Chihuahua, Barrancas del Cobre cuts through a 25,000-square-mile rugged section of northern Mexico's Sierra Madre Occidental. Four times larger and 280 feet deeper than the Grand Canyon, Barrancas del Cobre has resisted the taming of man. However, with new technology, more and more people are getting to experience its wonders. Today, tourism has become rather highly developed.

The Barranca del Cobre, at 4,225 feet deep, is but one of the canyons. The Urique, formed by the Río Urique, is the deepest at 6,107 feet. Other main canyons, all deeper than the Grand Canyon, include these:

- **Barranca de Batopilas:** 5,850 feet deep, formed by the Río Batopilas
- **Barranca de Candameña:** 5,688 feet deep, formed by the Río Candamena
- **Barranca de Chínipas:** 5,200 feet, formed by the Río Chínipas
- **Barranca de Huápoca:** 5,265 feet, formed by the Río Papigochi
- **Barranca de Septentrión:** 5,200 feet, formed by the Río Septentrión
- **Barranca de Sinforosa:** 5,948 feet, formed by the Río Verde

These canyons link three main rivers that flow through the length of the Sierra Madre Occidental to Los Mochis and the Gulf of California. Snow often covers the canyon rims while on their floors, palm and citrus trees as well as tropical flowers flourish. The Sierra Madre is home to the Tarahumaras, a population of approximately 50,000 indigenous inhabitants; thus, it's also referred to as the Sierra Tarahumara, covering 58,000 square miles. Archaeologists believe these indigenous people settled in the canyons thousands of years ago. These indigenous people have proven they have more endurance than marathon runners. In fact, the Tarahumaras have been known to run down wild deer on foot.

≡ FAST FACT

Though the Tarahumara call themselves *Rarámuri*, which means "Light Feet," Jesuit missionary Juan Forte misunderstood it to be *rarahumares*, then wrote it as Tarahumaras in his journal in 1607.

The majority of Tarahumaras now live in huts made with logs or rocks and mud, rather than caves as their ancestors have for the last 400 years. Though some men still wear loincloths, others have begun wearing pants with a leather belt, a bulky-sleeved shirt, and leather sandals tied with leather thongs. Women wear brightly colored skirts

and embroidered blouses. They weave fine wool blankets that help keep their families warm during the harsh canyon winters, as well as delicate baskets of pine needles.

💼 TRAVEL TIP

By respecting the customs and traditions of the Tarahumaras, you'll be rewarded by a handshake, a smile, and possibly an invitation into a private home. You'll find plenty of opportunities to interact with them. All local tour operators include a variety of walking and hiking tours to the caves and cabins of the Tarahumaras, where they'll welcome you with a cup of *tesgüino*.

The Copper Canyon isn't a solitary destination. Rather, it's a collection of sights and sounds, from the most tropical vegetation to the most incredible vistas in the world strung together between Los Mochis in the south and Chihuahua in the north by the Ferrocarril Chihuahua El Pacifico (Chihuahua El Pacifico Railway), more commonly known as El Chepe.

At its southern end lies the city of Los Mochis, meaning "place of turtles," located on Bahía de Topolobampo, the third-largest bay in the world. Built during construction of the railway, Los Mochis is a quiet town known for its crops of cotton, alfalfa, sugarcane, rice, and vegetables.

Next up the line fifty-miles from Los Mochis lies the small town of El Fuerte (The Fort). Founded in 1564 by Don Francisco de Ibarra, a Spanish conquistador who was the first to explore the Sierra Madre, El Fuerte became the gateway to the last frontiers of the territories of California, Arizona, and Sonora. Today, the town's cobblestone streets and picturesque squares help make it a wonderful starting point for a canyon excursion.

 TRAVEL TIP

While in El Fuerte, be sure to pick up a booklet containing a guided walking tour of the historic district. In two hours you can visit the *zócalo,* church, and city hall, plus a couple of colonial mansions.

Further up the line is Témoris, a mining town and railroad station. Here, three levels of viaducts, bridges, and tunnels converge on the Barranca de Septentrión, often mistaken for the Barranca del Cobre.

The departure point for Barranca de Urique, the Cerro del Gallego overlook, and the town of Cerocahui—forty-five minutes over rough road—is Bahuichivo. The short distance between Témoris and here is the most impressive part of the train ride. Thirty-seven bridges span canyons and waterfalls, and eighty-six tunnels burrow through mountains on three levels of track along the entire route. Those who stay at one of the new hotels on the Canyon's rim get off the train at the Posada Barrancas station. And less than two miles up the track stands the station at El Divisadero Barrancas, located on the rim of the Barranca de Urique, which is also mistaken for the Barranca del Cobre. Easy walking trails lead off along the rim to various lookouts.

The next stop heading north is the town of Creel, a town of 7,000 and the center of the action in the Copper Canyon. Sitting at 7,514 feet against a backdrop of pine forests, it's the high sierra at its best. It's also the departure point for hiking or biking excursions into nearby canyons.

The largest group of Mennonites in the world—approximately 50,000—live in Cuauhtémoc, the next stop. They produce hand-made embroidered fabrics and delicious white Cheddar-style cheese known as Chihuahua cheese.

Finally, the train arrives at the northern end of the line in Chihuahua, the capital city of the state of Chihuahua, Mexico's largest state. This colonial city reflects the modern side of Mexico with its shopping malls and *maquiladoras* (assembly plants). But its historic side reveals the intrigues of the Mexican Revolution leader Pancho Villa, a baroque-style cathedral, and several art museums.

Best Time to Go

Winter brings heavy snows to the rims of the canyons, but the floors become dry and dusty.

In July and August, daily afternoon rains make for lush vegetation and muddy conditions. The best time to visit the Copper Canyon is during September and early October after the summer rains, when rivers and spectacular waterfalls return to life. During the day, temperatures in the canyons range from 70 to 90°F, while high above on the mesas, they hover around 70°F. At night, temperatures can fall to 25 to 35°F. While you can visit the mesas during the summer, you should stay out of the lower canyons as the temperature can reach 100°F or more.

Cuisine

Since much of the Barrancas del Cobre lies above 5,000 feet, food here is simpler than other places in Mexico. A main staple of the cuisine is beef. Sample meat-filled corn *gorditas*, plus classic *burritos* made with a special *asadero* cheese tortilla, and beef tacos smothered in Chihuahua cheese. And don't forget *barbacoa* (barbecue), the speciality of the *Norteña*. The Tarahumaras are best known for their stews that combine fried meats, onions, and potatoes. They also eat beans, zucchini, tortillas, and wild herbs and roots.

Tarahumaras drink *tesgüino*, a fermented mixture of corn with a combination of leaves, roots, and grass seeds added. Once mixed, they ferment this concoction for twenty-four hours, and the result is a liquid rich in vitamins, minerals, and calories that they drink to excess during religious ceremonies called *tesgüinadas*.

Cautions and Safety Concerns

In the warmer months, rattlesnakes and scorpions can be a problem on canyon trails, even heavily traveled ones. Be sure to carry a snake-bite kit if you go hiking or biking. And shake your shoes and clothing for scorpions.

Getting Around Copper Canyon

Gravel and paved roads provide access for buses, for-hire, and private vehicles to formerly isolated villages. But be careful on these two-lane roads. Though much improved in recent years, you'll come upon slow-moving vehicles, speeding livestock, and lumbering logging trucks. Between Chihuahua and Creel, gas stations remain sparse. Second-class-only Estrella Blanca buses from Chihuahua to Creel cost about $25 per person but take nearly five hours.

Seeing Copper Canyon by Train

The Ferrocarril Chihuahua al Pacifico (Chihuahua al Pacifico Railway), the Copper Canyon's rail line, shouldn't be missed. Called "the most dramatic train ride in the Western Hemisphere," it took over ninety years to complete. Inaugurated in November, 1961, this extraordinary train ride takes you over 408 miles of track with thirty-nine bridges and through eighty-six tunnels in fourteen to seventeen hours. The sheer excitement of traversing the Puente de Chinipas (Chinipas Bridge), hundreds of feet above a watery gorge, can only be balanced by the slow rocking portion of the train ride. The train travels through the Barranca de Septentrión—the only canyon through which the railroad actually passes—negotiating the ride's steepest grades and most stunning landscapes by a series of tunnels and bridges.

≡FAST FACT

The Chepe train stops for only a few minutes at each station, so if you plan to hop off and take photographs, be sure you listen for the warning whistle telling you it's time to board the train.

Your adventure begins as you board the Chepe train, departing at 6 A.M. from either Los Mochis in the south or Chihuahua in the north. Each train arrives at its final destination at 10:25 P.M. local time, though there are frequent delays. Be sure to take along some toilet paper, which sometimes runs out, and some bottled water.

 TRAVEL TIP

To get the most scenic views in full daylight, it's better to take the train from Los Mochis to Chihuahua and sit on the right side of the aisle. In fact, the most scenic part of the trip runs from Los Mochis to Bahuichivo, as your train climbs nearly 5,300 feet through rugged deep canyons and mountains.

Tickets may be purchased through local or U.S. travel agents or at the station itself beforehand. The entire trip from end to end will cost you about $132 on the Primera Express train, with reclining seats, air conditioning, and heating, plus smoking-bar and dining cars, and about $66 on the Clase Economica (coach) train, also with air conditioning, heating, and a snack bar. However, the coach train, which leaves an hour later, has no smoking onboard and doesn't arrive until 1:30 A.M. If you plan to stay at any of the stops along the way, you'll need to purchase separate tickets for each segment. Reservations are essential (in Los Mochis, ✆668-812-0853; in Chihuahua, ✆614-415-7756).

Seeing Copper Canyon by Car

Another scenic way to reach Copper Canyon is by car. From Chihuahua, you can head southwest on Highway 16. The roads, now paved all the way to El Divisadero, allow you to travel through scenic ranching and agricultural areas and mountains dotted with log cabins, railroad car homes, logging camps, and old mines. You'll pass through the Mennonite community of Cuauhtémoc, passing through beautiful orchards along winding mountain roads on your way to the quiet lumber town of Creel. Here, you may continue exploring the canyons on foot or catch the south-bound Chepe train for Bahuichivo.

Family-Oriented Hotels

Though no hotels cater strictly to families, your hotel will be secondary to your outdoor adventures. Some newer hotels are quite luxurious. All hotels at station stops in the canyon area can make arrangements for tours to sites within the canyons.

El Mansión Tarahumara (Tarahumara Mansion)
Reservations: ☎617-415-4721, ✍*www.mansiontarahumara.com.mx*
Delicately balanced on the rim of Urique Canyon, this medieval-looking hotel offers sixty individual stone cottages, each with fireplace and large rustic rooms, as well as an indoor heated pool and jacuzzi. The dining room serves delicious family-style meals, included in the rates.

The Lodge at Creel Best Western Hotel and Spa
Reservations: ☎800-528-1234 (U.S.), ✍*www.thelodgeatcreel.com*
As the newest hotel in Creel and one of its nicest, this stone-and-log lodge offers twenty-eight rooms with all amenities, including an excellent restaurant and a full spa.

Hotel Divisadero Barrancas
Reservations: ☎641-410-3330, ✍*www.hoteldivisadero.com.mx*
This picturesque fifty-five-room lodge features stone construction, fireplaces in the rustic rooms, and great vistas from its dining room and bar. Rates include three meals per day.

Hotel Misión de Cerocahui
Reservations: ☎800-896-8196 (U.S.), ✍*www.mexicocopper canyon.com*

This hotel's forty-five large rooms opening onto a central courtyard have no heat, but they do have fireplaces and electricity.

Hotel Santa Anita

Reservations: ☎800-896-8196 (.U.S.), ✎*www.mexicocoppercan yon.com*

A 133-room luxury hotel in Los Mochis, part of the Balderrama hotel chain, with one of the best restaurants in town, offers a bus to the train station.

Posada Mirador

Reservations: ☎800-896-8196 (U.S.), ✎*www.mexicocopper canyon.com.*

Set in an apple orchard at the canyon rim, this bright pink hotel's sixty-three rooms, each decorated in light wood with modern fixtures, have breathtaking views. Rates include all meals, served family-style.

Something for Everyone

The natural beauty of the Barrancas del Cobre will enthrall you. Whether you'd rather see it from the comfort of a first-class train seat, on the back of a horse, or on foot, you'll find the area offers abundant opportunities for adventure on many levels.

Things to Do

One of the most enjoyable ways to experience Barrancas del Cobre is to stop at El Divisadero Barrancas (The Viewpoint), the stop before Creel traveling east. Here, the pure, crisp air, combined with the inspiring view that extends more than 100 miles across the Copper Canyon, makes for a fantasy come true. El Divisadero Barrancas, Copper Canyon's highest reachable point, rises more than 7,700 feet above the canyon floor, affording spectacular views of the Urique River and the Urique and Copper canyons from this natural overlook.

≡FAST FACT

If you're traveling from Los Mochis, you can expect to arrive at El Divisadero Barrancas at about 2:30 P.M. Coming from Chihuahua, you'll arrive about 1:30 P.M.

Upon disembarking from the train, you're catapulted into Divisadero's colorful open-air market. You'll be amazed at the abundance of handmade baskets, wooden dolls, jewelry, and even violins sold here. The vendors, including the local residents and the native Tarahumaras, swoop down in one great mass to set up their stands for approximately forty-five minutes each day before the scheduled train stops. *Regateando*, or bartering, is highly encouraged at the market. You'll only have fifteen minutes to perform a market sweep and see the view. The touristy market almost overpowers the view of the canyon—but not quite.

The Bahuichivo station is the stopping-off point for Cerocahui, a village of less than 1,000 set in a valley filled with apple orchards. Jesuit missionary Padre Juan Maria de Salvatierra built a mission church here in 1680, but it wasn't until 1940 that another Jesuit priest, Padre Andres Lara, actually founded the town. Across from his church, he built the Tarahumara Indian Boarding School for girls, which you can visit. From Cerocahui, it's an easy day trip to Barranca de Urique and a Tarahumara cave home, from which you buy baskets, on a dirt road 7,500 feet above the village. Nearby is the Cerro del Gallego Urique overlook, from which you'll get an almost 360-degree view of the canyons, as well as the village of Urique along the river below. If you travel further on, you can visit the church, cemetery, and old kiln in the silver-mining town of Urique, surrounded by coffee and fruit trees and fields of corn and peanuts.

Share a few words and break bread with a Mennonite family in Cuauhtémoc. Chihuahua al Pacifico Tours (☎614-437-0057) and Tarahumara Tours (☎635-456-0065) offer tours of the Campo Menonitas (Mennonite Camps) for about $35 per person, including stops at a cheese factory and the Mennonite Museum and Cultural Center, plus a family-style lunch in a Mennonite home.

Chihuahua has figured prominently in Mexico's history. The most popular historical attraction is the Museo de la Revolución (Museum of the Revolution), housed in the former home of hero/outlaw Pancho Villa. Formally known as Quinta Luz, in honor of his only legal wife, the museum contains the bullet-ridden car in which Villa died under fire in an ambush, plus cartridge belts, guns, and uniforms. Admission is $1 (open daily 9 A.M. to 1 P.M. and 3 to 7 P.M.). The Museo Regional de Chihuahua, one of the most beautiful museums in town, occupies a restored 1910 mansion, Quinta Gameros, furnished in the art nouveau style with stained glass windows. You'll enjoy the building, used for social gatherings, as well as the exhibits of art, Chihuahua history, and the Mennonites of Cuauhtémoc. Admission is $2. (Open Tuesday to Sunday, 10 A.M. to 2 P.M. and 4 to 7 P.M.)

For the Kids

Unlike other Mexico destinations, the Copper Canyon doesn't offer any activities just for kids.

 RAINY DAY FUN

Drive fifty-three miles south of Chihuahua to Delicias to visit the Museo de Paleontología, containing the largest collection of fossils in Mexico (☎639-474-4068). If the sun comes out, take your kids to El Delfin water park.

But exploring together as a family is not only fun, it's safe and educational for your children.

Ecotourism

Tucked away within the Copper Canyon are some of the most isolated places you'll ever see. The canyons offer a multitude of hiking, rail, walking, climbing, and canyon trekking opportunities, all guaranteed to satisfy your family's desire for adventure.

More than any other region in Mexico, the Copper Canyon provides spectacular hiking. Much of the area remains true wilderness, so you shouldn't hike alone. Several operators offer three-to-six-day hiking tours, depending on the type of tour you desire. Typically, they cost from $300 to $750, including most meals, guides, lodging accommodations, and transfers to the point of origin. As with most excursions, the variety and level of challenge varies tremendously.

If you're a devoted hiker, you can take hiking tours into the most remote areas of the canyons where you can camp far from civilization. Or you may choose to leave on day excursions to different areas before returning each evening to the same lodge.

One of the most dramatic hikes is to Parque Cascada de Basaseachic, the only national park in the northern Sierras. Cascada de Basaseachic, falling 807 feet to the canyon floor, is Mexico's second-highest waterfall. You'll begin in the village of Basaseachi and follow a trail that takes you across sparkling streams, up steep slopes, and then down nearly 1,000 feet below to the base of the falls. It's best to see the falls at the end of the rainy season in September, when the volume of water is greatest.

From Cerocahui, you can take a three-and-a-half-hour hike to the old Sangre de Cristo gold mine. Or you can walk two miles round-trip to Las Cascaditas (Little Waterfalls) in rainy season. You'll see a sawmill, an old cemetery, and some Tarahumara ranches. If you just want a view of the village, you can take another two-mile hike to El Valle del León (The Valley of the Lion).

From Creel, you can ride or hike to the Valle de los Monjes (Valley of the Monks), a series of unusual rock formations that look like hooded monks, or to the Valle de los Hongos (Valley of the Mushroom Rocks), an area of mushroom-shaped rock formations. Nearby lies Lago Arareco (Arareco Lake), a horseshoe-shaped lake ringed by pine woodland and boulders near the village of San Ignacio de Arareco, where you can visit La Misión de San Ignacio. Or you can hike to the bottom of Barranca de Tararécua and spend some time soaking in the ninety-degree waters of Balneario de Recowata (Recowata Hot Springs).

 **TRAVEL TIP**

To access many of the trails around Creel, you'll need to pay a small fee, usually $1 to $1.50, to the local *ejido*, a government-established community cooperative.

Some of the best mountain bike trails exist around Creel, with loose rock, breathtaking climbs, and dramatic descents, providing mile after mile of thrills. There are also plenty of old logging roads and tracks to bike within the canyons. If you're a beginner, the road through San Ignacio *ejido* will offer plenty of challenges. Or you may opt for a smoother ride along the road to Balneario de Recowata. The best local person for information on bike riding in the Barrancas del Cobre is Arturo Gutierrez (☎635-456-0248, ✎*www.umarike.com.mx*). You can rent a bike from him for $15 for a half day, $20 for a full day, and can purchase area trail maps. He also rents climbing equipment.

Though made for rock climbing, there aren't many prepared bolted routes within the canyons. The area's volcanic topography offers interesting climbs ranging from overhung to vertical.

Experienced guides, contacted through local guesthouses, charge $15 to $25 per day plus the cost of food. If you're staying at a hotel, you could pay as much as $50 per day for a guide. The following are some of the most reputable outfitters:

- **Copper Canyon Hiking Lodges:** ☎800-776-3942 (U.S.), ✎*www. coppercanyonlodges.com*
- **Safari Aventura:** ☎614-410-1338
- **The 3 Amigos Canyon Expeditions:** ☎635-456-0036, ✎*www. the3amigoscanyonexpeditions.com*
- **Wilderness Outfitters:** ☎602-882-5341 (U.S.)

If you'd rather go exploring by horseback, you can rent horses for $6 to $8 per hour through most of the canyon hotels.

Special Rail Tours

If you wish to travel the Copper Canyon route in luxury, you can spend two days and one night aboard the opulent South Orient Express, operated by DRC Rail Tours (✆800-659-7602, of Houston, Texas). The fully restored train runs seasonally from October to November and March to April and features lavish turn-of-the-century-style passenger cars, all-glass vista domes, elegant bars, and world-class gourmet cuisine, included in the price.

Still another option for luxury train travel is The Sierra Madre Express, offered by Tauck Tours (✆800-468-2825). Combining five Pullman cars, observation lounges, and deluxe staterooms, you'll spend two of seven nights of an all-inclusive eight-day package aboard the train.

Visit Botapilas

An overnight trip with local tour operators to Barranca de Batopilas from Creel will take you on a descent from cool pine forests to the semitropical zone, where tropical fruits grow, to the mining town of Batopilas at the bottom of the canyon. You can also take a bus, which takes six to eight hours, from Creel to Batopilas for about $7. Or you can hire a private car at your hotel in Creel.

TRAVEL TIP

Four miles beyond Batopilas at Satevó stands the red brick Mision de Satevó, built between 1760 and 1764, whose padres ministered to the groups of indigenous people and settlers working in the mining communities through 1910. The church's unusual construction features three domes and four half domes connected by a vaulted ceiling arching three stories above the empty chamber.

Batopilas thrived between 1880 and 1910 and was the second town in Mexico after Mexico City and the third in North America to receive electricity. Ruins of the Hacienda de San Miguel provide evidence of the grandeur and mystery of this colonial mining village hidden in one of North America's deepest canyons. Swaying palm trees and whitewashed houses with tropical gardens line cobblestoned streets. Daily temperatures can be as much as 30°F warmer than on the canyon rim, so dress accordingly. You'll see ranchers on horseback and pigs and goats wandering the streets.

Time to Relax

If you feel the need for a massage or facial, plus aroma- and hydrotherapy, you'll find them at the Lodge at Creel (✆635-456-0071).

Shopping

Creel, the trading center of the Barrancas del Cobre, offers everything from handmade jewelry to musical instruments, baskets, and pottery. You'll find Tarahumara handicrafts—dolls, violins, bead necklaces, wool rugs, woven purses and belts, and pottery—at several handicraft shops, including Artesanías Misión, Casa de las Artesanías, and Artesanías Tarahumara. At Divisadero's market, Tarahumara women and children work together to craft beautiful woven pine-needle baskets, belts, and wooden figures.

Time to Eat

Simple restaurants serving down-home–style foods have sprung up everywhere. Also, nearly all the hotels provide meals for their guests.

Local Dining Suggestions

- **El Farallón:** This restaurant serves all varieties of fresh seafood in a nautical setting (Obregón 593, Los Mochis, 668-812-1428).

- **El Caballo Bayo:** Steaks, burgers and fries, and sandwiches fill an American menu, served in bright surroundings (Avenida López Mateo 25, Creel, ✆635-456-0136).
- **La Parilla:** This is *the* place to go for Chihuahuan beef, with a *menu turistico* that includes soup or salad, steak, and potatoes, or try several of the twenty-one kinds of tacos (Calle Victoria 420, Chihuahua, ✆635-415-5856).

 **TRAVEL TIP**

While you may be tempted along the way to buy homemade tamales, tacos, and *empanadas* from Tarahumara Indian women at each of the stops along the route, it's best to eat only in restaurants.

Dining Precautions

Even though the Copper Canyon may be developing for tourism, it's best to not eat food sold by individual vendors. Eat in established restaurants. Bottled water is available everywhere—twenty-liter jugs cost as much as two-liter bottles. So buy a couple two-liter bottles and refill them. It's high and dry here, so you'll need to stay hydrated.

Where to Go After Dark

The only place to go after dark within the canyons is the Disco Cascada in Creel.

Cancún

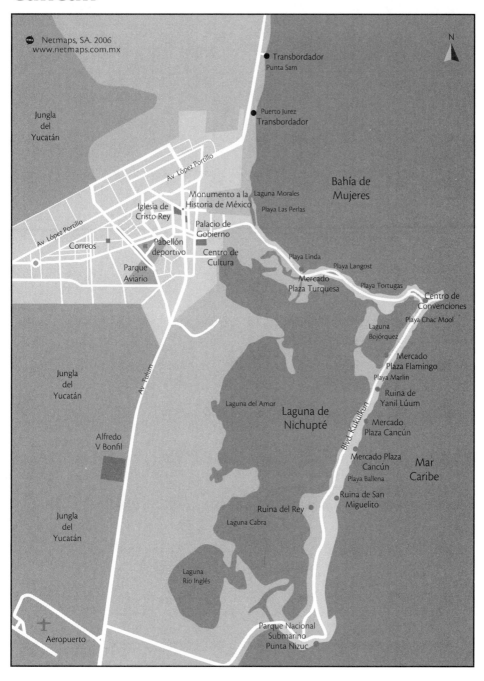

Netmaps, SA. 2006
www.netmaps.com.mx

N

Transbordador
Punta Sam

Jungla
del
Yucatán

Puerto Jurez
Transbordador

Av. López Portillo

Bahía de
Mujeres

Monumento a la   Laguna Morales
Historia de México
Iglesia de   Playa Las Perlas
Cristo Rey
Palacio de
Gobierno

Av. López Portillo

Correos   Pabellón
deportivo   Centro de
Parque   Cultura
Aviario

Playa Linda

Playa Langost

Mercado   Playa Tortugas
Plaza Turquesa

Centro de
Convenciones

Playa Chac Mool

Laguna
Bojórquez

Jungla
del
Yucatán

Av. Tulum

Mercado
Plaza Flamingo
Playa Marlin

Laguna del Amor   Ruina de
Yanil Lúum
Laguna de
Nichupté

Blvd. Kukulkan

Mercado
Plaza Cancún

Alfredo
V Bonfil

Mercado Plaza
Cancún   Mar
Playa Ballena   Caribe

Ruina de San
Miguelito

Jungla
del   Ruina del Rey
Yucatán   Laguna Cabra

Laguna
Río Inglés

Aeropuerto

Parque Nacional
Submarino
Punta Nizuc

Mexico

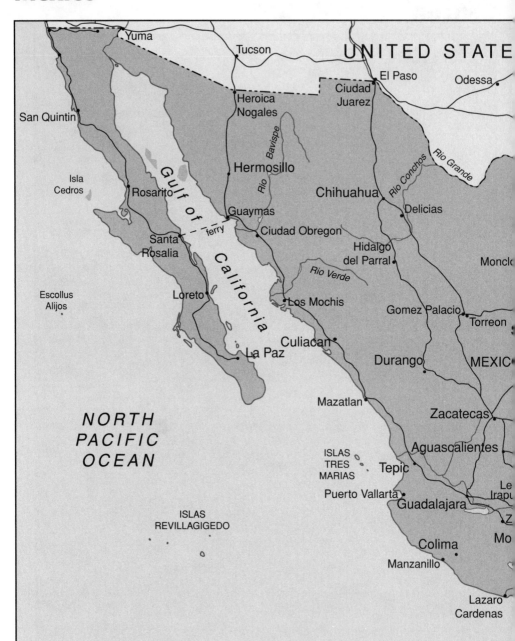

Yuma
Tucson
UNITED STATE
El Paso
Odessa
Ciudad
Juarez
Heroica
Nogales
San Quintin
Bavispe
Rio
Rio Conchos
Rio Grande
Isla
Cedros
Hermosillo
Rosarito
Chihuahua
Delicias
Guaymas
Ciudad Obregon
Santa
Rosalia
ferry
Hidalgo
del Parral
Monclo
Rio Verde
Escollus
Alijos
Loreto
Los Mochis
Gomez Palacio
Torreon
Culiacan
La Paz
Durango
MEXIC
Mazatlan
Zacatecas
NORTH
PACIFIC
OCEAN
ISLAS
TRES
MARIAS
Tepic
Aguascalientes
Le
Irapu
Puerto Vallarta
Guadalajara
Z
ISLAS
REVILLAGIGEDO
Colima
Mo
Manzanillo
Lazaro
Cardenas

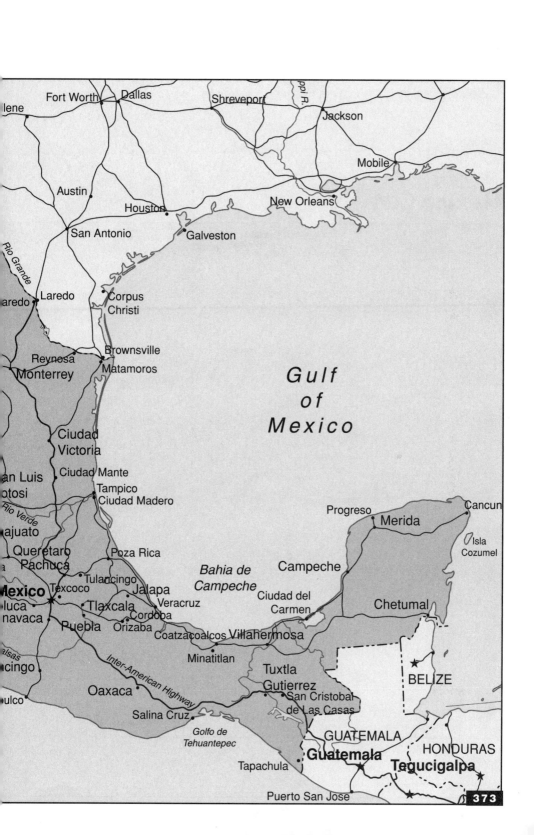

lene
Fort Worth • Dallas
Shreveport •
Jackson •
Mobile •
Austin •
Houston •
New Orleans
San Antonio •
Galveston •
Rio Grande
aredo • Laredo • Corpus Christi
Brownsville
Reynosa • Matamoros
Monterrey •

Gulf
of
Mexico

Ciudad Victoria •
an Luis otosi •
Ciudad Mante
Tampico • Ciudad Madero
Rio Verde
ajuato •
Progreso • Cancun •
Merida •
Queretaro • Poza Rica •
Pachuca •
Campeche •
Bahia de Campeche
Isla Cozumel
Mexico • Tulancingo •
Texcoco • Jalapa
luca • Tlaxcala • Veracruz •
navaca • Cordoba •
Ciudad del Carmen
Chetumal •
Puebla • Orizaba
Coatzacoalcos • Villahermosa
alsas
cingo • Minatitlan •
★ BELIZE
Inter-American Highway
Tuxtla Gutierrez •
ulco • Oaxaca • San Cristobal de Las Casas
Salina Cruz •
GUATEMALA
Golfo de Tehuantepec
Guatemala ★ HONDURAS
Tapachula • Tegucigalpa ★
Puerto San Jose •

Mexico City

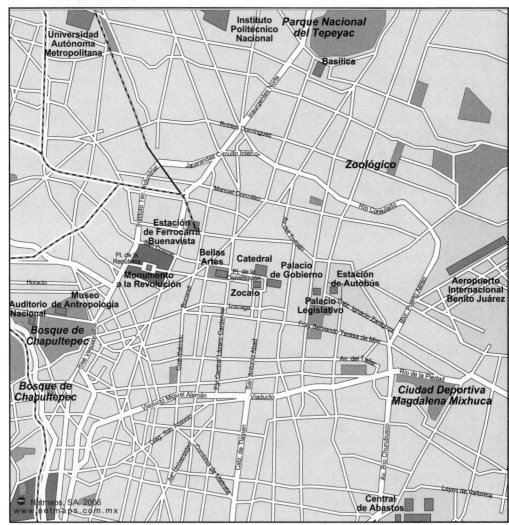

Universidad Autónoma Metropolitana

Instituto Politécnico Nacional

Parque Nacional del Tepeyac

Basílica

Zoológico

Robles Domínguez

Insurgentes Norte

Jacarandas Circuito Interior

Manuel González

Río Consulado

Instituto Tec. Industrial

San Cosme

Estación de Ferrocarril Buenavista

Pl. de la República

Av. del Trabajo

Bellas Artes

Catedral

Pl. de la Constitución

Palacio de Gobierno

Estación de Autobús

Horacio

Monumento a la Revolución

Bucareli

Zocalo

Izazaga

Palacio Legislativo

Calz. Ignacio Zaragoza

Blvd. Puerto Aereo

Aeropuerto Internacional Benito Juárez

Museo de Antropología

Auditorio Nacional

Bosque de Chapultepec

José Vasconcelos

Cuauhtémoc

Eje Central Lázaro Cárdenas

San Antonio Abad

Fray Servando Teresa de Mier

Av. del Taller

Río de la Piedad

Bosque de Chapultepec

Viaducto Miguel Alemán

Viaducto

Diag. San Antonio

Cumbres de Maltrata

Calz. de Tlalpan

Av. Río Churubusco

Ciudad Deportiva Magdalena Mixhuca

Leyes de Reforma

Av. Imsurgentes

Central de Abastos

Netmaps, SA. 2006
www.netmaps.com.mx

Familiar Spanish Phrases

MEXICAN SPANISH IS TO Castilian Spanish what American English is to British English. Though many of the words are the same, they sometimes sound different. Also, some Mexican words and place names have evolved from ancient cultures and have become part of the everyday language used today.

A Friendly Hello

Like many other peoples, the Mexicans really appreciate when you try to speak their language—no matter how much you butcher it. Everyone will greet you with a smile even when you say a simple "*Hola*" (hello). And if you go so far as to say "*Buenias dias*" (Good day), you'll receive a like greeting and a smile in return.

To help you receive those Mexican smiles, I've prepared a short list of some basic greetings, preceded by a simple explanation of Spanish pronunciation. While many people who work in tourism can speak English, it's ever so nice to say just a little in their language. You'll be glad you did.

Basic Spanish Pronunciation
Pronounce Spanish vowels as follows:
a as in father
e as in yet
i as in greet

o as in open
u as in loot

Pronounce Spanish consonants as you do in English. But keep these differences in mind:

b and *v* are always pronounced as *b*
c before an a, o, or u is always pronounced as *k*
c before an e or i is always pronounced as *s*
ch is always pronounced as in *chin*
g before an a, o, or u is pronounced as in *go*
g before an e or i is pronounced as in *hey*
h is always silent
j is pronounced as *ach*
ll is pronounced as in *million*
ñ is pronounced as the ny in *canyon*
q is always pronounced as *k*
r is pronounced as in *right*
rr should be trilled
x (in Indian words) is pronounced as *sh*
x after an e or i is pronounced as *h*
z is always pronounced as *s*

Everyday Phrases

Good morning	*Buenos días*	*Bway*-nohs *dee*-ahs
Good afternoon	*Buenas tardes*	*Bway*-nohs tahrdehs
Good night	*Buenas noches*	*Bway*-nohs *noh*-chehs
How are you?	*¿Cómo está usted?*	*¿Kohmoh ehstah oostehd?*
Hello	*Hola*	Ola
Hello (on phone only)	*Bueno*	Bway-*noh*
So long	*Hasta luego*	*Ahstah* loo-eh-goh
Goodbye	*Adiós*	*Ah*-deeohs

Please	*Por favor*	Pohr fah-*bohr*
Thank you	*Gracias*	*Grah*-seeahs
Thank you very much	*Muchas gracias*	*Moo*-chahs *grah*-seeahs
You're welcome	*De nada*	*Day* nah-dah
Pleased to meet you	*Mucho gusto*	*Moo*-choh *goos*-toh
With pleasure	*Con mucho gusto*	Kohn *moo*-choh goo-stoh
How do you say ___?	*¿Cómo se dice ___?*	*¿Koh*-moh seh *dee*-she ___?
Yes	*Sí*	See
No	*No*	Noh
Okay	*Bueno*	*Bway*-noh
All right	*Bien*	*Bee*-ehn
What time is it?	*¿Qué hora es?*	*¿Keh* ohrah ehs?
Excuse me	*Perdóneme*	Pehr-*dohn*-ney-may
Excuse me (when walking in front of someone)	*Con permiso*	Kohn per-*mee*-soh
Excuse me (interrupting speech)	*Discúlpeme*	Dees-*cool*-pe-me
I'm sorry	*Lo siento*	Loh see-*ehn*-toh
I am well	*Estoy bien*	Ehstoy *bee*-ehn
What's happening?	*¿Qué pasa?*	*¿Keh* pahsah?

I don't understand	*No entiendo*	Noh ehntee-*ehn*-doh
Where is ___?	*¿Dónde está ___?*	*¿Dohn*-deh eh-*stah* ___?
When?	*¿Cuando?*	*¿Kwahn*-doh?
What?	*¿Que?*	¿Kay?
What do you wish?	*¿Qué desea usted?*	Keh dehss-ehah *oos*-tehd
I want	*Yo quiero*	Yoh kee-*ay*-roh
I would like	*Quisiera*	Keyh-see-*air*-ah
Do you have ___?	*¿Tiene usted ___?*	*¿*Tyah-nay oos-*ted* ___?
The check, please	*La cuenta, por favor*	Lah *kwehn*-ta pohr fah-*bohr*
It's good	*Hace buen*	Ahseh *boo*-ehn
It's bad	*Hace mal*	Ahseh mahl
Weather	*tiempo*	tee-*ehm*-poh
How much is it?	*¿Cuánto cuesta?*	*¿Kwahn*-toh *kwess*-stah?
It's too expensive	*Cuesta mucho*	*koo*-ehstah *moo*-choh
Please take it	*Me lo llevo*	Meh loh lee-*ay*-voh
Where is the restroom?	*¿Dónde está el baño?*	*¿Dohn*-deh ehs-*tah* ehl banyo?
I feel sick	*Me siento mal*	Meh see-*ehn*-toh mahl
I need a doctor	*Necesito un doctor*	Neh-seh-*see*-toh oon *dohk*-tohr

Bring me	*Tráigame*	Tra-*hee*-gah-meh
Speak slowly	*Hable lentamente*	*Ahb*-leh lehn-tah-*mehn*-the
Do you speak English?	*¿Habla usted inglés?*	*¿Hah*-bla oosted een-*glehs*?
Is there someone here who speaks English?	*¿Hay alguién aqui qué hable inglés?*	*¿Ahy ahl-gee-ehn keh ahbleh een-glehs?*
To the right	*A la derecha*	ah lah day-*ray*-chuh
To the left	*A la izquierda*	ah lah ees-ky-*ehr*-dah
More	*Más*	Mahs
Less	*Menos*	May-noss
Small	*Pequeño*	Peh-*kehn*-yo
Quick	Rápido	*Rah*-peedo
More slowly	*Más despacio*	Mahs des-*pah*-cheeoh
Hot water	*Agua caliente*	Ahgwa kah-lee-*ente*
Cold water	*Agua frio*	Ahgwa *free*-oh
Here, please	Aqui, por favor	Ah-key pohr fah-*bohr*

Glossary

THE FOLLOWING LIST OF WORDS are some of those you'll come across on your trip to Mexico. Some of them are strictly Mexican Spanish terms or Spanish words used in a different context in Mexico. Others are indigenous words that have become a part of Mexican Spanish.

a la plancha
fried

abuelo
grandfather

abuela
grandmother

A.C.
antes de Cristo (before Christ); equivalent to B.C.

adobe
sun-dried mud brick used for building

aduana
customs

aeropuerto
airport

agave
family of plants, including the maguey, used to make tequila

agua fresca
fruit-flavored water

agua minerale
bottled carbonated water

agua purificada
purified water

agua sin gas
bottled uncarbonated water

al carbón
barbecued

Alameda
name of the formal parks in
Mexican cities

alberca
swimming pool

alfarería
potter's workshop

alfénique
baroque architectural
decoration resembling sugar-
paste candy

almuerzo
lunch

alt íz
a Moorish rectangular frame
around a curved arch on
Mexican buildings

Altiplano Central
plateau stretching across north
central Mexico

amate
paper made from tree bark

Angeles Verdes
Green Angels, bilingual
government-funded mechanics
who patrol Mexico's major
highways

antojitos
Mexican appetizers or
substantial snacks, like tacos or
tamales

arroyo
dried-up stream or riverbed

asado
roasted

artesanías
folk arts or handicrafts

atrium
enclosed yard of a large church
or cathedral

audiencia
an executive panel set up by the
Spanish king to rule Mexico in
the sixteenth century

autopista
expressway

avenida
avenue

azúcar
sugar

azulejo
decorated ceramic tile

bahía
bay

balneario
natural hot-spring bathing resort

baluarte
defensive wall or bastion

barbacoa
barbecued meat

barrio
poor neighborhood of a town or city

basura
rubbish or trash

boca
the break in a barrier island where the ocean meets a lagoon

boleto
ticket

boleto
boarding pass

bosque
grove of trees or forest

botana
light snack

burro
donkey

caballero
horseman, but can also be used on men's room doors

cabaña
cabin or simple beach shelter

cacique
Aztec chief

café con crema
coffee with cream

café de olla
coffee with cinnamon and sugar

café con leche
coffee with steamed milk

café negro
black coffee

calandría
nineteenth-century horse-drawn carriage

caldo de pollo
chicken broth

calle
street

callejón
alley

callejonada
alley walk, usually behind a small band, with alcoholic refreshments en-route

calzada
grand boulevard or avenue

camarín
a chapel beside the main altar in a church, containing ceremonial clothing for statues of saints

camarones
shrimp

camionera
bus terminal

campesino
farm worker

cantina
a small Mexican bar where women are traditionally not allowed

capilla
chapel

capilla abierta
an open chapel used in early Mexican churches for saying Mass to crowds of unbaptized Indians

carne
meat

casa de cambio
place where currency is exchanged

caseta de larga distancia
public telephone (also caseta de teléfono or caseta telefónica)

cazuela
clay cooking pot

cena
late-night snack or dinner

cenote
a limestone sinkhole filled with rainwater and used for ceremonial purposes in the Yucatán

cerro
hill

cerveza
beer

ceviche
fresh raw fish marinated in fresh lime juice, garnished with chopped tomatoes, chiles, and onions

chac-mool
pre-Columbian stone sculpture of a belly-up figure used in sacrificial ceremonies

chac
Mayan rain god

charreada
Mexican rodeo

charro
Mexican cowboy

Chilango
citizen of Mexico City

chinampas
Aztec gardens built from lake mud and vegetation

chultún
man-made cistern used to collect rainwater and found in the Puuc hills of the Yucatán

churrigueresque:
heavily ornamented Spanish-baroque architectural style found on many Mexican churches

cigarro
cigarette

clavadistas
cliff divers

colectivo
van that picks up and drops off passengers along a predetermined route

colegio
junior college or preparatory school

colonia
neighborhood of a city

combi
a Volkswagen van

comedor
a sit-down stall in a market or a small restaurant

comida
dinner (eaten at midday)

comida corrida
fixed-price midday meal

conde
the title of count

conquistador
early Spanish explorer-conqueror

convento
Mexican convent or monastery

cordillera
mountain range

correos
post office

crema
cream

criollo
person of Spanish descent born in New Spain

cuchara
spoon

cuchillo
knife

cuota
toll

curandero
an Indian shaman healer who used herbs and magic to cure diseases

D.F.
Distrito Federal (Federal District)

damas
ladies

D.C.
después de Cristo (after Christ); equivalent to A.D.

de lujo
deluxe

delegación
a large urban governmental subdivision in Mexico City comprising many *colonias*

desayuno
breakfast

descompuesto
broken, out of order

dulcería
candy shop

efectivo
cash payment

ejido
a government-sponsored
community with shared land
ownership

embarcadero
quay, jetty, or boat launch

enramada
thatch-covered open-air
restaurant

entrada
entrance

entremeses
hors d'oeuvres or also theatrical
sketches performed during
the Cervantino festival in
Guanajuato

equipales
barrel-shaped rustic chairs and
tables made from wood and
leather

equipaje
luggage

escuela
school

estación de ferrocarril
train station

evangelistas
people who type for others who
cannot read

ex-convento
former convent or monastery

familia
family

farmacia
drugstore

feria
fair

ferrocarril
railroad

fonda
a small restaurant or food stall
in a market

FONATUR
*Fondo Nacional de Formento del
Turismo* (National Foundation
for Tourism Development)

fraccionamiento
a subdivision or housing
development that's like a *colonia*

fuente
fountain

fuerte
fort

gachupines
a derogatory term for the
Spaniards sent from Spain to rule
Nueva España

garnachas
small fried tortilla topped
with chicken or pork, onions,
avocado, and chopped
tomatoes

guía
guide

glorieta
traffic circle

gorditas
thick fried-corn tortilla, slit/
stuffed with a variety of meats,
cheeses, tomato, lettuce, and
onion

gringo
Mexican slang for white North
American

grito
the shout (the Grito de Dolores
or call to independence by
Father Hidalgo)

gruta
cave or grotto

guarache
woven leather sandal (also
huarache)

guardería de equipaje
luggage storage room

guayabera
man's shirt with pockets and
appliquéd designs on the front
(also *guayabarra*)

Guera de la Casta
War of the Castes, a bloody
nineteenth-century Mayan
uprising in the Yucatán
peninsula

hacendado
hacienda owner

hacienda
large estate

helado
ice cream

henequén
fibers from the maguey plant
used to make rope

hielo
ice

hombres
men

horchata
refreshing drink made of ground
rice, ground almonds, and sugar

hoven
waiter

huarache
see *guarache*

huevos
eggs

huipil
Indian woman's short-sleeved
embroidered tunic of various
lengths

Huizilopochtli
Aztec god

iglesia
church

llegada
airport gateway

INAH
Instituto Nacional de Antropología e Historia, the Mexican government agency in charge of archaeological sites and museums

indígenas
inhabitants of all-native descent who speak their native tongue

infante
baby

ISH—impuesto sobre hospedaje, the lodging tax on the price of hotel rooms

isla
island

IVA
impuesto de valor agregado, a 15-percent sales tax added to the price of many items, including hotel rooms

ixtle
maguey fiber

jaguar
panther and symbol of the Olmecs

jai alai
the Basque game *pelota*, brought to Mexico by the Spanish

jaiba
crab

Jarabe Tapatío
a courtship dance in which a girl and boy dance around the boy's hat (Mexican hat dance)

jardín
the main square in central Mexican towns (literally "garden")

Jarocho
resident of Veracruz

jefe
boss or political leader

jipijapa
local name for a Panama hat in the Yucatán

jorongo
small poncho worn by some indigenous men

jugo
juice

Kukulcán
Mayan name for the plumed serpent god Quetzalcóatl

la cuenta
the restaurant check

la ermita
a hermitage, usually a church

Lada
abbreviation for *larga distancia*

Ladatel
the long-distance telephone
system operated by Telmex

ladino
the same as *mestizo*

laguna
lagoon or lake

lancha
fast, open, outboard boat

larga distancia
long-distance phone

leche
milk

libramiento
free or regular highway

licenciado
university graduate, abbreviated
as "Lic." and used before a
person's name

licuado
drink made from fruit juice,
water or milk, and sugar

limón
Mexican lemon (small green
half-lemon, half-lime)

llave
key

lonchería
a lunch counter or food stand

machismo
an exaggerated sense of
maleness

madre
mother

maguey
a type of agave with thick
pointed leaves growing straight
out of the ground

malecón
waterfront promenade

mantequilla
butter

mañana
tomorrow or some time in the
future

maquiladora
assembly plant in a Mexican
border town

mariachi
small ensemble of musicians
playing traditional ballads
on guitars and trumpets for
weddings and other celebrations

marimba
wooden xylophone-type
instrument that's popular in
Veracruz and the Yucatán

mariscos
seafood

marisquerías
open-air seafood restaurants

matachine
ceremonial dance procession

mercado
market

mescal
an alcoholic drink distilled from
the fermented hearts of the
maguey plant (also *mezcal*)

Mesoamerica
ancient Mexican cultures

mestizaje
Mexico's mixed-blood heritage

mestizo
person of mixed Indian and
Spanish ancestry

metate
shallow stone bowl with legs
used for grinding corn

migración
immigration

mirador
a lookout point

molletes
a *bolillo* (a crusty hard roll with
a soft center) cut in half and
topped with refried beans and
cheese then broiled.

Mudéjar
a Moorish architectural style
brought to Mexico by the Spanish

muelle
pier

mujeres
women

municipio
a small Mexican local-
government area

museo
museum

Nahuatl
the language of the Aztecs

nao
Spanish galleon

niño
child

nopal
prickly pear cactus, cut in
strips and served as a vegetable
(*nopalitos*)

norteamericanos
people from the United States

Nte
abbreviation for norte (north),
used in street names

Nueva España
New Spain

ostiones
oysters

Ote
abbreviation for oriente (east),
used in street names

palacio municipal
town or city hall

palacio de gobierno
state capitol or state house

palapa
thatched-roof beach shelter

pan
bread

pan dulce
sweetened bread, pastry

PAN
Partido Acción Nacional
(National Action Party)

panadería
bakery or pastry shop

panga
small fishing boat

parada
bus stop

parque
park

parque nacional
national park, a protected area
banning development and
exploitation

parroquia
parish church

paseo
boulevard or pedestrian street

pastel
cake or pie

Pemex
Petroleos Mexicanos (Mexican
Government–owned petroleum
corporation)

peninsulares
those born in Spain and sent by
the Spanish government to rule
the colony in Mexico

periférico
bypass or ring road

pescado
fish

pesero
small vans in Mexico City

petate
a palm or reed mat

peyote
a hallucinogenic cactus

pimienta
pepper

pinacoteca
art gallery

pintos
traditionally painted dancers

piñata
decorated clay pot or papier-
mâché mold filled with sweets and
gifts and smashed open at fiestas

plancha
plate

plata
silver (sometimes used to mean silver plate)

playa
beach

plaza
town square

plaza de toros
bullring

plazuela
small square or plaza

Poblano
person or thing from Puebla (literally, in the style of Puebla)

pollo
chicken

Porfiriato
Porfirio Díaz's reign as president-dictator of Mexico for over 30 years

portales
arcades

postre
dessert

presidio
military fort or garrison

PRI
Partido Revolucionario Institucional (Institutional Revolutionary Party)

primera classe
first class

propina
tip

Pte
abbreviation for *poniente* (west), used in street names

pueblo
town

puerto
port

pulque
a thick milky drink made from fermented maguey juice

punta
point of land

quechquémal
Indian woman's diamond-shaped embroidered shoulder cape with a head opening

quesadilla
flour tortilla stuffed with melted white cheese and warmed (Mexican toasted cheese)

queso
cheese

quetzal
crested bird with brilliant
green, red, and white plumage
highly prized by pre-Columbian
cultures

Quetzalcóatl
plumed serpent god of pre-
Columbian Mexico

quinta
a country house

rebozo
long woolen or linen shawl
covering the head or shoulders

Recibo de Equipaje
baggage claim

refresco
soft drink

Regiomontaño
person from Monterrey

reja
wrought-iron window grille

reserva de la biosfera
biosphere reserve

restaurante
restaurant

retablo
an altarpiece or a small painting
on wood or tin, placed in
a church to give thanks for
miracles

retorno
cul-de-sac

río
rive

s/n
sin número (without number),
used in street addresses

sacbe
ceremonial avenue between
great Mayan cities

sal
salt

sala
waiting or exhibition hall

salida
exit

salsa verde
sauce made with green tomatillo
and pureed with hot peppers,
cilantro, garlic, and onions

salsa Mexicana
chopped tomatoes, onions, and
cilantro with a small amount of
oil, put on restaurant tables

sanatorio
hospital

sanitario
restroom

serape
blanket with an opening for the
head which is worn as a cloak

segunda classe
second class

Semana Santa
Holy Week or the week before Easter

servicios
toilets

servilleta
napkin

sierra
mountain range

sin carne
without meat (vegetarian)

sin numero
s/n (without number) used in addresses without street numbers

sitio
taxi stand

Solomonic
spiral Spanish baroque columns

sopa
soup

sopa clara
consomme

sope
a small tortilla spread with refried beans and topped with crumbled cheese and chopped onions

stelae
Mayan standing carved-stone monuments that tell a story about an era (fifty-two years)

supermercado
supermarket

Sur
south

taco
filled tortilla

talabartería
shop where they make and sell saddles

taller
shop or workshop

taller mecánico
a car mechanic's shop

talud-tablero
stepped building style with alternating vertical (tablero) with sloping (talud) sections

tamal
meat rolled with masa, then wrapped in a corn husk and steamed (plural is *tamales*).

Tapatío, Tapatía
resident of Guadalajara; anything having to do with Guadalajara

taquería
place where you buy tacos

taquilla
ticket window

taza
cup

té
tea

té negro
black tea

telar de cintura
backstrap loom used by Indian
women

teleférico
cable car

templo
church (which took the place of
pre-Columbian temples, a place
of worship)

tenedor
fork

teocalli
Aztec sacred precinct

tequila
a liquor produced from blue
agave plant

Tezcatlipoca
pre-Columbian god, the lord of
life and death

tezontle
a pink, porous volcanic rock
that the Aztecs and Spaniards
used for building

tianguis
weekly open-air Indian market

tienda
store

típico
characteristic of a region

Tláloc
the pre-Columbian rain god

topes
speed bumps

torta
sandwich

tostadas
crispy fried tortillas topped with
meat, tomatoes, lettuce, onions,
avocados, and cheese

transbordador
ferry (also *barca de transporte*)

turista
Moctezuma's revenge

UNAM
*Universidad Nacional
Autónoma de Mexico* (National
Autonomous University of
Mexico)

universidad
university

vaso
glass

vía cuota
toll road

viaje
trip

viajero
traveler

vino
wine

vino blanco
white wine

vino tinto
red wine

virreinal
viceregal period from 1521–1821
when a Spanish viceroy ruled
Nueva España

voladores
the Totonac Indian ritual in
which men, suspended by their
ankles, whirl around a tall pole

zócalo
main plaza or square of a
Mexican town

Zona Rosa
a tourist area of hotels,
restaurants, and shops in
Mexico City

Place Pronunciations

BECAUSE MANY PLACE NAMES in Mexico originated in the Nahuatl (Aztec) language and not Spanish, or the Spaniards altered them to be able to pronounce them in Spanish, they're difficult to pronounce. The following list will help you pronounce place names included in this book:

Acapulco
Ah-kah-*pool*-koh

Ajijic
Ah-hee-*heek*

Atontonilco
Ah-tahn-tahn-*eel*-koh

Bahuichivo
Bah-*wee*-chee-voh

Barranca del Cobre
Bahr-*rohn*-kah dehl *Ko*-bray

Barranca del Urique
Bahr-*rohn*-kah Yoo-*ree*-kay

Batopilas
Bah-to-*pee*-las

Cabo San Lucas
Kah-bo Sahn *Loo*-kas

Cancún
Can-*koon*

Cerocahui
Sehr-roh-*kah*-hui

Chapala
Cha-*pah*-lah

Chapultepec
Chah-*pool*-teh-pek

Chichén Itzá
Chee-chen *Eet*-zah

Chihuahua
Chee-*wah*-wah

Cholula
Cho-*lool*-lah

Coatepec
koh-*wah*-te-pec

Colima
Coh-*lee*-mah

Coyoacán
Koi-yo-wah-*kahn*

Cozumel
Kah-*zoo*-mehl

Creel
Kreel

Cuauhtémoc
Khwa-*tay*-mok

Cuernavaca
Kwer-nah-*vah*-kah

Divisadero
Dee-*vees*-sah-dehro

Dolores Hidalgo
Dohl-lohr-res Hee-*dahl*-goh

Dzibilchaltun
Dzee-beel-*chah*-toon

Guadalajara
Gwad-dah-lah-*hah*-rah

Guanajuato
Gwah-nah-*hwah*-toe

Guerrero
Gay-*ray*-ro

Isla Mujeres
Eesla Moo-*her*-rayss

Ixtapa
Ees-*tah*-pa

Izamal
Ees-sah-mahl

Jalapa
Hah-*lah*-pah

Jalisco
Hah-*lees*-koh

La Paz
Lah *Pahz*

La Antigua
Lah Ahn-*tee*-gwua

Los Cabos
Lohs *Kah*-bos

Manzanillo
Mahn-san-*knee*-yoh

Manzanillo
Mahn-zawn-*ee*-yo

Mazatlan
Mah-saht-*lahn*

Mérida
May-ree-dah

Mexico
May-hee-co

Michoacán
Meeh-choh-ah-*kahn*

Mitla
Meet-lah

Monte Albán
Mon-tay Al-*bahn*

Monterrey
Moan-ter-*ray*

Morelia
Moh-*reh*-lyah

Morelos
Moh-*rehl*-los

Mulegé
Moo-leh-*hay*

Oaxaca
Wah-hah-kah

Patzcuaro
Pahtz-*kwar*-ro

Playa del Carmen
Pleye-yah dehl *Kar*-men

Puebla
P*weh*-blah

Puerto Vallarta
Pwer-tow Vah-*yar*-tah

Querétaro
Kay-ray-*tah*-ro

Quintana Roo
Keen-tanah *rooh*

San José del Cabo
Sahn Ho-*say* dehl *Ka*-boh

San Àngel
Sahn *Ahn*-hell

San Miguel de Allende
Sahn Mee-*gehl* day Ah-yen-day

Sinaloa
Seen-ah-*loh*-ah

Taxco
Tahs-koh

Tenochtitlán
Ten-*otch*-tit-lan

Teotihuacán
Teh-oh-tih-wah-*kahn*

Tequisquiapan
Teh-kees-*keyah*-pahn

Tlaquepaque
Tlah-kay-pah-kay

Tula
Too-lah

Uxmal
Ooch-mal

Veracruz
Veh-rah-*kruz*

Xel-ha
Shell-hah

Xochimilco
Zoch-ee-*meel*-koh

Yucatán
Yoo-kah-*tahn*

Zacatecas
Zahc-kah-*tek*-kas

Zempoala
Zem-*pwoah*-lah

Zihuatanejo
Zee-*whah*-tan-eh-hoe

Index